Nar

Nānā I Ke Kumu

(LOOK TO THE SOURCE)

Volume I

Mary Kawena Pukui
E.W. Haertig, M.D.
Catherine A. Lee

Published by Hui Hānai
An Auxiliary of the
QUEEN LILIʻUOKALANI CHILDREN'S CENTER
1300 Halona Street, Honolulu, Hawaii 96817

Hui Hānai is grateful to the Dolores Furtado Martin Foundation for making this 2022 reprint of *Nānā i ke Kumu (Look to the Source)*, Vol. I, possible. We extend a special mahalo to Mrs. Martin's children, Mrs. Māhealani Riley and Mr. Watters O. Martin Jr., for their support of our publishing efforts.

Published by Hui Hānai
P.O. Box 1552
Honolulu, Hawaiʻi 96806

First published, paperback and hardbound editions, 1979.
Paperback Vol. I reprinted 1992, 1994, 1996, 2001, 2002, 2003, 2004, 2005, 2009, 2020, 2022;
Paperback Vol. II reprinted 1992, 1994, 1996, 2001, 2002, 2003, 2005, 2009, 2017, 2021.

(*Nānā i ke Kumu*: Helu ʻEkolu, Vol. III, was published in 2020 by Liliʻuokalani Trust; reprinted in 2020.)

LIBRARY OF CONGRESS CATALOGING IN PUBLICATION DATA
Pukui, Mary (Wiggin) 1895–1986
Nānā i ke kumu (Look to the source)
(A Queen Liliuokalani Children's Center publication)
In English
Bibliography: v. 1, pp. 207–213; v. 2, pp. 317–325.
1. Hawaii — Social life and customs.   I. Haertig, E.W., joint author.   II. Lee, Catherine A., joint author.   III. Title.   IV. Title: Look to the source.   V. Series: Queen Liliuokalani Children's Center.
A publication.
DU624.5.p85   996.9   72-93779

ISBN 978-0-9616738-0-2 (v. 1)
ISBN 978-0-9616738-2-6 (v. 2)

Printed in China

This volume was prepared in cooperation with the Hawaiian Culture Committee of the Queen Liliuokalani Children's Center. It is published through the efforts of *Hui Hānai*, an auxiliary group organized in 1969 to assist in carrying out the objectives of the Queen Liliuokalani Children's Center.

Culture Committee members:
Betty A. Rocha, MSW, ACSW, Chairman
William Apaka, Jr., MSW, ACSW.
Marian C. Haertig, M.A.*
Grace C. Oness, MSW, ACSW.
Richard Paglinawan, MSW, ACSW.

*Marian C. Haertig, psychological consultant, died just as this volume was completed. Her professional insights, warm enthusiasm and encouragement were a constant inspiration. To Marian we say, with sadness, *"Mahalo"* and *"Aloha."*

Foreword

Nānā I Ke Kumu ("Look to the Source") is dedicated to the families and children of Hawaii. It is a source book of Hawaiian cultural practices, concepts and beliefs which illustrate the wisdom and dignity contained in the cultural roots of every Hawaiian child.

The Hawaiian lived for many years isolated from the rest of the world, with a viable culture that met the needs of a thriving, industrious and religious people. Then came the foreigner with his technology and Judeao-Christian culture. He saw the native beliefs as pagan and inferior, and superimposed his culture. In order to gain acceptance, avoid ridicule and disapproval, the Hawaiian gradually adapted to Western ways. However, he secretly hung on to some of the beliefs and ways of his own culture. The confusion in his sense of identity which resulted exists today. For many Hawaiian families today, only the negatives, often in garbled fashion, have persisted. This is complicated further by mergers or conflicts of Hawaiian convictions with other ethnic or religious precepts. Forgotten are the positives in the culture, such as: the importance of the family *('ohana);* the respect for seniors *(kupuna);* insuring harmonious interdependence within the *'ohana* through regular family therapy *(ho'oponopono);* dealing with each successive layer of trouble *(mahiki);* forgiving fully and completely *(mihi);* and freeing each other completely *(kala).* It is this knowledge that the Hawaiian needs to recapture.

The objectives of this work are to provide factual information as accurately as possible in a subject that reaches back to unwritten history and legend, to clarify Hawaiian concepts, and to examine their applicability to modern life.

Volume I culminates seven years of weekly meetings of study and research by the Culture Committee of the Queen Liliuokalani Children's Center, a child welfare agency created by the Deed of Trust of Her Majesty Queen Liliuokalani, to provide services to children of Hawaiian and part-Hawaiian ancestry. This committee was started when, in our work with children and families, many Hawaiian concepts, beliefs and practices emerged. Our staff, confronted by these deeply felt beliefs, felt uncomfortable, and as a result avoided discussion and exploration, even though this hampered successful work in resolving family conflicts. This pointed to our need to learn and understand the authentic Hawaiian culture in order to increase our effectiveness in helping those we serve.

We are fortunate that Mrs. Mary Kawena Pukui, associate of the Bishop Museum, translator and author, agreed to be our *kumu* (this also means teacher). Her belief in our sincere wish to help our people and her recognition that cultural information was of great value, were the motivating factors behind her sharing her knowledge with us. She did express her concern that the concepts in this book not be misused or misunderstood to cause her people embarrassment. (For example, she was once severely criticized for writing an article on *ho'oponopono.*) She believes the Hawaiian needs to understand and appreciate the soundness and beauty of his culture. We are deeply indebted to the contributions of Mrs. Pukui. Without her, this work could not have been done.

In Mrs. Pukui we found the ideal *kumu*. Born in two cultures, she grew up knowing both. In her mother's family line were *kahunas;* in her father's background were the ways of New England. *Hānai'd* as an infant to her maternal grandparents, she was reared to be the family senior. This involved memorizing the old chants, rituals and customs, and learning the meanings and purposes of them. She spoke Hawaiian to her parents and grandparents; at school in Honolulu she was once punished for speaking her ancestral language; later, with Dr. Samuel H. Elbert, she compiled five editions of the definitive *Hawaiian-English, English-Hawaiian Dictionaries.* Mrs. Pukui's childhood acquaintance with Hawaiian customs is reflected in her *Polynesian Family System in Ka'u.* Through the years she enlarged this knowledge by interviewing aged Hawaiians in other regions and other islands, by wide reading, and by translating the work of earlier Hawaiian historians. Today, at 77, she continues to travel and interview, recording her material for the Bishop Museum.

In 1960, the University of Hawaii named Mrs. Pukui an honorary Doctor of Letters.

Throughout *Nānā I Ke Kumu,* Mrs. Pukui is the primary source of all information on Hawaiian culture not otherwise documented.

Dr. E. W. Haertig, the agency's psychiatric consultant, and the late Mrs. Marian Haertig, psychological consultant, have not only contributed greatly in pointing out the parallels or contradictions that exist in Western thought and psychiatric tenets, but also were the morale builders in this project. This stemmed from their firm belief in the value of this work and its use to all who work with Hawaiian people.

Throughout *Nānā I Ke Kumu,* Dr. Haertig is the primary source of psychiatric and medical information unless otherwise noted.

In 1969, Catherine A. Lee, a writer with a background in health education and East-West cultures, was employed. She added to the material accumulated by the committee. It is Mrs. Lee who undertook the difficult task of culling out and condensing the reams of material collected in seven years. We are grateful to her.

Many staff members, particularly those on this committee, provided case material, as well as examples from their own lives, which assisted greatly in making our understanding of Hawaiian concepts more meaningful. Some members, early in our work, felt hesitant about working with this material. Those of Hawaiian ancestry admitted their own fears in relation to some concepts. They now agree that their involvement in the development of this source book has been a key to a better understanding and appreciation of their Hawaiian heritage.

To the readers of this book, our hope is that acceptance or rejection of Hawaiian beliefs is based on understanding, not on old prejudices or current fads. *Nānā I Ke Kumu* is in a sense a bridge linking Hawaii's past and present. How much of the old one wants to carry across that bridge is each person's individual decision.

Betty A. Rocha
Chairman, Culture Committee

Authors' preface

Having completed the rather lengthy delivery of this book, we now yield to a not-uncommon impulse—that of discussing the birth pangs.

In other words, we want to talk about how *Nānā I Ke Kumu,* Vol. I., was written.

The material came from weekly meetings of the Hawaiian Culture Study Committee, recorded and transcribed for a seven year period; the references listed in the Bibliography, and numerous interviews and conferences among the three of us. With the Committee, we selected the major topic listings. To do this we asked some simple questions:

Has the known, identified concept or custom had some effect on lives of Hawaiians within the last ten years? Have Center clients or associates asked for information or showed concern about this specific topic? Or, has the topic been implicitly referred to in dreams recalled or other communications from the unconscious? Or, has the Hawaiian idea or custom influenced lives and been the subject of concern and inquiry—even though the person concerned no longer recalled the Hawaiian term that described it?

If so, then the topic was included. Other terms used within topic discussions were either listed separately or indexed for reference purposes in the Hawaiian Table of Contents. Some terms referred to briefly in this volume will be included in major topic listings in Vol. II, now in preparation. Vol. II will discuss concepts, practices and attitudes concerned with sex, hostility and aggression, child care, guilt and shame, prayer and religious beliefs.

This book is intended primarily for members of the helping professions who work with Hawaiians. These persons include physicians, psychiatrists, nurses, psychologists, social workers, community leaders, the clergy and the various technicians and aides within these groups. We have deliberately avoided the style and jargon of the professional journal. Essential medical and psychiatric terms are explained for readers in other fields.

Because of this focus on a helping-counseling readership, case history material is included, sometimes with suggestions for possible remedial approaches. Identities are disguised; all names are fictitious; most case illustrations are fragmented or are composites.

These case examples may be helpful to readers in the various helping professions. To other readers, case illustrations may give an unbalanced and negative view of the Hawaiian in the present day. For case histories come from troubled and in-trouble Hawaiians. Case examples can be doubly negative because they tell much about the troubled person's difficulties and deficiencies and little about his healthy, positive qualities. Case histories do not come from the many Hawaiians who have adjusted successfully to an imported culture. They do not come from the Hawaiians who, secure in their own self-image, safe in their own reasonable success, prosperity and happiness, are in a position to give rather than receive assistance, counsel and leadership.

There are many references to supernatural or mystic occurrences. Though psychiatric parallels or interpretations, necessary to the purpose of this book are often given, the authors do not consider it their prerogative either to agree or disagree with the preternatural character of the incidents. These mystic experiences have been reported as accurately as possible. Their inclusion in this volume is essential. Hawaiian life and thought cannot be understood without knowing about them.

Perhaps we should list what *Nānā I Ke Kumu* is *not* intended to be.

Our attempt was not for scholarliness, nor for research in the scientific meaning of the term. These have been avoided in the design, staffing and procedures of the study group. Instead, the effort has been to capture the freshness, the intimacy and the "aliveness" of Hawaiian ideas put into action.

In short, this does not purport to be a scholarly nor scientific work. Rather, we hope it is a source book on life as it has been—and often is—still lived.

The book is not a reference work on the Hawaiian language. If a word listed has 16 meanings, but only six denote feelings or behavior or thought patterns, then we listed only those six. For the most part, we have disregarded the Hawaiian plural form and written the commonly used English plural form. *(Akua* becomes *akuas).*

Nānā I Ke Kumu is not a compilation of Hawaiian herbal medicines or physical therapeutics. Monographs on these subjects already exist.

Essentially, we have tried to clarify distorted beliefs, suggest the rationale behind Hawaiian ritual, and convey some of the poetic imagery of ancient rites and their underlying concepts. One way to discuss the purpose and function of a Hawaiian custom is to look for parallels or contradictions with apparently similar customs of other societies. Usually, we drew such comparisons with the Western Christian world. We regret we could not extend this to a comparative study of other great cultures, such as those of the East.

Mary Kawena Pukui
E.W. Haertig, M.D.
Catherine A. Lee

Acknowledgments

The Culture Committee of the Queen Liliuokalani Children's Center is indebted to many individuals, too numerous to list, who have contributed in a variety of ways during the conduct of this study. These include the office workers, the aides, the ministers, lawyers, educators, doctors, nurses, social workers and others who shared their knowledge and expressed their enthusiasm about the work. These include, too, the Center's Advisory Board, a group of interested and dedicated persons who gave of their time and knowledge without compensation. To them goes our *Mahalo nui loa.*

We are grateful to our trustees, Gordon May, Mrs. Clorinda Lucas and the First Hawaiian Bank, represented by Charles Dole. Without their approval none of this work could have been undertaken. Their support reflects not only their belief in us and the value of our Culture Committee, but also their farsightedness. We have only to look at the recent interest in ethnic study programs and in various Hawaiian cultural arts now being widely taught to know that this work is wanted and needed.

We owe special thanks to Myron Thompson, former director of Queen Liliuokalani Children's Center, who recognized the need for this cultural information. To our present director, Masaru Oshiro, a very special thanks, as he has never wavered in his belief in the value of our project.

To our clerical staff and to Blanche Takata, our secretary, we express praise and gratitude. Mrs. Takata handled the numerous tedious tasks and did the volumes of required typing which form so important a part of manuscript preparation.

Hawaiian topic index and reference guide

Bold face type indicates terms or concepts listed and discussed as separate topics. References which define terms or provide some significant information within topic listings are in light-face type. Hawaiian terms merely repeated or used in translated conversations are not indexed.

Nānā i ke kumu
Look to the source

Ask, ask the high-priest,
E ui, e ui i ke kahuna nui,
Generations new, generations past.
I na hanauna hou, na hanauna i hala.

Who is the flower above there?
'Owai ka pua i luna?
What is the work of that god?
He aha ka hana a kēlā akua?

O, generations, O.
E na hanauna, E.
Generations spread again
Na hanauna laha hou
Quickly over the plain.
Me ka hiki wawe, i ke kahua.

Ask, ask the high-priest,
E ui, e ui, i ke kahuna nui,
Generations new, generations past.
I na hanauna hou, na hanauna i hala.

Excerpts from ancient chant, "The Deluge"

'aha'aina and ho'okē'ai—fasting and feasting.

'aha'aina—feast; feasting. Feasts were held for purely human comfort and enjoyment and/or to commune with and seek the help or pardon of the gods. In its supernatural context, a pre-Christian concept.

    Deriv: *'aha,* meeting; gathering; assembly.
            'aina, meal.
            Literally, "meal gathering".

ho'okē'ai—to fast; fasting. Usually a prayerful fasting to gain supernatural help and find solution to a problem. A post-missionary concept.

    Deriv: *ho'o,* to make; to cause; to do.
            kē, shun; avoid; abstain from; refuse.
            'ai, food.
            Literally, "shun food"; "abstain from food".

'aha'aina and ho'okē'ai
A Study of Contrasts and Similarities

'aha'aina
the feast

Before Christianity was brought to Hawaii, both religious occasions and human milestones were observed with feasting. Food, often scarce, was precious. What was precious was symbolically offered to the gods. Also, eating was pleasant. Man felt closer to his fellow man when the *'ōpū* (belly) was being filled. And though the gods were awesome and powerful, they had all the natural appetites and frailties of man. Therefore, would not man and god feel a warm rapport if they ate together?

It seemed so. For the feasts of old Hawaii—and often ordinary meals as well—carried a feeling of eating with and communing with the gods.* This went beyond a ritual offering of the spiritual essence *(aka)* of the food. The god or gods were not offered their portion and then mentally retired to their shelves. A sense of their presence remained throughout the eating. The gap between man and god was indeed narrowed, and the gods were thought more receptive to mortal requests for help or forgiveness.

And so, Hawaiians feasted among themselves and with the appropriate gods on such occasions as the birth of the first child, a child's first birthday, when a young person finished making his first fish net, woven mat, or tapa, or when he caught his first fish.

'aha'aina make
funeral feast

When a relative died, a feast comforted the mourners. This was held immediately after the funeral, and was called the *'aha'aina make* or "feast of *(make)* death". Some Hawaiian families still observe this custom.

---

*Hawaiian men customarily made offerings of food to the household gods during meals in the *hale mua* or "men's eating house". Effigies of the gods were kept here.

1

'aha'aina waimaka
feast of tears

One year later, the *'aha'aina waimaka** or "feast of tears" was held. This was neither an occasion for mourning nor a ritual meal. It was a party for those who the previous year had shed tears together and were now happy together. Early Hawaiians seem to have sensed that the process of grief is normally completed in a year.

Feasting invoked the goddess *Laka* when hula students were graduated. *Lono,* the god who made things grow, was present when feasting marked a boy's exit from the female world of his mother and his entry into masculine life. (See *kā i mua*.)

The dedication of a *heiau* (temple), or an ordinary house, of a canoe or a fish net—all these called for feasting. So did the end of a *kapu* (taboo) season and the harvesting of crops.

'aha'aina kala hala
feast of forgiving

And if man seriously offended a god, he sought forgiveness, not by subjecting his body to hunger, but by invoking his god in the important *'aha'aina kala hala* (literally, "feast to forgive wrong").

In the pre-Christian days of religious feasts, the Hawaiian and his gods were linked by a human-and-supernatural tie, the *aumākua*. Once living forebearers, the *aumākua* were ancestor gods, divine, but still very much *'ohana* (family) members. Thus the Hawaiian feast reinforced both the tie between man and gods and the human bonds of living family. The feast was both a part of religion and a part of the total *'ohana* way of life.

Today the gods are rarely present at the feast, and the *'aha'aina* as a religious observance has almost disappeared. But, let's underline that *"almost"*. As recently as 1969, after a construction worker was accidentally killed on the job, his co-workers held what was surely a ritual *'aha'aina*. A black pig, traditionally most favored by the gods, went into the *imu* (earth oven). But before that some of the blood of the pig was poured on the earth in what may have been a more or less garbled version of early sacrificial offerings.

This is the exception to 20th Century custom. Feasting today is usually a purely human affair—a *lu'au* for family, for employees of Big Business, or for the tourist. The menu is much like that of the old *'aha'aina,* but the symbolism of the food is usually forgotten. Only the tradition-conscious Hawaiian remembers that:

The *pua'a* (pig) had long been the preferred sacrifice to the gods. Taro leaves were a vegetable symbol of the pig; the *āholehole* fish, considered a *pua'a kai* "sea pig", also symbolized and could be a substitute for the real *pua'a*.

Taro, substance of poi,† goes back to the legendary origin of the Hawaiian race. For the first Hawaiian was said to be born as a taro.[1]

Limu kala (seaweed) symbolically unbound or loosened man from wrong doings and mutual hostilities that marred human and human-with-god relationships.

---

*wai (water) + *maka* (eye)—"eye water" or "tears."

†Staple food in the Hawaiian diet.

Chicken *(moa)*, always pleasing to the gods, was once used as the most specific of food offerings. A speckled fowl was sacrificed to gain release from insanity *(pupule)*. A Plymouth Rock was the specific offering for a sickly, whining baby.[2]

Ti leaves, used as tablecloths even in modern *lu'aus*, invoked protection of the gods and purified man from contamination.

The gods may have been deposed and the food symbolism forgotten, but when modern Hawaiians hold an *'aha'aina* much of the spirit of old Hawaii yet lives. Usually dozens of family members, friends and neighbors get together to provide and prepare food, in the mutual helpfulness known as *kōkua* or *laulima* ("many hands"). And certainly, in the eating, drinking, singing and talking together, the ties of man to fellow man are strengthened in the mutual regard and love summed up as *aloha*.

In any culture or time, feasting entails more than surface conviviality. Eating together in leisure and relaxation makes the unconscious a little more accessible. (This does not necessarily apply to the business lunch!) External pressures of work, worry and responsibilities lessen or are laid aside for a time. While the physical "inner man" is being satisfied, the psychological "inner man" to some extent emerges. People know each other on a some-what deeper, more honest level, when they "wine and dine" together. Among Hawaiians, already finely attuned to human relationships, the feast may be a more than ordinarily effective means of getting to know the real person behind the social-conventional facade.

NOTES AND REFERENCES

1. Hawaiian mythology tells that Wakea and Papa ("sky" and "earth") gave birth both to islands and children. The daughter, Ho'ohokuokalani, mated with her father, Wakea. She gave birth first to Hāloa, a child born as a taro. Later she delivered Hāloa, the "younger brother", born as a man. Mystically, man and taro, were the same.

2. Hawaiians believed in "magic by association" of words, appearance or even sound. The speckled fowl was called *pulepule*. *Pulepule* was also a synonym for *pupule* (insane). There-fore, this was the chicken sacrificed to cure a *pupule* person. Use of the Plymouth Rock had an even more intricate rationale. The chicken looked like the Hawaiian goose, the *nēnē*. The real *nēnē* was so named because the syllables sounded something like the bird's cry. A whining, "fussing" baby gives a "nēnē, nēnē, nēnē" sound. Therefore, sacrifice a Plymouth Rock, the "nēnē chicken", to cure the baby.

This meaning-upon-meaning is what makes literal translation of Hawaiian phrases difficult— if not impossible.

ho'okē'ai
the fast

On the last day of March, 1820, the brig *Thaddeus* ended almost a half-year's journey at Kohala, Hawaii. The first organized Protestant missionaries had arrived to teach the "Sandwich Island natives" a new faith and a new way of life. Other missionaries—Catholic, Mormon, representatives of various Protestant sects—followed.

In the years of conversion, Hawaiians were introduced to a new tenet: the religious fast.

It was a startling precept—that the new God actually liked to have men be hungry! For Hawaiians had always invoked their gods by feasting. To go without food deliberately—if anyone had ever considered anything so foolish —would certainly have displeased the gods. The gods themselves were ritually fed. And when humans ate, Hāloa, god of taro, hovered over the *poi* bowl! *Ho'oke ai?* Abstain from food? *'Ano 'e!* (How odd!)*

Yet, converts did accept fasting. Some enthusiasts gave up all religious feasting and substituted the fast. Others, fence straddlers of their day, fasted first, and then had a feast.

Now, in 1971, fasting to ask God's help is common practice with Hawaiians. This is especially true in the Pentecostal faiths, in the small, locally-established Protestant sects with Hawaiian congregations, and among Mormons. Sometimes a minister fasts for someone in his flock. Always, fasting is accompanied by prayer.

A Mormon elder, a Hawaiian, says:

"In fasting, we give the spirit a chance to have ascendance over the body. Sometimes a fast is only for a few meals. If you have a very sick person in the house, you fast all day for him . . . or two or three days . . . A fasting person can say in his prayer, 'I come before Thee in fast.' . . . No, you don't tell the whole world you're fasting. You can fast and go about your normal business. You can fast and enjoy life. You don't have to go around dragging your beard!"

In contrast with this matter-of-fact short fast is the vigil described by the Hawaiian minister of the church her family founded. She tells that:

"When my *hānai*** daughter was in an accident and the doctor said he didn't know if she would live, I went into fast . . . asking if it was my mistake or her real parents' [mistake] that had caused this . . . in the Bible I found out that it was my mistake.†

". . . so for seven days I stayed in the church, night and day. I never went out to eat or drink water. On Saturday I came out and had a meal. I went back in on Sunday and stayed another week. I did this for three weeks. When I went in, I weighed 257 pounds. I lost 67. And she pulled through . . . I gave God thanks. I put my mind so strongly in His love, and I trusted Him . . . He wouldn't refuse me."

"Were you ever weak or giddy?" she was asked.

"No. The psalms are my standbys. I started on the First Psalm, and every day I read and studied a certain psalm, and I began to not crave food . . . Oh, sometimes at night I would dream that someone had brought me water . . . or a whole tray of food. I would eat and drink in my dream. Next morning I would feel full."

"You mean you never felt hungry?"

"When I began to, I would open my Bible and read it. Then I wouldn't feel hungry at all."

She then told the parable of the loaves and fishes. The 12 baskets of bread that remained after the miracle she compared to the people who came "hungry for the Word and physically hungry, too." The actual, nourishing bread they received was also the spiritual "bread of life—the Word of God."

Thus, in her own fasting, "God provided the Bread of Life" that satisfied both the soul and the hunger pangs of the body.

Without use of such metaphors, numerous Hawaiians, lay and clergy, speak of "fasting and praying when we need Divine guidance".

---

*Literally, "An odd one".

**Hawaiian style adoption. Binding in everything but legal sense.

†Finding passage at random and interpreting it as answer. See *wehe i ka Paipala*.

Why should a food-loving, pleasure-loving people who once fed their gods adopt anything as ascetic and self-denying as fasting?

Explanation is, at best, speculative. One fact that sparks speculation is that fasting and feasting have certain similarities. Fasting, like feasting, brings the unconscious closer to conscious thought and expression (see 'aha 'aina, the feast). In both, outside influences and distractions are lessened; one's "inner" thoughts are more likely to be expressed. Dreaming is more vivid and prolific.

Both these dreams and conscious thoughts give more information about one's real wishes, urges, loves, fears and conflicts. For the "feaster," full, fat and content, warm feelings for his fellow feasters usually emerge. (Or, hostility, if, deep-down he really hates the man across the table.) For the fasting person, "buried" thoughts of parents, bygone loves, a forgotten experience—these are only a few examples—may surface. In the religious fast, the mind is already attuned to the supernatural. Previously repressed thoughts are therefore likely to appear as God-given help, or may even find climax in an ecstatic religious experience.

Fasting and feasting also have in common a mind-and-body feeling of satiety with pleasure, calm content—or even euphoria. These feelings come with changing body chemistry.

In the first stages of fasting, the body metabolizes its stores of sugar. This process lasts approximately 48 hours. During this initial sugar-metabolizing period, all the miseries of hunger are felt.

Then comes relief.

After the stored-up sugars are used, the body starts to metabolize fats (and, at first, very small amounts of protein). As the fats are metabolized, chemical products of this metabolic process appear. These are collectively titled "ketone bodies." They are appetite suppressants and "mood lifters." As the ketone bodies build up sufficiently, hunger pangs disappear. The fasting person feels nicely full. He also feels happy, perhaps buoyed up on a tide of well-being.

In an extended fast, physical deterioration results as protein is used up. But, if water intake is adequate, fasting after the first 48 hours is not just physically and emotionally bearable, but is a pleasant or even ecstatic experience.

The minister who reported her long fast expressed this parallel course of changing body chemistry and psychological-spiritual euphoria. Some of her statements are significant: "I had plenty of fat to use up." And, "The Word of God fed me and I didn't feel hungry."

We can speculate that Hawaiians may have adopted fasting as a dramatic proof of conversion. For, in refusing food, they cast off the old gods so closely linked with food.

We have no sure "answers". Merely theoretical surmises. However, it seems evident that fasting contradicts a basic Hawaiian philosophy that chose pleasure rather than pain, self-gratification rather than self-denial.

The early Hawaiian made his contact with the supernatural through satisfying, rather than depriving himself of food. And if the gods demanded human offerings, the defeated enemy and the kauwā (slave caste) were killed. Self-sacrifice in ritual suicide was not practiced. Penitential starvation and flagellation were unknown. Self-mutilation was pupule (insane) behavior.[1] There were no mutilating rites in puberty. The body was to be fed, massaged, molded to beauty, taught the arts of love—and, in general, enjoyed.

If, in the past, fasting was an obvious, observable way of disclaiming old gods and old ways associated with them, it does not always follow that the modern, fasting Hawaiian denies his cultural past. Among Center clients and associates[2] are many Hawaiians who fast. These include persons who believe "being Hawaiian is bad" and persons who are genuinely proud of being Hawaiian. The fast is today simply an accepted religious practice.

NOTES

1. Self-mutilation. In extreme grief over the death of a beloved *ali'i,* mourners once might knock out teeth, scar their faces or in rare instances scoop out their eyes. This, sometimes accompanied by wild, lawless behavior and the uncovering of the genitals, was done because the mourner was believed *"pupule"* or "crazy" with grief.

2. Ministers of various faiths met with the Hawaiian Culture Study Committee; others were interviewed by the writer. In addition, relatives of Hawaiian staff members recounted their experiences and views on fasting.

'ai—eat, to eat, eating; food, particularly *poi* or vegetable food. Meat and fish were originally called *i'a.* Also to destroy. To consume.

Deriv: unknown

A clue to the needs and values of early Hawaiian culture comes in Mary Pukui's statement, "we have not a single word for 'time' but many for food and eating."

There was good reason for prizing food and the *piha ka 'ōpū* or "well filled belly." Hawaiians enjoyed feasting; they also knew and dreaded hunger. Prayers to prevent famine were said.[1] Hungry experience taught the wisdom of storing food.

Mrs. Pukui tells that "in Ka'u my people dried sweet potatoes and stored them in refuge caves against war and drought." An account that apparently makes legend from a basis of truth tells of the navigator king Makalii who "... during a season of great fertility sent his messengers all over the country and collected all the food they could get and stored it up in [his] storehouses..."[2] Even in peaceful, happy times, obtaining food, whether taro from the patch, or fish from the sea, demanded time, patience, prayers and ritual on the part of commoners. Only the *ali'i* (aristocracy) had food furnished them.

So important was *'ai* that the gods were ritually fed, and feasting was a religious as well as a social rite. This is discussed under *'aha'aina.* A thief in early Hawaii was an *'aihue,* one who snatched food from someone else. Literally, *'ai* (food) *hue* (light-fingered; to filch). And if someone was "sick and tired" of something, he was *'aikena,* from *'ai* + *kena* (satisfied, satiated). He was "fed up."

Eating (and drinking) could indicate social, religious and sexual status. *'Awa,* the ceremonial liquor and social relaxant, was reserved for *ali'i* (aristocracy) and *kahunas* (priests; doctors) only, though this distinction was often disregarded.[3]

Eating segregated the men from the women—and the men from the boys. Women could not eat with the men, nor did little boys until after the ceremony that marked their entry into man's world. (See *kā i mua*). Women and little boys were not allowed pork, for the pig *(pua'a)* was the favored sacrifice of the gods. At one time, women were denied the yellow coconut, most varieties of bananas, the *ulu* and *kumu* fish, and some other sea foods.[4]

It was this sex-segregated food *kapu* that set the stage for Hawaii's first dramatic denial of the old religion. For this *kapu* was believed straight from the gods. When Kaahumanu openly ate with Liholiho in 1819, her act was public symbol of a clear break with the gods, and the beginning of a new social order.[5]

Less dramatically, food and plenty of it, was tied in with approved appearance and social standing. An ideally beautiful women had "a face as round and full as the moon." An early description of a king's daughter read, "she was not very big, *but* she had pretty features."[6] Royalty might be as fat as Princess Ruth who was known to eat 13 *haupia* pies at one sitting.[7] Mothers worried when their daughters were thin and gave them medicine to fatten them.[8] Only the men ever reduced, and that was done to get themselves in fighting trim. Possibly, one purpose of the *Makahiki* games was to get the warriors in shape for battles to come. In fact, the only mention of reducing we have seen applies to men:

"People in the old days liked *'awa* as a means of reducing weight. When a man saw himself growing too fat and subject to illness, the best thing was to drink copiously like the gods and like those possessed of the spirit until the skin scaled . . . buy a large quantity to drink and eat nothing between meals."[9]

At any rate, a look at the sketches of early Hawaiians by Choris makes it pretty clear that while warriors cultivated muscles and kept agile for warfare, pounds, curves, and dimples remained a girl's best friend.

If pounds were approved, so were the methods of putting on pounds. Hospitality was the rule; stinginess was beyond contempt. *"Kāhea 'ai. 'Ai a ma'ona"* ("Come in and eat, eat all you want") was the accepted greeting, even to comparative strangers.

ho'i no 'ai i kou kahu
Go back and destroy your keeper

'Ai, the verb meaning "to eat," carried a figurative second meaning of "to consume" or "to destroy" in the sense of causing death. The meaning took on supernatural connotations, for this death-dealing destruction was done by spirits often sent through the mystic spells of a sorcerer.

One of the most useful of Hawaii's early ritual phrases was *"ho'i no 'ai i kou kahu,"* meaning "go back and destroy—really kill—your keeper." This was said to the spirit sent by a sorcerer to inflict illness or death. This phrase was based on the cultural conviction that a blameless person need not accept a sorcerer's spell but could return it to its sender. From the sorcerer's viewpoint, any harm he sent out might well boomerang back on him. Or, to put it in a timeless and universal context, anyone who directs hostility and instigates harm to another person, usually sets into motion a chain of counter hostilities which eventually rebound.

7

'aihamu
to kill recklessly

'Aihamu denoted in general a lack of discrimination. Literally, 'aihamu meant to eat left-over food or thrown out food scraps. This was done not because of thrift, but because the person lacked fastidiousness. He was disgustingly greedy. In its more often used figurative meaning, 'aihamu referred to destroying or killing recklessly and without judgment or discrimination. 'Aihamu was wanton murder. The word often referred to a sorcerer (kahuna 'anā'anā) who killed without reason. The "discriminating" sorcerer killed on an assignment basis. His black art was directed at a particular person or persons, not to wholesale destruction. For a fee, he would destroy an enemy. If he "wiped out" many persons for the sheer lust of killing, his behavior was called 'aihamu.

'ai akua
eat for a spirit

'Ai akua or "eating for a spirit" was believed to be done when a human was possessed (noho) by a spirit who wanted food. In these cases, Mrs. Pukui recalls, the mortal consumed unbelievable quantities of food. A canoe-ful of fish! A whole barrel of poi at one sitting. The enormous amounts of food made 'ai akua clearly different from mere over-eating. Mrs. Pukui believes the tradition of 'ai akua resulted from seeing bereaved persons eat unusual amounts in the days when ordinary meals were already large.

In a 1968 'ai akua mention, one mother said that her son was possessed by the spirit of her recently deceased husband. "He is eating for his father's spirit," she told the social worker.

In this particular example, the son had seemingly developed a voracious appetite after his father's death, apparently as a response to grief and generally disturbed family relationships. Today when 'ai akua is related by clients, very probably eating has become "comfort in crisis." Or, as in this case, the woman, deprived of her husband, may have simply transferred her attention to her child, either plying him with food or merely taking fresh notice of his ordinary eating habits. The "spirit" eaten for, seems actually to have been the "spirit of unrest" in the household.

'ai in the 1970's

How important is food to the Hawaiians in the 1970s? The reader's answer may vary, depending on how long ago he attended a Hawaiian luau, and how much of the delicious food he ate at that time! Obviously, good food and plenty of it is still a part of the good life. The specific rituals associated with 'ai may be virtually forgotten. The conviction that food is good, fat is approved, and hospitality is demanded lives on. Hawaiian clients still greet the social worker with a cheerful, "Mai, mai, komo mai (Come in, come in). Mai e 'ai! (Come and eat!)"

One young social worker from the mainland refused the invitation. Word soon filtered back to him: "He is ho'okano. He is stuck up—he thinks he is too good for us and our food." There followed a lesson in the etiquette of eating as the Hawaiians see it.

Said Mrs. Pukui, "When anyone is invited to eat, he is expected to take something. The Hawaiians believed that a person who refused to eat their food was $p\bar{i}$ (stingy). They believed that anyone who was unable to accept was also unable to give."

Advised an experienced social worker married to a Hawaiian, "When a client offers you food, take something. Take a token bite or two, or a cup of coffee. To flatly refuse Hawaiian hospitality is a genuine insult."

Today, non-Hawaiians are particularly concerned about the health hazards of the Hawaiian love of food. How much this concern is justified is open to debate. One Island-born, non-Hawaiian physician says bluntly, "Hawaiians are dying off because of their eating habits." Many physicians are concerned about the high incidence of hypertension, strokes, heart and arterial vascular diseases among overweight Hawaiians. On the other hand, Kanae Kaku, M.D., statistician-epidemiologist, Regional Medical Program, says:

"I am not entirely sure that obesity in the Hawaiians is directly connected to blood vessel diseases. It may be more associated with the Hawaiian physique. A Hawaiian policeman or fireman, for example, may look big and stout, but this may be based on bone structure and physique."

When the Hawaiian must diet for the sake of his health, both he and his physician face a four-star, class A problem! The Hawaiian may politely and cheerfully shrug off diet advice. A Department of Health nutritionist reports that Hawaiian women respond to diet instructions with: "But my husband likes me fat." "But it's good to eat lots of food." Jerry Conover of the Hawaii Heart Association is convinced that some obese Hawaiians who show evidence of heart disease would prefer a heart attack to reducing. Warnings that they must diet are often answered with: "I like eating." "Food is good."

Donald Char, M.D., Director of the Student Health Service, University of Hawaii, says, "the Hawaiian will stay temporarily on a diet because of a friendly, person-to-person relationship with his doctor. When this relationship is diminished, he falls off his diet. Anyone is apt to do that, but the Hawaiian has a special problem. The dieter gets no support at home." Dr. Char suggests two approaches to be used with youthful dieters. One, especially for boys, is a camp for dieters, with sports and vigorous exercise, and a training table regime. For girls he suggests homemaker type clubs, which would meet where kitchen facilities were available. Girls would actually plan and cook low-calorie meals. Nutritionists and fashion experts to help supply motivation for slimness should all be low-key consultants, not platform lecturers. The camp and the club would supply group spirit and support. Everyone would be learning together to diet. The Center's psychiatric consultant suggests qualitative rather than quantitative diets, the substitution of good tasting, low-calorie foods rather than the withdrawal of food. Positive suggestions to put pleasure into dieting are needed. For the joys of 'ai are many; Hawaiians are not about to give them up. Or, as one Hawaiian responded when his doctor warned him he must diet if he wanted to live.

"So maybe I die, if I no stop eat. More better I die happy."

REFERENCES

1. Beckwith. *Kepelino's Traditions of Hawaii*, p. 18.

2. Titcomb. *Kava in Hawaii*, p. 107.

3. Ibid, pp. 1, 2, 6, 138, 237.

4. *Kepelino's Traditions of Hawaii*, p. 64.

5. Kamakau. *Ruling Chiefs of Hawaii*, pp. 219-228.

6. Fornander. *Collection of Hawaiian Antiquities*, Vol. 4, p. 504.

7. Personal informant, 1961.

8. Pukui. *Polynesian Family System in Ka'u*, p. 93.

9. *Kava in Hawaii*, p. 121.

aka —

Deriv: unknown

The word has at least four meanings that may have significance in the behavioral sciences. *Aka* can mean:

1. Knuckles of hands or joints.
   Pilikia (trouble) or *ma'i* (sickness, discomfort) in the *aka* could be an old Hawaiian's description of arthritic pains.

2. An embryo in early development stage, or a just-hatched fish which is still transparent and somewhat resembles an embryo. (Loss of an embryo through miscarriage may be background for old belief that *mo'o* [fish-like or "water spirit"] infants were born from human-supernatural union.)

3. The essence of anything, in the spiritual rather than material form. When food was offered to a god, it was understood that the god would be nourished by the *aka,* and a mortal would later eat the food. The ritual phrase was *"O ke aka ka 'oukou e ke akua, 'o ka 'i'o ka mākou,"* "Yours is the essence, O god; ours the material part." Rituals and reasons for feeding gods are discussed under *akua, akualele, 'unihipili,* and *'aha'aina.*

4. A shadow. In a sense, a living person's spirit. Also, very close to the concept of a shadow, a reflection glimpsed in the water or a ghostly image seen in moonlight.

The feeling that one's shadow was a visualization of one's own personality, living spirit or mystic essence was demonstrated in many beliefs of old Hawaii.

In one view, man's shadow contained some of his *mana* (spiritual power). No one, commoner or lesser *ali'i* (aristocracy), dared let his shadow fall on the highest ranking, *kapu* (sacred) chief, possessor of greatest *mana.* Nor could the *kapu* chief risk letting his shadow fall on anyone else, lest its tremendous *mana* destroy or harm him. One of the slave caste *(kauwā)* could not let his shadow fall on anyone who was not *kauwā,* for some people considered his *mana* repulsive. Others thought the *kauwā* had no *mana* at all, and the touch of such a shadow was an insult.

Even certain plants sacred to Lono were grown in a clearing where no other plant cast a shadow. (This may have come from observing that certain plants flourish in direct sunlight.)

These old beliefs concerning one's *aka* have, so far, not been mentioned by Center clients. We include them here because much of Hawaiian belief that is not openly discussed does hold a place in the unconscious. This has been brought out in dreams and in such experiences as *noho* (possession).

akakū, hihi'o and 'ūlāleo—visions and supernatural voice or sound.

akakū—vision, or to see a vision; also trance or reflection, as in a pool or mirror.

Deriv: *aka,* shadow; image; also spiritual essence.
ku, to stand, stop or halt (and 15 other meanings).
Literally, *akakū* is a "standing or halted shadow." A shadow was given great mystic significance in old Hawaii. The *akakū* type of vision can be seen in daylight and when one is completely awake.

hihi'o—vision; also dream as described below.

Deriv: unknown.
The *hihi'o* vision is the fleeting one seen in the just going to sleep (hypnagogic) or just awakening (hypnapompic) states. Because the *hihi'o* is seen in this half-awake, half-asleep state, the term is also defined as dream, but not the sound asleep dreaming called *moe'uhane.*

'ūlāleo—supernatural voice or sound; the hearing of such a voice or sound.

Deriv: *'ula,* spirit or ghost; sacred.
leo, voice or sound.
Literally, "spirit voice" or "sacred sound."

Uncounted centuries ago, so goes the legend, the goddess Pele heard the beat of ghostly drums, an *'ūlāleo* which led her from Puna, Hawaii, to Kauai.

Sometime in the late 1700s, one account tells, Kamehameha the Great saw a *hihi'o.* In this vision, he was given three additional *inoas* or names.[1]

In 1970, a 22-year-old Hawaiian, sitting in his beloved, souped-up "dragster," had the following experience:

"I was just taking it easy. It was broad daylight—about two in the afternoon—and I was wide awake. All of a sudden, my father [dead 10 years] came up and spoke to me. He told me to straighten up. Make a man of myself."

Such are a few of Hawaii's *akakūs, hihi'os* and *'ūlāleos.* They are kin to, but not identical with, the ghosts and demi-gods, giants and other *'e'epa* (strange and inexplicable) beings that made up a mystic population of old. The ghosts and *kupuas* (demi-gods), and to some extent, the giants, have been laid to rest somewhere in spirit land. The visions and voices are today just as existent, lively and eloquent as ever. At least this is true in the Hawaiian communities the Center knows.

Center case reports for 1969-70 are filled with accounts like the following:

"I had this vision of grandmother . . . I knew she was telling me to change my ways."

"I heard a voice. It told me my grandson should be named _____."

"After _____ [husband] died, the children would hear his footsteps . . . _____ [a daughter] saw him three times."

"Every time my husband and I quarrel, grandfather comes to me. He beckons me. Tells me to come to him. But my husband holds me back, so I can't go."

The examples distinguish the *akakū, hihi'o* and *'ūlāleo* from their preternatural brotherhood of things envisioned and heard. Both ghosts and giants used to appear in rather malicious play. One ancient folktale tells of summoning up "ten bald-headed ghosts" for a battle of wits more grim than playful.[2] And in the 20th Century, a part-Hawaiian reports that "my uncle got drunk and giants pushed him into the ditch."[3] And always, on the nights of Kane was heard the ghostly marching tread of long-departed chiefs.[4]

visions warn
and advise

In contrast, most of the visions and voices that clients report are the Mary Worths and the Dear Abbys of the spirit realm. They are the advice-givers. The dispensers of guidance, cautions, or at least significant messages usually interpreted as warning or counsel. The vision or voice is a *hō'ailona* or portent which leads to the revelation-like understanding of the message *(hō'ike)*. (See listing titled *hō'ailona* and *hō'ike.*) These visions and voices occur for a purpose.

In addition to being purposeful, visions and voices of today share other characteristics. A study of Center case reports from 1965 to September, 1970, provides the following generalizations:

Hawaiians of all
ages see visions

Clients of all ages and of both sexes report these visual-aural experiences. Even children too young to talk are thought to see visions. As a Hawaiian minister explained to parents in one case, "Little children are especially susceptible to seeing things."* Hawaiian tradition tells that dogs also may see visions.

known dead are
usually seen

A vision is nearly always of a known, identified person, who in life had been emotionally close to the visionary. A vision of a living person is rarely reported. Traditionally, this was believed possible, though it was rare and often a faked experience.[5]

A voice may be either known or unknown. The unidentified voice is sometimes thought to be that of an *aumakua* (ancestor god). This follows traditional belief.

grandparents most
often envisioned

Visions of a grandparent or grandchild are reported slightly more often than visions of parents or child. This is in keeping with Hawaii's old *hānai* (adoption-like) practice. In this a grandparent was given a grandchild, and the relationship that resulted was stronger than that of parent and child. Customarily, grandparents also took over the education of all grandchildren.

---

*Children have a "special talent" for experiencing as sensory perceptions the moods and tensions of those around them. The younger the child, the keener is this ability. A very young baby senses his mother's nervous-emotional states in how she holds him, the sound of her voice, and other, more subtle ways. The child that screams in wide-eyed terror is responding not to "seeing something" but to sensing tensions in others. This sensory reception of human stresses and anxious response can also be noticed in pet animals.

A vision is seen as an almost-real presence, rather than a nebulous wraith. Clothing, appearance and mannerisms are often described in detail. The phrases, "I saw Grandma" or "Kimo appeared," are used more often than "I saw a vision of Grandma" or "Kimo's spirit appeared."

visions of Pele

The only Hawaiian deity envisioned in these present-day cases is the volcano goddess, Pele. Clients say they have seen Pele as a young, beautiful woman, an old, distraught woman, a woman dressed in red, or a woman dressed in white. This is in accord with legends that tell of Pele's delight in traveling in various forms. Pele in white has traditionally been interpreted as a warning of sickness; Pele in red as a coming volcanic eruption.

In a very few cases, clients have told of seeing the Christian God, sometimes alternately with traditional Hawaiian visions. Adults involved had joined at various times Catholic, Protestant and Eastern faiths, and alternately stressed or denied their Hawaiian heritage.

The Christian God or Hawaiian *aumakua* or perhaps both may have been seen in what is often called the "universal vision." This is the vision onlookers ascribe to the dying. Approximately a century ago, Kamakau wrote:

death visions
past & present

"I have seen . . . a man smiling, and his cheeks dimpling with laughter, and if you asked him the reason for his happiness, he would tell how the door of heaven had opened, and a wondrous beauty not seen in this world had been revealed, and that he heard many voices calling him to go there. For such a person, the *'ao aumākua* [most personalized ancestor gods] were ready to welcome him . . . at whatever place was prepared for him in this *aumākua* realm by the 'guardian angels' and the *luna aumakua* [overseeing guardian spirit]."

(Kamakau, like many early converts to Christianity, bent and twisted Hawaiian gods to fit Western spiritual imagery. Turning the named, ancestral *aumākua* into the nameless, unrelated guardian angels was often done.)

Kamakau's observations are echoed in late 20th century accounts of death-visions: "_____ smiled and said, 'They are coming for me!'" . . . "Mama called out, 'Where are you taking me? Yes, I'm coming,' and then she dropped dead." . . . "Tutu sat up in bed and said, 'Look! The relatives [*aumākua*] are waiting for me!' and then she was gone." These are typical reports. The facial expressions are described as "happy," "peaceful," "filled with joy," "contented." No description suggests religious ecstasy.

animals, objects
seen in visions

Occasionally, animals or objects are seen in present-day visions. "Pele's little white dog" is sometimes described. Clients may interpret any type of envisioned dog as being Pele's spirit. This agrees with traditional belief that gods could change from human to animal, plant or mineral form. (See *kino lau*). Sometimes the dog is thought to be the spirit of a deceased human. This has historic precedent; giving a cat this spirit significance does not. Early Hawaii did not have cats.

When an inanimate object is envisioned, it is given symbolic meaning. A Hawaiian staff member with a gift for reporting as well as rapport gives this account of a 1970 visit with a non-client Hawaiian family. During dinner, the staff member had talked about a planned trip to another island. She relates:

"After dinner, _____ called me aside and told me in Hawaiian that she had a vision while we were eating . . . She had seen a little box on my shoulder. Then the box fell off.

"This means your pathway will be clear. There will be no *ku'ia'* [meeting of obstacle, either physical or mental] she told me.

"'Oh, thank you!' I said. 'I am so grateful. So glad.'"

reactions to visions

Reaction to a vision or mystic voice follows—with a few dramatic exceptions—an almost typical pattern: The vision or voice itself seldom frightens; the message may. Anxiety is apt to be present when the message is not understood. For example, the following account from a woman who frequently visited her dead son's grave:

"When I was almost there, I saw him . . . young and well. Oh, I was so upset! I threw myself on the grave and said, 'What's wrong? What is it? What are you trying to tell me?'"

More often, the vision that does not convey a specific message is interpreted as, "This was Mother's love coming through to me" . . . "He was sending his love and strength."

death portent frightens

Fright at seeing a vision often stems from the belief that the vision "has come for me" or from a confused mixture of Hawaiian and Christian, old and new beliefs. (Let's postpone any discussion of subjective fears or wishes and look at Hawaii's traditional vision-beliefs.) Tradition says that a vision may mean the viewer is going to die. However, the vision almost never was thought to *cause* the death. The spirit of the loved dead did not—as one frantic teen-ager thought—turn into an "evil spirit. A demon come to get me!" Here, Christian concepts of the devil were garbled with Hawaiian beliefs.

visions often bring solace

As a rule, both the vision and the message bring comfort and solace. The "ghost horror" of other cultures does not seem to exist. Why be afraid of Grandfather, just because he is dead? He is still very near and very dear to us. Such is the prevailing sentiment.

More often than not, Hawaiians interpret their own visions. They seek other's interpretation of dreams. Just because a patient or agency client talks about his visions or voices does not mean he wants to be "cured" of them. A recurring vision may be loved and cherished (or should we say a loved and cherished vision is apt to recur?). But no matter what was seen or heard, whether vision or voice brought reassurance or apprehension, all Hawaiian visionaries share the same trait. They want, even need, to talk about the experience.

So, for a page or two, let's forget the viewer-of-visions and concentrate on the listener: The social worker, nurse or physician on the other side of the desk.

How does he respond to talk of mystic visitations?

Sometimes with a feeling of unease or even embarrassment.

The non-Hawaiian listener may wish the vision would just go away. This seems to have operated in one case in which the advice given was to "keep busy and forget about it."

Or, almost unintentionally, the listener may simply shift the conversation to another topic.

Or perhaps the visionary himself can be wished away with the magic-in-triplicate of the referral.

vision or hallucination?
Hawaiian diagnostic tests

Or, the professional worker may ask himself: Is this person psychotic, seriously neurotic, or is he merely following his cultural heritage? Is this vision-seeing, voice-hearing simply normal Hawaiian behavior?

Hawaiians of the past asked substantially the same questions. They knew that a visionary might or might not be mentally normal. In fact, they had their own diagnostic methods to distinguish the rational from the irrational person. To do this, they first looked at the vision itself. Was it a "true" (culturally normal) vision? Or was it a "wrong" vision (pathological hallucination)? Mary Kawena Pukui summarizes the criteria:

"When one person in a group sees a vision or hears a voice, but nobody else does—or even senses it—then it is not a true vision or voice. It came from inside the person's own mind.* The person is probably *hewa hewa* [odd; eccentric] or maybe *'ōpulepule* [slightly or temporarily crazed].

"But if everyone sees or hears or senses a presence, then the voice or vision is a true one. It is *there*. Right there with the people."

If one saw a vision when he was alone, there were other ways to distinguish true mystic presence from hallucination. Again, quoting Mrs. Pukui,

"A vision that nobody else can understand is a wrong vision."

Other criteria depended heavily on hindsight:

"When a voice tells a person to climb a cliff, and the person climbs and falls and gets hurt, then this is not a true vision. Or, when strange lights lead a fisherman on to places where there are no fish, this is not a true *'ūlāleo*. The person just imagined the voice and the lights."

Which brings Mrs. Pukui to the general guideline:

"A true vision or voice does not harm. It comes to tell you something or to advise and help."

old criteria
still useful

These criteria of old remain surprisingly useful today. One reason is that they entailed much more than judging the vision. Studied along with the vision was its effect on the visionary's safety, well-being and peace of mind; its ap-

---

*In old Hawaii the word would have been *na'au* (intestines). Intellect and emotions were thought to exist in the intestines, rather than in brain or heart.—M.K.P.

propriateness to what we now label his "life style;" and whether the vision was a comprehensible one with a helpful purpose, or simply a confused and confusing experience of sight or hearing.

The many present-day cases in which a grandparent or parent appears and gives advice, warning or comfort are obvious examples of the comprehensible, usually non-pathological visions. And when others see or sense that "Grandma is with us," the balance swings even more over to the culturally normal. Even if this is group response to the power of suggestion (hō'upu'upu), it is operating within the context of Hawaiian life.

Hawaii's criterion that a vision everyone can understand is a true (benign) one finds a close parallel in modern diagnostic judgment. The center's psychiatric consultant explains:

"When a vision is rather clearly and readily comprehensible in terms of what is known about the person, and about the person seen in the vision (presuming such knowledge is adequate and accurate), then in all probability this is not a psychotic manifestation. Nor even necessarily a neurotic one, though hallucinatory experiences may come in some of the neuroses.

"Whereas, if a vision is relatively unintelligible in the light of the person and his life, it is much more likely to be a symptom of something seriously wrong."

vision reveals
unconscious

To the professional worker, the normal vision or voice is comprehensible in yet another sense. It is fairlyrtransparent and has little distortion. In contrast, the pathological hallucination has much distortion and disguise. It is difficult to "read"—more difficult than a dream. However, the culturally normal vision gives a fairly direct pathway to the unconscious.

What the unconscious frequently reveals is grief. A dead person is seen. The message from the unconscious may be as clear as "Please come back. My life is so empty without you!"

Sometimes revealed is the simple "guilty conscience" at disapproved behavior: "Father appeared and told me to make a man of myself." "Grandma came and told me to change my ways."

Often the love-hostility-guilt blend that is a normal part of grieving is expressed and finds some assuagement in the vision. The dead returns in love and friendship with the message that no grudge is held; no ill-will is felt.

The simple need for reassurance in personal crisis may take the form of a vision. This is common in illness with its emotional regression to childhood. A typical account: "Father always comes when I am sick. He tells me not to give up. He tells me I will get well."

Sometimes the veil between unconscious wish expressed in a vision, and conscious, stated thought is thin indeed. The report that "Grandfather appears ... He tells me to come to him" was followed by "Sometimes I wish I could go with Grandfather."

The wish to return to ancestral ways may have been a part of the following 'ūlāleo experience. A non-client, a middle-aged woman active in Hawaiian civic and social circles, tells:

"I had been very ill, and I was terribly depressed. One day I went to sit beside the stream near our house. I was sitting there, not thinking of anything in particular, when I heard my grandfather say, 'Something is the matter with you. You're sick.' Then he said, 'Girl, you are looking at your medicine.' I turned around, but nobody was there. Then Grandfather repeated, 'You are sick and your medicine is in front of you.'

"I looked down, and all I saw was the water running over the rocks, and the *limu** flowing. I knew Grandfather had come to help me, so I started thinking and thinking about what his message meant . . . then I knew. The *limu* was the medicine."

The woman then gathered *limu,* and for five days ate nothing but the plant. She drank only black coffee.

Both vision and interpretation were, with one marked exception, very much in the Hawaiian pattern. Grandfather's appearing, use of *limu* as medicine, and the ritual "five" all follow ethnic prototypes. Only the woman's decision to fast did not. Fasting is a Christian import. Perhaps this is a good place to point out that neither vision nor resulting action must be "one hundred percent Hawaiian" to qualify the visionary as mentally normal. The woman in this instance is intelligent, rational—and notably attuned to her Hawaiian background.

(This incident illustrates common pre-conditions of a vision. Water running over rocks, the flow of the *limu,* the mind not focused on "anything in particular"—the total mesmeric situation was ideal for hearing a voice or seeing a vision. Self-hypnosis certainly may have been involved. The idea of taking *limu* for medicine may have been a recovery of forgotten information from the unconscious.)

In contrast to this normal, very much Hawaiian vision, are visions—often recurring ones—that are a hodge-podge of religious-cultural and other ideas. These visions are more likely to be psychotic or neurotic hallucinations. For example, one client often has the virtually "standard" vision of Grandfather. She also sees "blood dripping down from the ceiling," and tells that, "I was lying down and the devil jumped right on me!"

However, even a mixed bag of variegated visions does not by itself provide a diagnosis. Psychiatry and medicine remind us that a diagnosis is made on a syndrome, not on a symptom. This holds true whether the decision is "Yes, this person is psychotic," or "No, this person, eccentric though he seems, is not psychotic." With a truly Hawaiian person, close to his cultural roots, his visions may not even be symptoms, in the strict sense of the term.

---

*Any kind of plant that grows in fresh or salt water. Most often used to mean seaweed.

Visual or auditory hallucinations or both are usually present in schizophrenia. But also present are many other indications of personality disorganization, such as disorientation, disturbances of function, various kinds of bizarre thinking, and various disturbances of affect (emotions). The individual may become infuriated for no apparent reasons. Or, he may become extremely happy or giggly* or grief-stricken—all for reasons that are meaningless to anyone else.

In a psychosis, hallucinations do not appear until the beginning of a psychotic break. At about this time, others may sense a personality change in the individual. Another personality seems to take over. This is close to what Hawaiians perceived in one who was *noho* (possessed by a spirit). In schizophrenia, the "lost" personality is replaced—but the replacement is apt to be disorganized and not integrated.

Or, what may be sensed instead is an almost complete absence of emotion or affect. Others may feel that here is a person "in a cocoon" or "frozen in a block of ice."

On the other hand, the person not psychotic but seeing what Hawaiians call "true" visions makes a quite different impression on others. One senses a fairly normal range of emotions. This may be somewhat limited, simply because the person is absorbed in his visionary experience. But the severe deadening or absence of emotion is not perceived.

The non-psychotic visionary also demonstrates little or none of the inappropriate emotions, "far out" thinking, or functional disturbances, or if he does, physical factors may be the cause. His actions and emotional responses make sense to others. So do his visions—*if the observer is informed about Hawaiian visions!*

(One of the most misunderstood Hawaiians of the present day may be the old gentleman on a neighbor island who sees "balls of fire in the sky." "Grandpa's crazy" say his descendants. Perhaps he is senile. He is not a Center client so we do not know. However, his visions might be culturally normal ones. They might be the "flying gods" described under *akualele* or the "*aumakua* lights" often called "lights of Kane," seen when *aumakua* accompanied the marching chiefs on the nights of Kane. [See footnote #4.] Or, perhaps the "menehune lanterns" of Kohala legend. Or the Big Island's "lights of Pele." Or, with mixed ethnic background, the Japanese or Okinawan equivalent of *akualele*. Any of these might be visions or natural phenomena given either widespread or regional visionary significance, or hallucinations.

Occasionally, a vision may be an almost totally absorbing interest. This may occur in an individual who is psychotic, and in one who is not. The "takeover" of the vision can look deceptively like an aspect of schizophrenia.

**case history of Lila:
not a schizophrenic**

A case in point:

Psychiatric evaluation was requested for Lila (fictitious name), a 12-year-old Hawaiian girl, *hānai'd* into a family still very close to their Hawaiian heri-

---

*In Oriental tradition, grief or bad news may be accompanied by smiles, giggles or open laughter. What to the Western mind is the most inappropriate response is to the East culturally fitting.

tage. Lila was referred to the Center because of difficulties in school. Her achievement had dropped sharply. She had intermittent periods of being withdrawn, unfriendly and "closed in on herself." Alternately, she was gregarious, even aggressively so. According to her teachers, Lila was "daydreaming" or "wool-gathering all day." Lila told her caseworker a different story.

"Grandfather is buried in that cemetery," she said, pointing out the direction. "When I look out the window at school, I can see his grave. Then Grandfather comes. I see him standing right on his grave . . . Sometimes we talk. Grandfather tells me he loves me . . . Sometimes he asks me to come with him."

The caseworker first suspected that Lila had an especially dramatic alibi for not paying attention in school. When she was alert and friendly, she did a lot of "grandstanding" to gain attention. However, he visited the school and found that for most of the day Lila sat where she could see the grave. He then believed Lila was hallucinating her grandfather, and suspected schizophrenia. It was then a psychiatrist was consulted.

Comments the psychiatrist:

"On the surface it looked as if the girl was so tied to her grandfather that she was hallucinating his presence, and sliding into a schizophrenic, private world containing only the two of them. Other elements, such as the periodic occurrence of the vision-seeing days, suggested the possibility of an organic brain condition. A few times, the youngster also said she had 'seen and talked with God,' and that she had 'almost' killed herself so she could join her grandfather. In cold type these claims read pretty much like pathological indications. Actually, they seemed to be the inventions of an adolescent seeking love and attention. It was the girl's reports of seeing her grandfather that had the ring of sincerity.

"I went over the girl with the proverbial 'fine tooth comb.' She was given a full battery of projective psychological tests. An EEG* examination showed no brain damage or epilepsy. I found no decompensation in the psychiatric sense.[7] Nothing pointed to a true schizophrenic process, or to any kind of grave, progressive personality disorder. The problem seemed to be one of prolonged mourning and accompanying moderate depression.

"The girl was, of course, 'tied' to her grandfather—tied in the entanglement of unfinished grief work which she fit into the most typically Hawaiian pattern—seeing visions at the grave. What was needed was help in working this grief through."

From the caseworker's file come notes on how Lila was encouraged to talk about her grandfather and, even more importantly, about the fact that he was dead and departed forever. In weekly sessions, it became clear that Lila believed her grandfather's indulgent, permissive, gift-giving (and perhaps somewhat seductive) expressions of affection were the only ways to show love. She took any refusal of material or emotional request as a personal rejection. Specific examples of her mother's affectionate care were pointed out. Gradually, Lila stopped talking about her visions. Her schoolwork showed improvement. By the time her family moved away and the case was closed, Grandfather had indeed gone to his rest, as far as we know, permanently.

---

*Electroencephalograph. Electrical impulses of the brain (brain waves) are recorded in graph form.

(Other cases of incomplete grief work within the Hawaiian context are discussed under *'unihipili,* a recalling of the dead; *noho,* possession by the spirit of the dead; *hō'ailona* and *hō'ike,* sign and revelation; and *make, kanu* and *kaumaha,* death, burial and grief).

hallucinations
in hysteria

The case of Lila points out the need to evaluate many factors before the visionary Hawaiian can be diagnosed as psychotic or not, and his visions pronounced benign or pathological. The same "see the forest, not only the tree" approach helps distinguish Hawaiian normal visions from hallucinations of the intensely hysterical* person. Hysterical hallucinations are more transparent and "readable" than those of schizophrenia, but less so than the culturally normal vision. The hallucinations of hysteria may include those of taste, smell and touch, as well as sight and hearing. In general, the hysterical hallucination is likely to be accompanied by, or alternate with, other symptoms, such as hysterical paralysis, anesthesia, blindness, loss of voice, or disturbances in other body functions.

is psychiatric
consultation needed?

We hope these last few paragraphs may be useful to the nurse or caseworker in an isolated area. It is this person who must answer the initial questions: Should any intervention be taken in this vision-viewing? Is a psychiatric consultation indicated?

One way to answer questions is to ask more questions. To wit:

Is the person disturbed about the visions? Are the visionary experiences affecting personal functioning? Damaging family relationships? Or—somewhat surprisingly—enhancing them?

One current case brought a "hands off, do nothing right now" decision. Involved is a 75-year-old widow whose deceased daughter appears frequently in a certain picture frame. The older woman enjoys and is comforted by these visions. By age and inclination, she is comfortably "set" in her ways and ideas. Also in the home is the adolescent granddaughter, the daughter of the deceased woman. The girl is not frightened or nervous over the idea of visions. The caseworker's chief concern is that the girl might feel her grandmother is "shutting her out" because of the absorbing visions, or that her dead mother is rejecting her in favor of visits with Grandma. Currently neither seems to be happening. The girl accepts her grandmother's explanation that "Your mama comes to see me to find out how you are." For the worker, it is a "watch and wait" situation. For the time being, the vision is certainly not a disrupting influence.

The case of Mrs. H————— makes an interesting contrast:

A middle-aged widow, Mrs. H————— was deeply disturbed by repeated visions of her dead husband. She believed the family was under a curse *('ānai),* and thought her husband appeared to carry out this curse.

"He's coming back to take the boys [three sons] away from me . . . one by one," she told the caseworker.

---

*Hysterical is used in its clinical meaning, not in the "scream, cry and go out of control" popular sense of "having hysterics." However, hysterics of this type can occur in clinically defined hysteria.

Mrs. H_____ exemplifies a truism: Hawaiians are most apt to be upset about a vision—or any other Hawaiian mysticism-tinged experience—when
they garble tradition.

Mrs. H_____ erred in two respects: In traditional belief, the dead,
envisioned or not, did not pronounce curses or carry them out. And, when
they "claimed" the living, this had the quality of coming to welcome and
escort to eternity someone already destined to die. Traditional stories of a
spirit actually killing are rare, and not in this context of family relationships.
(See footnote #4, Nights of Kane.) Here Mrs. Pukui's statement that "visions
come to help, not harm" was especially pertinent. It was also suggested to
Mrs. H_____ that her visions really meant her deceased husband was
reminding her to get help in realistic problems of the boys' health and happiness.

Hawaiian tradition even includes a way to banish disquieting visions. The
idea is summed up as *kaukau,* literally "placing, placing." This is a kind of
lay-the-cards-on-the-table statement to spirit or vision—or to a living person.
Mrs. Pukui gives an example:

"You just say to the dead person something like, 'You are making the
children nervous. You love them. You don't want to worry them. So, please
stop coming back. Leave us alone and go to your rest.'"

Ideally, this was said over the grave. However, it could be said directly to
the vision in any setting.

The most common way to banish vision, lessen fear, or seek help in understanding the vision's message is to pray. Prayer *(pule)* in any language, to
Christian God or Hawaii's deities, has always accompanied Hawaiian action
and permeated Hawaiian thought. When the Hawaiian prays in moments of
fear, awe, or calm seeking of guidance, he follows a cultural precedent that
began long before the introduction of Christianity.

When the message of vision or voice is one of death or disaster, prayer
is believed either to avert the doom or diminish it. Death could be prevented;
critical illness could become less painful, curable and of shorter duration. In
Hawaiian terms, a *pule kala* (prayer to free; prayer of release) could *'oki*
(remove or sweeten) the force of mystically foretold harm. This applied to messages of vision or voice or dream. (See *'oki.*)

Clarifying tradition, giving a changed interpretation, or banishing the vision, are, of course, not much more than ways to alleviate immediate symptoms.
Mrs. H_____'s anxieties and guilts came from causes more complicated
and long-standing than her visions. However, Center workers have learned
they must often clear away a veritable thicket of garbled Hawaiiana before
anything more than symptomatic relief can get underway.

This thicket is usually filled with unorthodox offshoots of religious and
cultural beliefs from all the ethnic groups Hawaiians have mixed and married
with. A typically Hawaiian vision may be shaped to fit a Catholic, Pentecostal,
Mormon or Taoist framework—and embellished with bits of folklore from
here, there and everywhere!

It is the actual visionary experience that seems to be truly Hawaiian. It
may bring awe, peace, joy, or less often, fear. It does not bring horror. It is
not marked by exaltation and spiritual rapture. The experience itself seems

rather an extension into mystic realms of the Hawaiian closeness to family, and the Hawaiian tendency to seek advice rather than to forge ahead in individualistic, unsupported action.

The Hawaiian vision experience seems to be the slight parting of an already insubstantial curtain between the world of the living and the world of the spirits. And just behind that curtain, waiting his cue to appear with direct or disguised counsel or a message of love, is almost certainly a member of the family!

NOTES AND REFERENCES

1. Told in 1920 by Kapanokalani of Waikele, Ewa, Oahu. Translated and written (unpublished) by Mrs. Pukui. The account tells that Kamehameha was given the names *Ku-maka-ka-iaka'a* (Ku-with-open-eyes), *Ku-ka-'ili-moku* (Ku-snatcher-of-islands), and *Ku-nui-akea* (Large-and-wide Ku).

2. Fornander. *Antiquities of Hawaii,* Third Series, Vol. 6, p. 422.

3. Giants: Mrs. Pukui suggests that belief in mythical giants came from the fact Hawaiians sometimes actually grew to heights well over seven feet. She cites two present-day examples, one at Ka'u and one at Kipu-Kai, Kauai, in which skeletal remains suggesting extreme height were found.

4. Nights of Kane: The 27th night of the lunar month was *kapu* in its meaning of "sacred" to the god Kane. On this night, spirits of departed chiefs march over the pathways they trod in life. Anyone in the pathway of the marchers might be killed. The spirit of a relative could rescue him or the victim could save himself by stripping and lying flat in the path. This may account for the fear that visions can kill. (In the present day, Hawaiians report hearing marching feet more than seeing the ghostly chiefs.) Related by Mrs. Pukui and used in Beckwith-Kepelino's *Traditions of Hawaii.*

5. Vision of living person:
   "A sorcerer would tell a person, 'Today at noon . . . I saw your wraith . . . You are entirely naked . . . Your tongue was hanging out, your eyes staring wildly at me. You rushed at me and clubbed me with a stick . . . Your *aumakua* is wroth with you on this account . . . Now is the proper time . . . to make peace with me.' At this speech . . . the man consented to have the *kahuna* [in this case, sorcerer] perform the ceremony of *kala,* atonement, for him . . . This done, the *kahuna* said, 'I declare the ceremony perfect. . . . You will not die.' The *kahuna* then received his pay."—"Hawaiian Antiquities," D. Malo, pp. 112-2. Malo makes it clear this vision of the living was faked by an unscrupulous sorcerer.

6. Kamakau. *Ka Po'e Kahiko: The People of Old,* p. 50.

7. Decompensation in psychiatric sense: Term is borrowed from physical medicine. An example: When a damaged heart functions fairly well within safe bounds of physical activity, it is a compensated heart. What remains healthy and intact in the heart compensates for the damage. Over-exertion, illness, various stresses may push the heart beyond its limit-of-compensation. It can then no longer function reasonably well. It is a de-compensated heart. The personality, damaged in certain aspects, may also be compensated for by the healthy, intact elements. A person who has sustained and retained damaging outlooks, ways of doing things, ways of relating to others, for instance, may live fairly comfortably within somewhat limited demands and stresses. He functions in a compensated way. But if he pushes himself beyond his compensated capacities, he de-compensates. At this point, symptoms—acute depression, anxiety, psychosomatic distress, hallucinations are some—may develop. This may be described in such terms as "Decompensation is present" or "He is decompensating."

'aki'aki—a skin sensation usually interpreted to be a portent. This is a figurative extension of literal meanings: to "nibble as a fish does" and "a coarse grass."

Deriv: *'aki,* "nip and let go"; to "nibble".

'Aki'aki, as the word is used by Center clients, usually describes a sensation of the skin. This is often said to feel like "little nibbles" or "tiny, sharp pinches." Both descriptions are close to the literal meanings. *'Aki'aki* grass, stepped on with bare feet, gives this feeling of sharp little pinches.

To this intermittent "pinching" or "nibbling" feeling has been attached yet another meaning, that of malicious gossip or slander. This is the kind of character disparagement that is accomplished by small, continuing, accumulative remarks rather than one big lie or public statement.

'Aki'aki is reported as being felt while awake and in dreams.

This and other skin sensations are discussed under *'ili'ōuli.*

akua — god, goddess, supernatural spirit. Occasionally used to mean supernatural quality or even a human who has supernatural powers. *Akua* may, though rarely, refer to a corpse. Written with capital A, *Akua* refers to the Christian God. Deriv: unknown

The *akuas* were the impersonal gods of Hawaii, powerful, distant deities whose origins were lost in dim corridors of time. The *akuas,* like the gods of Greek mythology, combined supernatural qualities with many of the characteristic frailties of men. Accordingly, *akuas* could be vengeful, helpful or destructive, wise or capricious. This is in direct contrast to the Christian concept of all good and all evil, God and devil.

Akuas, again very much like gods of Western mythology, could take many forms *(kino lau),* appearing as a fish, a shark, a rock, a plant. They could mate with mortals and produce either normal human beings or *mo'o,* fish-like "water spirit" babies, or *'eho'eho,* rock-like babies. They could, in mysterious ways, bring forth *kupuas,* or demi-gods. Pele, the volcano goddess, carried in her bosom the egg that became her sister, Hi'iaka. *Akuas* could take possession *(noho)* of humans, totally or partially.

**four
major gods**

Many *akuas* were nameless; some were famous named gods or goddesses. The four major gods, believed to be worshiped as deities even before the migration from Tahiti to Hawaii, were:

Kāne, creator of man; heavenly father of all men, symbol of life, nature; god of fresh water and sunlight.

Lono, god of agriculture, clouds, weather.

Ku, god of war and chiefs, god of the forests, canoe making, fishing.

Kanaloa, the ocean god; god of salt water.

Trying to characterize the "famous four" by their own special *kuleanas* (areas of responsibility) is tricky. The four "traded duties" to an extent. They also took on multiple entities, with each entity worshiped as a separate deity. For example, in his function as god of canoe making, Ku became Ku-*alana-wao* or Ku-arising-in the forest. (Canoes were made of trees from the forest.) During the annual four months' *makahiki* festival, Lono became a separate personality, Lono-*i-ka-makahiki* or Lono-of-the-*makahiki.*

Both Ku and Lono are also considered gods of medicine. This is a logical extension of ideas. For Ku was primarily god of the forests; many of the healing herbs and vines came from the forest. Lono, as god of agriculture, extended his *kuleana* to the medicinal plants grown as agricultural projects. And with Ku and his goddess wife Hina, came the association of male and female properties in healing plants and in ritual. In the ancient myths, both went into the forest together; both were invoked equally when medicinal plants were gathered. Male and female were kept in balance (an idea quite close to the Chinese concept of balancing *yin* and *yan,* heat and cold or male and female).

With the coming of missionaries, efforts were made to fit Kāne, Ku and Lono into the concept of the Trinity and give Kanaloa the role of devil. The role-assignment "didn't take," but many early writings contain a conspicuous blank where Kanaloa's special *kuleana* is concerned.

Lesser, but still powerful gods included Ma'iola, god of healing; Kapo, goddess of sorcery; Pele, the volcano goddess; Laka, goddess of the hula. Pele and Laka are examples of deities who remain impersonal *akuas* but who are also personal *aumākua* to their human descendants. (See *aumākua).*

Abstract forces are more easily worshiped when they can be visualized as idols. And so Hawaii had carved wooden gods and earlier feather gods, said to accompany the first migration from Tahiti.

If it is possible to "short-change" mystic beings, then we have certainly done so. For there were hundreds of Hawaiian *akuas.* Some individual gods took on dozens of separate names and personalities. Pele's sister, Hi'iaka, was said to have as many as 40 different manifestations. It is impossible to list all the deities here.

(A convenient reference listing of Hawaiian gods is included in *The New Hawaiian Dictionary* by Mrs. Pukui and Dr. Samuel H. Elbert, published in 1971.—C.A.L.)

One conclusion about the gods seems possible. The *akuas* were distant, awesome deities, concerned with the mighty forces of land and sea, storm and calm, light of day and dark of night. As major gods, their help was invoked for major causes and great events. For the needs and solaces of daily life, Hawaiians called on their own personal ancestor gods, the *aumākua.* (It was Kanaloa who, by inhaling and exhaling, made the ocean tides, but if you got caught in an outgoing tide, you called on your *aumakua* for help!)

**the gods and
modern Hawaiians**

Occasionally, the modern Hawaiian still invokes the old *akuas.* One Hawaiian who openly states that he is a *kahuna* prays to Lono for guidance in healing and in the preparation of herbal medicines. This is within the old tradition. In at least one 1971 public meeting of Hawaiians, Lono was invoked before the preceedings.

Akua, as an unnamed impersonal god or merely "spirit" is more often mentioned. Explicitly or by implication, clients have said an *akua* has possessed them or someone in the family. Often *akua* was used when *'uhane,* the spirit of a human, was meant. *(Nahu akua* or "spirit bite" is discussed under separate listing.)

In general, the Hawaiian who today retains, emotionally, if not intellectually, his old beliefs, also retains the division between the awesome and the approachable deities. The *aumākua,* not the *akuas,* remain the personally significant supernatural beings.

REFERENCES

Beckwith. *Hawaiian Mythology.*

Emory. *Religion in Ancient Hawaii,* pp. 86, 87, 88

Kamakau. *Ka Po'e Kahiko: The People of Old,* p. 139.

Pukui-Elbert. *Hawaiian Dictionary,* University Press of Hawaii, 1971.

akualele—a "flying god" that was sent on destructive errands.

Deriv: *akua,* god or spirit.

lele, to fly, leap or jump as from a cliff.

Akualele or "flying god" goes back to the belief that certain gods took the form of balls of fire and flew through the air. Whether this belief arose from seeing actual shooting stars or glowing phosphorescence at night is anybody's speculation. However, legends say these gods entered the *kauila, nioi* or *'ohe* trees growing at Maunaloa on Molokai. These trees became poisonous only at the Molokai location; trees of the same family on other islands remained harmless. It seemed obvious that the gods inhabiting the Molokai trees were poison gods. "It is a wondrous thing how these trees became poisonous," says one account.[1]

Another legend tells that these trees on Molokai were descended from men, and, therefore, were inhabited by the spirits of men. One version relates a dream of seeing men marching to Maunaloa and turning into the trees. When the wood burned, it was thought to give off a smell of blood.

Another account, beginning with a dream, says that when the first tree was cut down, chips of wood touched the bodies of men, killing them instantly.[2]

At any rate, individuals on Molokai began to keep wood of the poison trees and fashioned images of it. Elaborate protective rituals were developed to keep men handling the wood from being poisoned (coconut water and *mimi* [urine] were both used).

With the making of god-images of the wood, the ritual of sending the poison god on death-dealing errands began. The image (or perhaps just a piece of wood) was scraped, always at night. This sent the *akua* or god out on its destructive mission. As the god sped through the night air, it was said to look like a "fireball."

Sending a god or spirit on an errand is called *ho'oūna* or *ho'oūnauna.* The term is a general one and does not refer specifically to *akualele.* Sending an ancestral spirit in *'unihipili* is also *ho'oūnauna.* (See *'unihipili*).

Associated with, but also not limited to *akualele,* is another phrase, *mālama pū'olo* or "keeping a bundle" for use in sorcery or spirit-sending. The "bundle," in the case of *akualele* the wood, was usually wrapped in tapa. The *kahu* or "keeper" of this "bundle" cared for, fed ritually and constantly called upon the spirit inhabiting the bundle. These were essential parts of the spirit-sending ritual. The fateful climax came when the keeper voiced the command for the spirit to fly on its errand. Thoughts had to be put into words before they took effect, either as sorcery spell *('anā'anā)* or human-to-human curse *('ānai).*

However, the keeper who sent the spirit out to do harm was endangering himself. The spirit or poison god might be returned with the ritual words, "go back and destroy your keeper." These rituals of sending and returning destructive forces recurred in Hawaiian belief. With *akualele,* another method of escaping harm could also be used. "Fireballs seen in the sky would burst and become harmless," says Mrs. Pukui, "if you swore at them—Hawaiian style!"

"Hawaiian swearing," she explains, "is not saying 'damn'; it's using words with nasty meanings." Sacrilegious swearing was unknown.

Keeping an *akualele* for supernatural errands seems much like *'unihipili,* keeping an ancestor's bones or personal possession as control-medium of the ancestor's spirit. The vast difference is that in *akualele* rituals, the keeper controlled an impersonal spirit for essentially harmful use. In *'unihipili,* the spirit was that of a close, dearly loved and fairly recently departed relative. This spirit helped or harmed as the keeper requested. The concept here is "recalling the beloved dead."

Belief in *"mālama pū'olo"* as a harmful practice is still related by Center clients. One client felt family troubles had increased after an old man moved in with the family. Said the client, "the old man's got something Hawaiian hidden under the bed." On advice of a *kahuna,* the client got the old man out of the house long enough to discover a *pū'olo* or "bundle" which she promptly burned.*

"I heard breathing sounds and cries of pain while it burned. And I think drops of blood came out of it!" said the client. "After the old man discovered the burning, he got mad and moved out."

This is an example of remedial action within the framework of Hawaiian cultural beliefs. The client was disturbed because she believed a traditional *pū'olo* was being kept, communicated with and ritually fed. To her this meant that a spirit, sinister and possibly not too quiescent, pervaded her home. With bundle and boarder both out of the house and the spirit consumed in flames, some very troublesome elements were removed. The client was better able to focus on her principal problems.

In some present day examples, walking sticks, canes or heirloom spears of *kauila* wood have been considered hosts to the poison god. These are not, as far as we know, wrapped in tapa or in any way made into a *pū'olo* or "bundle," though in at least one case, "spirit-feeding" lived on. Some instances show fear for the spirit in the wood; others almost affectionate attachment.

About three years ago, Mrs. Pukui was told the following during a visit on Molokai:

"N_____ died, and after death, nobody could stay in the house. Noises! Walking sounds! Everybody felt funny . . . uneasy. So N_____'s family searched and found a *kauila* cane high up over a window. They took the cane to N_____'s grave and buried it on top of him and said, 'Here is your cane. Take it with you and leave us be.' After that the house was all right. Everybody could sleep."

An almost opposite example—that of attachment—came to Mrs. Pukui's attention at Bishop Museum.

"A very nervous young woman came to the Museum and asked to see a spear her sister had brought in. After she identified it, she asked to come back with offerings . . . She came early the next day. With her was a small octopus,

---

*"You may also dispose of a *pū'olo* by throwing it in the ocean. After your throw it, never look back." M.K. Pukui

a *hīnālea* (type of fish), a *weke* (fish) and a small container of *poi*. After muttering a prayer she ate the food. Then she came smiling to me and said, 'The stick stays with you, but the spirit goes home with me.'"

The *weke* signified opening or removal, *hīnālea* meant "clearance" due to a play on the word *lea* (clear), even the octopus was once used to make sickness or sorcery "flee," "slip" or "slide out", Mrs. Pukui explained. The woman was ceremonially "freeing" the spirit so it could come back home.

The spear had belonged to the woman's older sister. During family parties, the younger sister had put filled liquor glasses near it and, unknowingly, fed the spirit. After the older sister's death, the spear was given to the museum. It was after this that the younger sister began to be tormented "night after night by something that said 'Go and get me.'"

The "spirit that was homesick" is one of several modern instances in which the original connotation of harm has been lost. Mrs. Pukui detected no feeling that *akualele,* instrument of death, lurked in the *kauila* wood. Rather, the spirit, like a lonesome, devoted pet, wanted to come back to its friend, companion and provider of "food."

If we put the woman's attachment to the spirit within the framework of behavioral sciences, something like this may be seen:

Dr. Haertig suggests two interpretations. Both, he stresses, are speculative and based on no personal professional knowledge of the case.

"In Freudian interpretation, the *kauila* stick or spear would be the obvious phallic symbol," he says.

"But in Hawaiian cultural belief, *kauila* wood and its spirit could be male or female. So I would wonder instead about the younger woman's association with her sister. The older sister died. Went away. Then the *kauila* wood was given to the museum. Went away. The *kauila* spirit the younger sister was trying to bring back home could be a kind of symbolic focus for the woman's need for and memories of the older sister. She may really have been trying to call back the sister—or at least all the values, memories and associations that her sister represented."

In a quite separate conversation with the editor, Mrs. Pukui recalled that the older sister had "been like a second mother" to the younger woman, and that the younger sister had addressed the *kauila* spirit as *tūtū!**

REFERENCES

1. Kamakau. *Ka Po'e Kahiko: The People of Old,* pp. 128-131.
2. *Journal of William Ellis,* pp. 52-54.

'anā'anā—evil sorcery; "black magic;" practiced by a *kahuna 'anā'anā.*

Deriv: unknown.

'Anā'anā, evil which could be illness, madness, loss of a specific body function, or death, descended on its victim through specific rituals conducted

---

**tūtū.* The word refers loosely to any woman of a grandparent generation, is used to mean "aunty" and also is an affectionate term for an older woman who guides and teaches younger persons.

by a sorcerer or *kahuna 'ana'ana* (trained master of sorcery). The *kahuna 'anā 'anā* must first gain possession of *kāmeha'i* or *maunu* (bait) closely associated with his victim. This could be hair, nails, body excretions, or a garment the victim had worn. All of these contained some of the *mana* (personal power) of the wearer. A sorcerer who obtained this "bait" could gain control over the *mana* and therefore over the victim.

To avoid *'anā'anā,* all possible *maunu* was carefully disposed of in secret. Co-author Pukui recalls, "When I was a little girl, my grandmother used to take special care of my hair. She'd take any that came out during combing and roll it up and bury it in a hidden place . . . watching over every little thing because it could become *maunu.*"

When the *kahuna 'anā'anā* had obtained the needed *maunu,* he first called on his gods of sorcery and then recited the particular prayer designed to bring about a specific doom. One example is the *pule 'umi,* literally "prayer to choke." For this the sorcerer had to recite, all in one breath:

"Faint, be faint, faint, faint.
Fall down, let him fall down, down, down.
Consciousness goes, it departs.
He gasps, gasps.
Now pinch him, strangle him,
Pinch his eyes to blind him.
His nose, pinch it, too.
His mouth, pinch it, close it.
His windpipe seize, choke, strangle!"[1]

In the geographically stable, closely knit communities of early Hawaii, word easily reached the victim of his doom. Before long, *hō'upu'upu* (planting a thought in another's mind) went to work. Under the "strangulation spell," the victim would attempt to eat the head of a live *manini* or *āholehole* fish. Both fish have sharp bones in the dorsal fin which, lodged in the throat, can cause strangulation. However, the victim, his air passage closing from fear and fish bone, could be saved by a counter-sorcerer called *kahuna pale* (*pale* means "to ward off"). The *kahuna pale* said the counter-prayer. The first few lines seem addressed to the fish, but because the human was sometimes called "two legged fish," this could be symbolic. Certainly the second part of the prayer was said directly *to* the victim. The prayer goes:

counter spell

"Though he chokes, yet he lives.
Strangles, yet he lives.
Oh fish, be softened, be cooked.
Be pliable, be very soft.
O, bones, be reduced to ashes.
Though you have swallowed a *manini*
And be choked,
Yet Life comes to the rescue.
Though you become crooked, a paralytic,
Yet Life comes to the rescue.
Though you eat of the *āholehole* and choke,
Life shall deliver you.
Though you be broken, paralyzed,

Life comes to your rescue.
And health be with you to the end of your days."[2]

This counter-spell, said to the frightened victim in a ritual-accompanied "doctor-patient" relationship, must have been vastly reassuring. It may have been hypnotic.

hypnotic cadence

In the following spell, this one to inflict harm, the hypnotic content and cadence come through clearly even in translation:
"Numbness, numbness, numbness, numbness,
Spreads, spreads, spreads, spreads,
Stiffens, stiffens, stiffens, stiffens.
Your head droops, droops, droops,
Bends over, bends over,
It droops, droops."[3]

For the victim who knew he was under a spell, rescue lay either in a counter spell or through *'oki,* severing or cutting off a spell by prayer. In current case histories, *'oki* sometimes includes both Hawaiian and Christian prayers.

What about the victim who did not know he was under a spell? In his case, the family and the "family doctor," the *kahuna lapa'au,* took over. The family gathered in *ho'oponopono,* the family conference which worked, through prayers and frank confession of error and restitution for wrong-doing, to find solutions to family crises. In the case of *'anā'anā,* the family joined in trying to help the victim remember what he might have done that would lead to sickness. The *kahuna lapa'au* examined the victim, praying to his *aumākua* (ancestor gods) for medical insight. There were causes and effects to investigate. Did the victim have a swollen hand, sign that he had stolen? This might mean that the one he had stolen from had employed a sorcerer to cast a spell on him. Prayer, detective work and a medical *kahuna* often discovered the spell in time for counter measures.

kuni ritual

If the victim died in spite of all efforts, the family could still take revenge through a counter ritual called *kuni.*

(The possibility has been raised that the victim who died may simply have been poisoned by a sorcerer. The *kahuna 'anā'anā* knew the deadly plant and fish poisons.)[4]

Kuni means to burn. As a revenge-ritual, it entailed taking hair or nails or clothing of the victim killed by sorcery. These were burned and the ashes scattered in the path where the sorcerer walked, or in the water where he bathed. This, with accompanying ritual incantations, sent the evil back to its originator, the sorcerer, and killed him. This could, and has, bred family feuds. The feuds could be *'oki'd* by prayer.

Kuni could be used as a double-purpose ritual. If the person (sorcerer or enemy) who caused a victim's death was not known, then the burning of hair or nails of the victim could be used as a divination ritual. In the flames, the counter sorcerer could see a vision of the death-dealer.

Such was Hawaii's practice of *'anā'anā.* (Being "prayed to death" is known in many cultures.) Harold M. Johnson, M.D., Honolulu dermatologist, wrote in *The Archives of Dermatology*, of *'anā'anā*-caused cases seen in 1944, and two in 1963.[5]

The late Nils P. Larsen, M.D., of Honolulu described two deaths that apparently resulted from *'anā'anā*. In these nearly identical cases, Dr. Larsen examined two youths who told him they would soon die because of death-spells. Dr. Larsen found each boy in excellent physical health. Yet each died shortly, and in each case, autopsy showed no physical cause for death.[6]

psychiatric,
medical views

Both cases inevitably invite medical and psychiatric speculation. Walter B. Cannon, M.D., former professor of physiology, Harvard Medical School, and H.A. Wilmer, M.D., faculty, Langley-Porter Clinic, University of California, both see *'anā'anā* and similar Voodoo-caused deaths as the result of intense fear affecting the adrenal glands and the heart.[7]

From the psychiatric point of view, Dr. Haertig wonders why these two *'anā'anā* victims so accepted their doom that their fear became intense enough to cause death. Suicide was not in the Hawaiian tradition. The two boys probably did not have a "death wish," but rather a feeling that they accepted death because, for some reason or guilt we do not know, they deserved to die. Apparently the two made no effort to use the remedial measures practiced in the Hawaiian culture. This remembering of the "punishment," the spells, curses and death, and forgetting the "remedies," prayer and *ho'oponopono*, for example, recurs among present-day Center clients.

In the present day, no Center client feels specifically doomed by *'anā'anā*, though many believe they are under a curse *('ānai)* which can be inflicted without sorcery. However, two current clients feel they have the *mana* or power of *'anā'anā*. Both fear they can harm others.

In the first case, the client is completely vague about the possible origin of her supposed power.

In the second case, the client knows the family line did include a *kahuna 'anā'anā*' She believes she inherited this power after the death of her grandfather, a kindly, thoughtful man whose sole vengeful act seems to have been cursing *('ānai)* an irresponsible, dishonest and unrepentant son-in-law.

For both clients, education in authentic Hawaiian beliefs to correct misconceptions might remove some measure of fear. Traditionally, a sorcerer inherited or passed on some of his specialized *mana* only through specific intent and ritual. This was most often done through *hā*. In this, a person who felt death approaching breathed into the mouth (or sometimes on the fontanel) of his chosen descendant and declared he was thus passing on his *mana*. The other method (used more often for less specialized powers) was to make a spoken declaration that he was passing on his *mana* to a specific, named descendant. Otherwise, *mana* went with its possessor in death. The client who believes her power came from the grandfather knows of no such ceremony or statement.

Also, the *kahuna 'anā'anā* may have acquired some of his special *mana* from a sorcerer ancestor, but traditionally, he could not put it in practice until after a rigorous training period. This training was climaxed by one supreme test. To prove his power, the hopeful *kahuna 'anā'anā* was required to kill a relative or split a tree or rock by mental effort alone.

Both fear-filled clients have badly garbled knowledge of Hawaiian beliefs. Each presents such an intricate web of fears, possible delusions and tangled personal relationships that any kind of "instant prescription" would be ludicrous.

But where both clients' misconceptions about 'anā'anā are concerned, knowledge of authentic practices may unsnarl at least one thread from this web.

REFERENCES

1. Pukui. Translated for committee.

2. Ibid.

3. Kamakau. *Ka Poʻe Kahiko: The People of Old*, p. 26.

4. Larsen. *Ancient Hawaiian Civilization*, p. 261.

5. Johnson. "The *Kahuna*, Hawaiian Sorcerer," *Archives of Dermatology*, Vol. 90, pp. 530-535.

6. Larsen. Personal communication to M.K. Pukui.

7. "The *Kahuna*, Hawaiian Sorcerer."

'ānai—to curse; put a curse on; a curse.

> Deriv: Not definitely known. Possibly from original meaning "to rub, grate, lay waste or destroy." *'Ānai* as curse was a destructive force which imparted a constant mental "grating."

In the old Hawaiian culture, putting a curse or *'ānai* on someone was done in a very direct manner. The curse was said directly *to* another person in a phrase that might be as simple as "Be forever accursed for your wrongdoing." The *'ānai* was not directed by devious means or through a third person. It did not require a sorcerer as did *'anā'anā,* the "spell" which doomed a person to trouble or even death.

**innocent can
refuse curse**

If the recipient of *'ānai* was innocent of the wrong-doing, he could refuse the curse and send it back to its originator. The phrase of refusal went, *"Hoʻi no kau me 'oe"* or "What you have just given me, so [return] to you." The whole significance lay in the innocence of the cursed one. A guilty victim could not send the curse back; the phrase was then useless, mechanistic ritual.

If the cursed one was indeed guilty, there were ways to have the curse lifted. One was to go directly to the sender of the curse, give evidence of sincere repentance and of righting the wrong, and ask him to *'oki* the curse. (Literally, *'oki* means to cut or sever; the curse is "severed" from its victim.) Here tradition demanded that forgiveness be granted and the curse lifted.

**ways to
lift curse**

The one who placed the curse might, of his own volition, decide to remove it. In this case he announced to the assembled family his intention of taking the curse with him in death, thereby removing it and cancelling all its residual unpleasantness forever. Where peace of mind was concerned, this was tantamount to removing the curse immediately.

If the originator of the curse died without making such a statement and the accursed one had not asked for and received forgiveness, then the 'ānai remained in effect.

The one cursed could have it 'oki'd through *pule kala* or "prayer of freeing or release." In this particular context, the *pule kala* is said directly to the corpse before burial.* The essence is something like "Now you are gone, take all curses [or the specific curse named] with you."

If this was not done before the corpse had been buried, there remained two other ways of lifting the curse. One was sincere prayer. The other depended on the senior member of the family.

As Mary Pukui describes it "the senior, acting from *aloha* for her descendants, could decide to take the curse—and, indeed, every possible curse that might exist—with her in death. The senior will discuss this with all the family members and make her intention clear. All members should agree that the curse should so go beyond the grave when the senior dies."

(Mrs. Pukui's choice of the feminine pronoun may reflect her personal intention of taking with her in death all curses or "residuals" that could possibly harm or merely carry on unpleasant memories for her descendants.)

Says Mrs. Pukui, "This *'lawe i ka wa make'* or 'take in time of death' is the best way to 'oki the curse. There's a feeling of absolute finality. The living ones feel they are no longer burdened with the curse or the anger, resentment and sadness connected with it. The air is cleared. And this clearing of the air . . . this lifting of anxiety begins when the senior member announces the intention. I have seen this happen. Peace of mind doesn't wait on actual death of the senior member. The curse is gone—even if the senior should live on another ten or twenty years."

These precise methods of lifting or severing *('oki)* a curse may be yesterday's traditions, but they remain essential knowledge in dealing with many troubled Hawaiians today. Belief that one has been 'ānai'd comes into almost half of the cases known to the committee. In fact, a case involving 'ānai stimulated the writing of this book.

The following examples, fragments or composites of actual cases, show the very real fears surrounding 'ānai:

The first example required only a little Hawaiian-style psychiatric first aid. An entire hula class of Hawaiian children believed they were cursed by the mother of one of the pupils. The mother had shouted an angry 'ānai during a class session. Her grievance: that the hula was being taught wrong. The class had nearly broken up as a result. In this simple case, the children were helped to realize that the hula, traditionally a religious rite, was under the protection of the gods. Therefore, learning the hula was not wrong, and the children were safe from any curse.

A far more complicated case involved a mother who felt her son, now age 9, had inherited a curse. The boy's father had been cursed by his own father and had definitely refused to mend his ways and ask to have the curse lifted. The grandfather died, leaving his son still unrepentant and under the curse.

---

*The concept that both destructive forces and emotional attachments could be taken in death and so removed, and the practice of talking directly to a corpse recur through Hawaiian traditions.

Soon after, the younger man died. The boy was then about two. From then on, the mother believed the youngster had inherited the *'ānai*. She not only believed this, she attributed everything from the boy's inferior school work to behavior problems to ill health to the fact that he was cursed and therefore "hopeless."

**no one can
inherit curse**

Here we called on Mary Pukui to answer the question, "In the Hawaiian tradition, could an innocent child inherit a curse?" Her answer was "No, though this is usually misunderstood."

What the child does suffer from, she explained, are the residuals of the curse. By a kind of emotional osmosis he takes in and becomes a part of *hihia,* the entanglement of negative emotions that pervade disturbed family life.

And whether you call it *hihia* or "emotional spill off" it certainly existed in this case. For seven years the mother, projecting a non-existent "curse" on her son, had also projected her conviction that the son, like his father, would "never amount to anything." The "curse" was, for the mother, both a projection of the boy's future failures and an alibi for his past failures. The son, sensing his mother's feelings, fulfilled her negative expectations.

With little or no childhood experience in small successes and achievements, the boy not only accepted what he called a curse, but to some extent welcomed it as excuse. If everybody knew he just couldn't make good, why make the effort of trying?

This "accept a projection—welcome an excuse" process is not always labeled *'ānai,* nor is it exclusive with Hawaiians.

**guilt feelings
in curse acceptance**

What is exclusive to Hawaiian tradition is the clearly spelled out provision that only the guilty need accept and suffer from a curse. This guilt was for specific wrongdoing. Knowing this may remove some of the "top layer" of anxiety for clients who believe they are under *'ānai* for all sorts of vague, diffused guilts and general feelings of being "worthless." (The line is thin between feeling "I deserve to be cursed" and "therefore I am cursed" between believing "I am no account and no good" and "therefore I must be punished for being no account and no good.") Here explanations of authentic Hawaiian beliefs or even use of traditional curse-removing measures may relieve fear. The "emotional subsoil" may then become a bit more accessible.

In two interesting cases, clients "invented" curses. One woman, highly emotional, and inclined toward mysticism, believed threats made to her by her ex-husband were a "curse." (This interpretation that threats or angry predictions have the force of a curse is discussed under *hua 'ōlelo.)* After the former husband died, she reported that his spirit kept returning and threatening to take the children away from her. She then began to believe that the curse, working through her, would harm the children.

At various times the client had been Catholic and Mormon. She had consulted *kahunas,* and reported "seeing visions."

With this woman, super-charged with mysticism and religious-ritual beliefs, logical explanation that no *'ānai* had been pronounced and accepted, did not seem indicated. Instead the immediate relief measure for her seemed to be prayer. Because she was currently a Catholic, she was encouraged in Catholic devotions.

The other "self-invented" curse was that of a teenage girl, we will call Mary, who was outgrowing and in the process of leaving a sister, "Jenny," and a close friend, "Sara."

At different times Jenny and Sara enacted dramatic, hysterical episodes during which they warned Mary that serious danger threatened her. The girls believed these episodes meant they were *noho* (possessed). Mary herself interpreted the warnings to mean she was under a curse.

In this case, all three girls were interested in their Hawaiian heritage and liked to talk about Hawaiian practices. The worker took this as her cue. Both *noho* and *'ānai* were explained. It then became obvious that the so-called "possession" episodes did not fit the cultural pattern of *noho*, and that the curse Mary believed she was under met none of the criteria of the traditional *'ānai*.

With garbled ideas straightened out, the worker could help all three girls understand their feelings about each other. They discussed the resentment and abandonment Jenny and Sara felt at Mary's breaking away from old emotional ties and, in fact, her actual moving away from the community. Here the worker used other Hawaiian terms and concepts as a springboard for discussion. One was *hō'upu'upu*, the implanting of a thought in the mind of another (which the dramatic displays of hysteria certainly did for Mary). The other was *hā'upu*, the thought that comes spontaneously to one's mind—and often comes in disguised form. (Was the warning of harm Jenny and Sara gave Mary a fear or was it a wish disguised as a fear?)

In the Center's experience with clients who believe they are under an *'ānai*, certain similarities are striking. Invariably, all the doom, dread and punishment associated with *'ānai* are remembered, believed and felt. All the freeing, forgiving, remedial beliefs and practices have been forgotten, were never known or have not been employed. The feeling "I deserve to be cursed" seems to be more prevalent and more powerful than the feeling "I deserve to be freed."

'ao'ao—a specific side or branch of relationship, whether human relationship or that of the *aumākua* or ancestor gods. All long-departed ancestors were to their descendants *aumākua* or family gods. However, *'ao'ao* were the specific ancestor spirits on one's maternal or paternal side of the family. The word can also mean side, boundary, team, or in later usage, a particular political party.

Deriv: unknown.
See listing, *aumakua*.

ao kuewa—homeless, hungry spirits of the dead.
Deriv: *ao*, in the region.
kuewa, wanderer.

Ao kuewa were the spirits of the dead who were doomed to wander forever within specific geographic areas. Here they chased moths and grasshoppers in a vain effort to appease hunger. This doom came to the spirit of mortals who in life had so offended their *aumākua* (ancestor gods) that they denied them a place in the happier eternity of *Pō*. Hunger was the Hawaiian concept of "hell." See *aumakua* and *Pō*.

aumakua, plural, **aumākua**—ancestor gods; the god spirits of those who were in life forebears of those now living; spiritual ancestors.

Deriv: *au,* period of time; current of time; era; eon.
   makua, parent; parent generation; ancestor.

There is a sea of time, so vast man cannot know its boundaries, so fathomless man cannot plumb its depths. Into this dark sea plunge the spirits of men, released from their earthly bodies. The sea becomes one with the sky and the land and the fiery surgings that rise from deep in the restless earth. For this is the measureless expanse of all space. This is the timelessness of all time. This is eternity. This is Pō.

In Pō *there dwell our ancestors, transfigured into gods. They are forever god-spirits, possessing the strange and awesome powers of gods. Yet they are forever our relatives, having for us the loving concern a mother feels for her infant, or a grandfather for his first-born grandson. As gods and relatives in one, they give us strength when we are weak, warning when danger threatens, guidance in our bewilderment, inspiration in our arts. They are equally our judges, hearing our words and watching our actions, reprimanding us for error, and punishing us for blatant offense. For these are our godly ancestors. These are our spiritual parents. These are our* aumākua.

You and I, when our time has come, shall plunge from our leina* *into* Pō. *If our lives have been worthy, our* aumākua *will be waiting to welcome us. Then we too shall inhabit the eternal realm of the ancestor spirits. We in our time shall become* aumākua *to our descendants even yet unborn.*

So with the *aumākua,*** Hawaiians of old resolved their own quest for a comprehensible immortality, satisfied their own desire to worship compassionate, approachable deities, and filled their own need for a standard of ethics more personal and more permanent than that incorporated in the chiefly edicts.

The concept of *aumākua* was a nearly ideal one. The Hawaiians lived within the close relationships of the *'ohana* (family or family clan); the *aumākua* remained members of the clan. The *'ohana* invested family authority in its senior members; the *aumākua* as spiritual ancestors were certainly seniors. With one's *aumakua,* a human-to-spirit communication was possible. One spoke to an *aumakua* through ritual and with reverence, but without the almost paralyzing awe the *akuas* or impersonal gods sometimes inspired. Therefore, an *aumakua* could also be a "spiritual go between," passing on prayers to the *akua.*

---

*Each island had cliffs or seacoast promontories called *leina* from which the spirits of men, after death, were believed to plunge into eternity.

**Sometimes the ancestor gods were called *kumupa'a.*

origin of aumākua

Praying to the *aumākua* as link to the *akua* seems logical. For one of the ways the first *aumākua* were said to originate was by the mating of *akua* and mortal. When a child was born to this union, the *akua* became an ancestor to a human line. He took on a dual role. As ancestor-god he became an *aumakua* to his descendants. Yet he remained *akua* or impersonal god to non-related humans. The dual role was sometimes referred to as *akua aumakua*.[1] Traditionally, even the major gods, Kāne, Ku, Lono and Kanaloa were both *akua* and *aumakua*. Union of powerful gods with humans is said also to have created the chiefs who ruled by "divine right." The major gods were more often thought of as *akua* only; the *aumakua* role seems to have been lost, except by Pele, Hiʻiaka and Laka. These three were usually accepted as both goddess and *aumakua*. Even today Pele is goddess to non-related Hawaiians and *aumakua* to descendants. To Mrs. Pukui she is *aumakua*.

Evidently in ancient times, there were not enough *aumākua* to go around, for prayers for acquiring an *aumakua* are recorded. One could pray for either a male or a female.[2]

family had many aumākua

This scarcity of *aumākua* was not to be permanent. Co-author Pukui memorized names of all her family *aumākua* as part of her childhood education. She learned a total of 50 names! With so many *aumākua*, the word *'ao'ao* was used to designate the spiritual ancestors on a specific side or branch of the family.

kino lau, many forms

Aumākua were also called *"po'e o ka pō,"* people in the night or dark, therefore, "invisible people." However, *aumākua* could assume visible, tangible forms because of their ability to take *kino lau* (many bodies; many forms). The *akua* also had this ability. *Aumākua* took the form of sharks, owls, mud hens, lizards, eels, and indigenous small field mice, caterpillars, even rocks and plants. They could change back and forth from animal to plant to mineral form. The *aumakua* that was a *pe'elua* or *'enuhe* (caterpillar) on land became the *loli* or sea-cucumber in the ocean. The *aumakua* inhabiting the body of a certain animal might also inhabit a plant that had either visual resemblance, similar characteristics (slippery, clinging, rough or smooth) or symbolic resemblance because of similar name. The *aumakua* in the mackerel or *'ōpelu* was also associated with a variety of the lobelia plant with leaves shaped and colored like the fish, and called *'ōpelu*.

kākū 'ai described

Traditionally, Hawaiians could transform a deceased member of the family into a special class of *aumākua*. This was done in the ceremony of *kākū 'ai*. Mary Pukui describes *kākū 'ai* as her forebears practiced it:

"... They would take the bones after the flesh was all gone, wrap the bones in red and black tapa, and take them to the volcano. Then the *kahuna* [priest] would prepare the *'awa* [Hawaii's ceremonial drink]... After the *'awa* had been poured into the crater, the bones were thrown down there. For generations, some of our folks were taken there. Later, others who were related to the sharks were given the *kākū 'ai* ceremony and their bodies placed in the sea. The *aumakua* shark was supposed to take the bundle of bones, cover it with a belly fin, and care for it until that bundle of bones somehow turned into another shark.

"The last time my people conducted *kākū'ai* rituals was when my great grandmother was taken to the volcano. From my grandmother on down, we had earth burial," Mrs. Pukui explains.*

A relative so transfigured became a particular type of spirit who served family *aumākua* within their own supernatural realm. For example, a relative consigned to the volcano became a flame spirit serving Pele. Living descendants did not call on these spirits for help. Though they were usually called *aumakua,* and sometimes loosely classified as *'unihipili,* they were generally considered unique spirit-beings.[3]

In other *kākū'ai* rites, a still-born or malformed live baby or a fetus could be returned to its *aumakua.* This is described in listing, *kākū'ai.*

For the early Hawaiians, the *aumākua* as invisible force or in tangible form were ever-present, permeating thought and action. The ritualistic care given the *piko* (umbilical cord) came, in part, from the knowledge that the cord had connected the baby with an living ancestor who after death would be a directly linked *aumakua.* The *kapu* (taboo) against hitting anyone on the head or face was intertwined with the belief that good spirits—and the *aumakua* was certainly a good one—entered the body by the head. The many *kahunas* of the healing arts prayed to their *aumākua* for diagnostic insights. The child was taught which specific *aumakua* to call on for help. And when one man became an expert canoe maker and another an especially skilled fisherman, this was due only partially to individual training. The training was superimposed on the *mana* (special power or talent) each had received from his *aumakua.*

aumakua warned
and protected

The *aumākua* also brought warnings of coming misfortune and deliverance from immediate danger.

If, for example, your family *aumākua* included the shark, you might have had an experience like this one, reported from the Puna District on Hawaii to anthropologist Martha Beckwith:

"... this one family ... had a supernatural helper or *aumakua* who appeared in the form of a particular shark. When any of the family go fishing, the shark appears. The *aumakua* obeys the voice of man. Name the fish you want and it will bring it. This family can never be drowned. If there is a storm and the boat capsizes, the shark appears and the men ride on its back."[4]

Or Mary Pukui's personal experience:

"... in our *'ohana,* we were taught to observe the owl. Owls were among the family *aumākua* ... If the owl cries in a strange way, *'eu'eu,* that means 'get out of here today.' When I was in Puna, an owl came and lit in a breadfruit tree and cried *'eu'eu.* I told the aunt I was visiting that I was going home right away, and I'm glad I did, because when I got home I found my *hānai* (foster child) was sick and feverish."

---

*For other accounts, see listing, *kākū'ai.*

The same *aumākua* could also punish. One way to bring certain retribution was to eat the physical form of one's *aumakua*. Co-author Pukui relates:

"There were things we could not eat because if we did, it would kill us . . . a cousin of mine defiantly ate a certain sea creature and said 'I ate the body of our *aumakua!*' He died a month later."

Though this death 30 days later cannot be considered an illustration, the late Nils P. Larsen, M.D., speculated that sudden death or illness after "eating one's *aumakua*" might be "clan allergies," family-line allergic sensitivities reinforced by the Hawaiian practice of intermarriage within the *'ohana*.[5]

illness was
punishment

Illness was often thought to be punishment sent from an offended *aumakua*. Breaking food *kapus* (taboos), bathing in pools that were *kapu,* violating the *kapus* of the menstrual period—all these could bring reprimands in the form of physical discomfort. So could behavior that impaired interpersonal relationships—greed, dishonesty, theft. Often there were "diagnostic clues." A swollen hand pained a thief until he made restitution. A sore foot told of "going where you were not supposed to be." An agony of pain in the scrotum betrayed the flagrantly unfaithful man. Psychosomatic ills were not limited to Western civilization.

The *aumākua* had many ways of expressing both warnings and displeasure. Says Mary Pukui:

dream warnings

"The *aumakua* makes its warnings, reprimands and guidance known in dreams, visions, physical manifestations, or just the nagging feeling that something is wrong. If you did something wrong unknowingly, you might be told in *hō'ike a ka pō* [revelation in the night, therefore a dream] or *hō'ailona* [sign or portent] while awake. This would be so you would know what you were punished for. Then you could correct your mistake."

This offer of a "second chance" suggests that the *aumākua,* even when displeased, were not vengeful. They forgave as well as chastised. Says one of Hawaii's earliest written accounts, ". . . if you have sinned against your guardian spirit [aumakua], with the root of the *awa* you could be forgiven. Then the anger of the guardian spirit would be appeased . . ."[6]

The *aumākua's* many helpful, constructive functions strengthen this supposition. One such function was giving mental or physical strength when it was needed. To do this the *aumakua* entered into or possessed *(noho)* a human, in varying degrees and lengths of time.

enabling
concepts

Three enabling-strengthening concepts are associated with the *aumākua: kīheipua, ho'oūlu ia* and *noho.*

Kī he i pua or *kīheipua** comes from *kihei* (shoulder covering) and *pua* (flower). It is the "flower shoulder covering" the *aumakua* places gently over the helpless, the child, the sick, the aged. Or to use a later meaning of *kihei,*

---

*The term *kiheipua* seems to be confined to the Ka'u area of Hawaii, but the concept is generally known.—M.K. Pukui.

a "shawl" of help and comfort. It is the influence of one's *aumakua* that temporarily enables a helpless person to function and help himself.

Mrs. Pukui gives this example:

"A woman may be sick and helpless in bed. Suddenly she feels strong. She feels her *aumakua* is there—right there! She can get up, wash the dishes, straighten the house, do what must be done. After she senses the *aumakua* has gone, she is weak and sick again."

Kiheipua comes by itself, the unsolicited gift of one's compassionate *aumakua*. A somewhat stronger possession that enables is *ho'oulu ia*. This can be prayed for.

Ho'oulu ia is literally the "making to grow." Still far short of total possession, *ho'oulu ia* is a kind of inspiration. Here is a surge of strength and control that gets a job finished. That turns an acceptable bit of work into a superior one. That transforms a mediocre artistic endeavor into a superior, even superlative one. Laka, goddess of the hula and an *aumakua*, was invariably called upon to inspire the dancer to a better performance.

"Laka takes mild possession. She is dancing through the dancer," explains Mrs. Pukui.

So strong was this sense of Laka *and* dancer becoming one during the hula, that the *lei* the dancer wore became *kapu*. The dancer should not give her *lei* away or put another *lei* on top of the one dedicated to Laka. For as Mary Pukui quotes one serious hula dancer, "It is *our lei*. Mine and my *aumakua*'s."

A third type of possession is the total—but not permanent—possession called *noho* or *noho ia*. Other spirits, notably spirits of the more recent, known dead could also take possession. (See *noho*.)

Noho by one's *aumakua* may supply the sudden burst of "superhuman" strength that enables a mother to lift a heavy log before it crushes her child, or the "second wind" that helps the exhausted swimmer make it to shore. In the benign *noho* of the *aumakua*, normal capability becomes spectacular.

agent of
'ānai (curse)

The *aumakua* also carried out the curse *('ānai)* one person put on another.

In the "relatives beyond death" concept of the *aumākua*, it was understood that even spiritual beings were not heroic, helpful or admonitory all the time. The *aumākua* also had that most beguiling quality, a sense of fun.

"*Aumākua* could be capricious, mischievous and naughty!" says Mary Pukui.

But even the tricks of a naughty *aumakua* were without malice. For example:

A dignified, usually quiet man all at once becomes "the life of the party." Then just as suddenly he stops, thinks, "what came over me!" and becomes his old, stuffy self. Explanation: his *aumakua* was having a little fun through him.

Without any previous plan, a woman out on an errand finds herself going just the opposite direction. The errand is forgotten and she visits some friends instead. Explanation: Her *aumakua* was having a small adventure through her.

judgment
after death

For all their appealing, human-like qualities, the *aumākua* remained figures of supreme authority. After death each mortal would know his *aumākua* as implacable judge and jury. For the *aumākua* had the power to punish or reward the released spirit, or even to send it back to the body.

eternity
called Pō

As tradition tells it, when the spirit left the body after death, it traveled along the roads and pathways of the bodily host's own island and on to a *leina* or "place of leaping." And from there the spirit plunged into the sea of eternity or *Pō*.

And there, to quote Mary Pukui, "the *aumākua* would be, ready to welcome those in life who had not offended."

revived after
apparent death

Not all spirits made this prompt leap into *Pō*. For some, the mystical acceptance into the *aumākua* was delayed by the *aumākua* themselves. These were the spirits who left the body prematurely in what were evidently "apparent deaths." Says Mary Pukui, "Sometimes when it is not yet time to die, the relatives stand in the road and make you go back. Then the breath returns to the body with a crowing sound, *o'ō-a-moa.*"*

Entry into *Pō* would also be delayed by living relatives who constantly recalled the spirit by practicing *'unihipili.* (See *'unihipili.*)

The true unfortunates were the spirits whose earthly existence was found unworthy. Explains Mrs. Pukui:

"Those who in life had offended and did not try to correct the offense disgusted the *aumākua*. The *aumākua* would not bother with them. These became *ao kuewa,* homeless, hungry, wandering spirits, chasing moths and grasshoppers for food."

Spirits neither delayed nor judged unworthy found the *aumākua* waiting, some say in ghostly canoes, near the *leina*. For the Hawaiian conscious of a well-spent life, here was the ultimate, expected benevolence of the *aumākua*. For the final great leap from Now into Forever is an awesome thing, and without the welcoming *aumākua* the mist-veiled waters of eternity would be chill and strange indeed.

welcome in Pō
for the worthy

This, then, was the reward for a good life! Eternity with those closest to the *'ohana*-loving Hawaiian, one's own ancestors. An eternal dwelling place in the mystic sea of *Pō,* and at the same time in the specific realm of family *aumākua,* whether water, or rock or sky or land or volcano.

The *aumākua* received their official dismissal notices more than a century ago when the Hawaiian people accepted the missionaries' Christian God.[7]

---

*The Hawaiian's knowledge of resuscitation was considerable. See *'o'ō-a-moa.*

But two questions persist:
Did the *aumākua* really go away? Or did they just go underground?

aumākua in
the present

For the majority of Hawaii's present multi-cultural population, the *aumākua* are forgotten or were never known. For some, *aumākua* is a still-vivid childhood memory. A middle-aged Hawaiian businessman remembers going out with his father to feed shark *aumākua*. Another, when irritated, mutters softly, "may your *aumakua* take care of [meaning punish] you!" And for a few persons the *aumākua* still quite literally exist. Says Mary Pukui: "I know families who even today make ritual offerings of young taro leaves and eggs to their *aumakua*."

For the Hawaiian and part-Hawaiian clients of the Center, and possibly their close associates, the *aumākua* have never quite disappeared. The "relatives" are still here, by implication. Many clients view dreams in the Hawaiian context as warning, experience waking visions or physical manifestations they interpret as portents, seek the significance of names (see *inoa*), use *ti* leaves to ward off trouble. Many have already consulted a *kahuna* (priest, healer) before they visit the Center, and at least one *kahuna* waits for guidance in a dream before deciding on remedial measures. In all these practices, the *aumākua* are traditionally present, even though the presence is today half acknowledged, or fully acknowledged but never called by name. Staff members speculate that clients most reticent about their *aumākua* may be the ones who more deeply believe in them and are influenced by their belief. This is in the traditional cultural pattern. As Mary Pukui points out, "Hawaiians didn't go around talking about their *aumākua*."

Clients who do mention *aumākua,* may say:

"I have *aumākua*. I don't exactly know which ones. They're just a presence. My *aumākua* have given me this *mana* [special power]. I have had it for 15 years. But since I turned to religion, the *aumākua* can't do anything. They're just there. The *mana* is there. But the *aumākua* can't interfere." (She meant interference to make the *mana* inactive.)

"I have a *mo'o aumakua*. My children are safe in water."

"I had this dream. I think it means I have a shark *aumākua*." (From a teenager).

More frequent are references to "spiritual" parents, ancestors or relatives, or statements that "my people are sharks" or "in our family we have *mo'o* people."

Since the time the *aumākua* (and *akuas*) were "put underground" more than a century ago, a mixed crop of beliefs has sprung from the fertile soil of religious-mystic concepts. The just-converted writers-translators of the mid-1800s attempted Hawaiian-Christian hybrids. From these writings came efforts to make the *aumākua* guardian angels. The two concepts refuse to merge. As Mary Pukui points out, the guardian angel "transfer" leaves out the dominant ancestor-relative concept in which one's close family *aumākua* or *'ao'ao* are known even by name. An *aumakua* is not just "a shark;" it is a specific named shark.*

---

*Not the name borne in life, but one acquired after becoming an *aumakua*. In contrast, the deified spirit of the recent dead (*'unihipili*) may continue to be "Kauane'a" or "Uncle Joe."

Today the most peaceful co-existence of *aumākua* and *akua* with the Christian God seems to be in prayers. Hawaiian and Christian prayers are sometimes said on the same occasion without any apparent conflict.

is aumakua
super ego?

Obviously a concept as pervasive and deeply felt as *aumākua* must contain universal elements, ideas and beliefs closely akin to those of man in other cultures and other eras. The near-parallel often cited is that of the *aumākua* with the Super Ego of Freud and the conscience of Christian belief.

Opponents of this theory see the early Hawaiians' sense of right and wrong as coming from the externalized controls of the *kapu* system. The view seems to make little distinction between the *kānāwai kapu ali'i* or chiefly, man-made laws, and *kānāwai akua* or laws of the gods. At its extreme, an early chiefly edict ordered a man killed if he changed his body position slightly during a long ritual. Only the chief's own counter-edict could spare the man caught moving. Here was a crime-punishment control which took in no internalized temptation to transgress and no realization of wrong doing. Conversely, a man who broke a *kapu* of *akua* or *aumakua* could be told by a chiding, nagging *aumākua* that he had done wrong, that he must repent, and right the wrong. The process comes pretty close to "having a guilty conscience" and "squaring things with one's conscience." The belief that one who felt innocent could refuse to accept a curse or send back a destructive spirit, and the soul-searching of the *ho'oponopono** (all involving the *aumākua*) suggest a deeply internalized consciousness of right and wrong, guilt and innocence.

Dr. Haertig, our psychiatric consultant, sees the *aumākua* concept as including but not limited to functions of the Super Ego or conscience. He says:

"It seems important that these are family gods with names. Even though these people are in such dim and distant past that nobody alive ever saw them, yet they seem a somewhat mystical and externalized form of deeply ingrained family traditions, family mores, standards and values. All of these have similar broad standards in many families, but each has its unique variances within each particular family. I think this goes beyond the ordinary, limited concept of Super Ego.

"The concept has a similarity to the Oriental feeling for family traditions, perhaps some connection with the Orient's ancestor worship. And certainly it has a counterpart in Western culture, especially in English families who have lived, often on the same land, where generation after generation of ancestors have lived and died. One such Englishman told me, 'I have this sense of an actual physical presence. I can feel my ancestors approving or disapproving my actions . . . almost see them nodding their heads in approbation or shaking their fingers sternly.'

"In the Hawaiian *aumākua* are mystic entities with names. Yet operationally they are experienced as principles, values, standards. Undoubtedly these values and standards were taught Hawaiian children directly by their living family seniors and eventually internalized. Yet it goes beyond that. It

---

**Prayerful family council to "set to rights" disturbed personal and family relationships. See listing.*

is the feeling of a long, shadowy line of ancestors who exercise the seniors' prerogatives of guidance and judgment. It is the actual, felt presence of family."

Or as one Center staff member, a Hawaiian who attended a Christian day school and later earned a graduate degree, says frankly,

"In the back of our minds, there's always the old. It does come back. You have a feeling that your ancestors are always here—always with you."

NOTES AND REFERENCES

1. Kamakau. *Ka Po'e Kahiko: The People of Old*, p. 28.
2. Ibid, p. 30.
3. This "special class" seems to have been the reason for confusing *aumākua* and *'unihipili* and even referring to *aumākua* as slaves who did the bidding of the living. It was the *'unihipili*, the spirit of the more recently deceased person that was believed to be summoned back to obey commands of its human keeper. In this belief, bones or body parts were kept and cherished, not put into volcano or sea.
4. Beckwith. "Hawaiian Shark Aumakua," p. 503.
5. Larsen. Personal communication with M.K. Pukui. Unpublished papers.
6. Fornander. *Collection of Hawaiian Antiquities*, Vol. 5, p. 608.
7. Though the old gods were publicly disavowed with the breaking of eating *kapus* before the first missionaries arrived, Kalakaua wrote: "While the abolition of the *tabu* system received the universal approval of the masses, the destruction of the gods and temples met with very considerable remonstrance and opposition . . . many gods were saved from the burning temples, and thousands refused to relinquish the faith in which they had been reared." King David Kalakaua, *Legends and Myths of Hawaii*, p. 438.

'e'eu—formication; a creepy, crawly feeling of the skin interpreted as a sign or portent. "It is the feeling that the hair on the head is standing up," says Mrs. Pukui.

Deriv: *'eu*, to crawl.
See discussion under *'ili 'ōuli*.

hā—a strong expulsion of breath; to exhale; to breathe; breathe upon; breath; life. As ritual, connotes the imparting of mystic powers through breathing on recipient.

Deriv: unknown.

Grandfather was dying, and the entire *'ohana* (family clan) was gathered around his sleeping mat. Soon the old man's spirit would leave his body to join the family *aumākua* (ancestor gods) in the eternity called *Pō*. But before this final moment, the patriarch, with almost his last breath, would impart his specific *mana*, his canoe-building talent, to a chosen descendant.

But now, *Kulikuli! Noho mālie.** (Hush! Be silent.) The moment has come. Grandfather motions his grandson, Kelala, to come closer. Summoning

---

Noho mālie. Literally, "Sit quiet."

his last strength, the dying man chants briefly. Then come the solemn words:

"To you, my dear and beloved *mo'opuna* [grandson], I give my *mana*. May this *mana*, the gift of the *aumākua* passed down through me, guide your hand so that your canoes may be as fleet as the *makani* [wind], as strong as *nalu nui* [high surf], and as bold in ocean's waves as the *manō* [shark]."

Bending down, Kelala places his mouth close to his grandfather's. The old man draws a deep breath, and exhales directly into Kelala's mouth.

"Through this *hā*, you have now received my *mana*," he says, and in peace and serenity meets death.

Such, in this fictionized but typical example, was *hā*, Hawaii's ritual in which *mana* in its specialized sense was passed on. This was not the general, diffused *mana* of power, charisma or authority. That was passed on by spoken declaration alone. This was not skill or proficiency, for skills came from training and practice. Rather, the *mana* of *hā* was a talent or natural aptitude. This *mana* might be hand-and-eye coordination for the craftsman. Insight, keen perceptions, hands sensitive to tactile messages for the various medical *kahunas* (doctor-priests). A "feel for the soil" for the farmer. Keen sight and a sense of direction for the navigator. Color sense, spatial perception, perfect pitch, bodily grace, a feel for rhythm, a natural singing voice—all these are examples of specific *mana*.

All these innate abilities were believed to be gifts of the gods, held in trust by man. And so *hā* was both a "last will and testament" and a religious rite. Hawaii had long observed the connection between breathing and life. (See *'o'ō-a-moa*). Long before the missionaries arrived, Hawaiians had invested the "breath of life" with a spiritual significance that closely paralleled Biblical, and earlier Hebrew references.[1] The idea of imparting supernatural endowments is the basis of *hā*.

The *hā* ritual could be done in several ways. The grandfather of our example could have spat into the young man's mouth. Or he could have exhaled directly on the *manawa* (anterior fontanel, or in infants, the "soft spot") of the young man's head.*

As a "last will and testament," *hā* had few surprises. Normally the entire *'ohana* had known for years exactly which person would receive the elder's specific *mana*. For example, Kelala had been his grandfather's *haumana* or pupil† since early boyhood, learning the canoe-building craft in a kind of master-apprentice system. And within hours of Kelala's birth, various *hō'ailonas* (signs) had been interpreted to mean the boy would follow his grandfather's profession.

This practice of *hā* seems to corroborate other Hawaiian tendencies to pre-cast a child's life role.[2] However, Mary Kawena Pukui reminds us that *hā* allowed for flexibility:

"The descendant could refuse the *mana*. Then the dying elder could *hā* on somebody else, or he could choose to take his *mana* with him in death. The elder could also change his mind about who would receive the *mana*. Usually if a junior family member refused *mana*, or the elder changed his mind, this happened years before death came. If Kelala had lost interest in canoe-making

---

manawa can also mean eternity.

†*haumana*, one who "takes in" food. Comes from the old practice of pre-masticating food for a child. Less literally, one who "takes in" knowledge from the elder. For various meanings and diacritical markings of *mana*, read separate section, *mana*.

44

as he grew up, then his grandfather would have given his boat-building *mana* to a second choice."

The only surprise in the *hā* came before the actual ritual. Before imparting his *mana,* the dying elder revealed his last bit of factual knowledge about his art or craft. Traditionally, teachers never told their pupils all they knew. Always, some bit of knowledge, some "professional secret" was held in reserve. Thus the teacher, whether in a grandfather-grandson relationship or more formally as, for example, instructor for an entire hula class, maintained his position as expert authority.

And so, before he *hā'd,* Grandfather told Kelala how to choose the best wood for a canoe.

"When the *'elepaio* bird pecks at a tree, this is a *hō'ailona.* A sign. For the *'elepaio* is the goddess of canoe-making. She is telling you not to use that tree. It will not make a good canoe."[3]

In the Hawaiian *'ohana,* the passing on of specific *mana* through *hā* filled a number of functions. It prevented any family doubts or disputes regarding who was entitled to the *mana.* Psychologically it was a kind of "passing on the torch" ceremony, infusing a sense of pride and dedication in the chosen descendant. Or, as Mary Pukui phrases it,

"The elder was sending the message, 'Now, I am going. You must carry on where I left off.'"

Outside the death-bed, family context, *hā* was also a ritual used by medical *kahunas.* The *kahuna* imparted his healing *mana* by breathing on the plants or other medical substances he used in healing. This was usually accompanied by prayers.

In the present day, the *hā* over medicines or ritual objects is remembered and sometimes practiced. The *hā* of the dying seems to be forgotten. And though some Center clients worry because they have "inherited bad *mana*" or "sorcerer's *mana*", they are vague as to *how* they acquired it. They know only fragments of their Hawaiian traditions.

In such cases, some surface anxiety may be skimmed off by pointing out that all *mana,* diffused power or specific talent, was traditionally passed down in deliberate, open ceremony, not by unknown, secret ways. Specific *mana* whether for beneficial use such as healing, or destructive use in sorcery, was transmitted by the person-to-person ritual of *hā.*

NOTES AND REFERENCES

1. Gen. 2.7; John 20.22; numerous other examples.

   A Hebrew creation myth has Yahweh (God) creating Adam from earth (adamah) and breathing life into him. S.G.F. Brandon in "Man, Myth and Magic" p. 537. Petty and Sons, Leeds, Eng.

2. Examples of pre-casting a child's role: The naming of a child for a dead sibling; attention to the pregnant woman's diet so what she ate might give the child certain characteristics; choosing a favorite child to take future family responsibility.

3. The practical and the mystic meet—as they so often did in old Hawaii. The goddess Lea, wife of Ku-mo-ku-halai (Ku-who-spreads-trees-on-the-land), took the form of the *'elepaio* bird and in her bird form told the canoe maker not to use certain trees. So goes the legend. The bird has very keen hearing. When it hears worms or insects inside a tree trunk, it pecks the tree to get at them. Such a tree is rotten inside.

haka—a person selected to be the medium in spirit possession seances.

Deriv: *haka,* meaning to perch, a perch; to roost or rest; a roost.

Literally, a *haka* was one on whom a spirit "perched" in order to possess *(noho)* him. The distinction between *haka* in its ancient and modern sense is that traditionally the *haka* was chosen to be a medium for ritualized, induced spirit possession. Currently the word is sometimes used for one possessed in spontaneous *noho* or, very loosely, to describe the medium in a modern, western spiritualistic session.

In early times, each *'ohana* or family clan had its *haka.* He was carefully selected. Often supernatural signs were detected even at birth to designate a future *haka.* From then on, he was trained in the seance rituals. The rituals, conducted with prayer and the offering of *'awa* (Hawaii's ceremonial drink) to the gods, invited the spirit to take possession of the *haka,* Once possessed, the *haka* then spoke in the voice of the spirit, counseling, answering questions and solving family problems and prophesying. Once a *haka,* always a *haka.* The special *mana* or mystic power he possessed was lost only if the *haka* violated an important *kapu* (taboo).

Also operating in the seance was the family *kahu,* or "spirit keeper" or "guardian." The *kahu* persuaded the spirit to take possession of the *haka.* (See *kahu*).

In this induced possession, the spirit was believed to be a family *aumakua* (ancestor god), or more commonly, the spirit of a known, recently deceased relative.

The psychological process of induced possession seems to be one of hypnosis, probably induced in the *haka* by the *kahu,* or auto-hypnosis on the part of the susceptible, hypnosis-habituated *haka.* In this hypnotic trance, unconscious identification with a deceased family member could emerge as the "spirit" of this member speaking.

The traditional Hawaiian seance with *kahu* and *haka* no longer exists. Spontaneous *noho,* with much the same hypnotic functioning, is still encountered. *Kahu* is currently used to describe other types of spirit keeping or spirit control. The connotation of being a chosen one is still attached to *haka.* A *kahu* who sends a spirit to possess another selects the possessed person as *haka;* a spirit who of its own volition takes possession chooses a certain human as its medium or *haka.* See detailed discussion of *noho* and separate listing for *kahu.*

hana ho'ohanohano—ritual; ceremony; usually, but not always, of a supernatural or religious character.

Deriv: *hana,* work.
  ho'o, causative prefix.
  hanohano, to honor, exalt, glorify.
  Literally, "work to honor."

The rituals of old Hawaii ranged from the ceremonials of religion and the incantations of sorcery, to formalized phrases that stated a curse, solemnized a vow or formulated a binding agreement; to what seems to the Western viewpoint, little more than social etiquette. The range was wide, for in Hawaiian culture, human affairs and mystical-religious concerns were often indivisible. For example, traditionally the Hawaiian, sent to get medicine, might gather it in the forest. His hapa-haole* grandson usually buys it at the drugstore. Both are purely mundane errands. But in past eras, the Hawaiian gathered his curative plants ritually, plucking five with the right hand and praying to the god Ku, then five with the left hand as he prayed to the goddess Hina. And so his errand became equally a religious rite.

Limiting Hawaiian rituals to a rigid definition, or arranging them in a numbered listing is nearly impossible. For in Hawaiian customs of living, the ceremonials, sacred or occult, kept popping up. They still do.

The Center staff finds that some Hawaiians and part-Hawaiians still practice the following rituals: the use of green *ti* leaves for protection; *pī kai,* ceremonial sprinkling with salt water; *kapu kai,* the bath for spiritual purification; *mōhai puhi,* the burnt offering; the ritual offering of the spiritual essence *(aka)* of food to a god or family *aumakua* (ancestor god); and *wehe i ka Paipala,* the post-missionary ritual of pointing at random in the Bible to find guidance. Each is described under its own listing. However, all have certain characteristics in common. They are all performed, not merely spoken. They are all used today to seek help or avert harm, and so are used by persons more or less worried and anxious. Because of these similarities, I asked our psychiatric counsultant to give some general comments on ritual. The following, with minor editing, is a transcript of the recorded interview:

Mrs. Lee: I'm wondering what you think about the *effect* of using rituals like *ti* leaves for the Hawaiian, lighting a holy candle when it's storming for a Catholic, or, until he was demoted, touching one's St. Christopher medal as the plane takes off. These can be spiritually comforting. Are they psychologically so?

Dr. Haertig: Are you talking about a "security blanket"?

Mrs. Lee: Yes—or a ritual tranquilizer.

Dr. Haertig: Of course, one of the many functions of a ritual, completely aside from its content, is that when you don't know what to do, it gives you something to do. In that sense it serves as a safety valve for anxiety. It brings a little sense of certainty into a condition of uncertainty; something familiar into what may be all or partially unfamiliar.

Mrs. Lee: With rituals of religious significance, how much of the religious comfort carries over to the psychological assurance gained?

Dr. Haertig: This is implied in nearly all such ritual that is socially acceptable.** You might finger your prayer beads—Occidental or Oriental—and this could have the anxiety-easing, "something to do" effects we talked about, plus religious effect. Or I should say the *religious-psychological* effect, a kind of taking *oneself out of oneself*—and more. The ritual puts you in touch with forces or powers greater than yourself. But when we get to the religious or mystical, it's pretty hard to leave content out of consideration.

---

*hapa, half; haole; Caucasian.

**prayers, once addressed to gods of sorcery, would be today socially unacceptable ritual.

Mrs. Lee: Just one more question, and then on to content. I keep wondering about the possible harm of constant resorting to ritual.

Dr. Haertig: Certainly, ritual, like anything else, can be misused. Ritual can be a substitute for positive action, and in that sense, an escape or evasion. Or ritual can go well beyond comfort and be an *enabling* thing. And here we do come to content. For depending on content and for that matter, ritual's content in personal and society's beliefs and customs, a ritual prayer can make you feel you have God on your side, or the *aumakua,* or the *aumakua* **and** the living *'ohana* all solidly with you and helping you. Then ritual can enable the troubled person to do what he needs to do. It's a positive force leading to action. Particularly in religious ritual, the "outsider"—you or I or the social worker from the mainland—can't begin to understand a ritual unless we know its content. At least from a psychological point of view, the things that are used in a ritual and what is done with them all have symbolic value. The symbolic value must be known to grasp the subjective significance. This is just as true for the one who practices the ritual. When he knows what he's doing, what the symbolism is, then the ritual puts him in touch with his own symbolic meaning and that of his society. And from the ritual he gains, in the psychological sense, an affirmation of belonging. He is not alone. Not facing his troubles all alone.

Mrs. Lee: Can you give an example—I mean of *symbolic* values in ritual content?

Dr. Haertig: One that comes to mind is *mōhai puhi,* the offering made by burning food. Or more specifically, *mōhai hua* when an egg is one of the foods burned. First of all the egg—the *hua*—symbolized the whole chicken. And the chicken itself symbolized various things, depending on the color of the feathers and sometimes whether it was cock or hen. A speckled fowl was the specific offering to remove madness or insanity. And here we come to the Hawaiian belief that a mystical-symbolic quality can be extended or carried over because of a similar word. Insanity is called *pūpule.* The speckled fowl was called *pulepule.* Obviously, a troubled person performing the *mōhai hua* ritual has to know the symbolism. Without knowing symbolic values, he would merely be following forms somebody taught him. He would gain little religious-psychological sense of belonging and affirmation.

Mrs. Lee: But when content *is* understood . . . when content and form are both deeply felt religious ritual, then can't a Hawaiian ritual move on to an even larger dimension? Can't performance of the ritual become a true mystical experience?

Dr. Haertig: I just don't know—anymore than I know whether religious ritual in Western faiths becomes a mystical experience . . . or when and in what degree it takes on this dimension. Nobody has proved or disproved the mystical phenomenon in any faith or culture. Where Hawaiian religious-mystical rituals and beliefs are concerned, it seems the Westerner's cue is simply to respect these, form and content, to understand their significance as both religious and psychological function—and perhaps stop there.

Mrs. Lee: You mean—beyond that—don't pry? Don't be nosey?

Dr. Haertig: Particularly as behavioral scientist dealing with client, yes. Only let's put that in Hawaiian. Don't be *niele!*

hānai—to foster, a foster child; to adopt, an adopted child.
Deriv: to feed; to nourish.

Hānai as it is most often used means a child who is taken permanently to be reared, educated and loved by someone other than natural parents. This was traditionally a grandparent or other relative.

Hānai is also a handy verbal short cut for many phrases that more exactly define the fostering relationships. The child is the *keiki hānai,* or merely *hānai.* A male adoptive parent is *makua hānai kāne* and a woman, *makua hānai wahine.* A variant term is *kahu hānai* (master or teacher of the *hānai*). *Hānai* can become an adjective to describe the adult who takes the child as, for example, "my *hānai* grandmother," or the child, as in "my *hānai* grandchild." The action of taking a child to foster is *lawe hānai,* but *hānai* alone is also used as active or passive verb, as in "I *hānai'd* this child;" or "I was *hānai'd* to my grandparents."

Hānai had a slightly different meaning among *ali'i* (persons of royal blood) who served, and were usually related to, a ruling chief. The idea was that the ruler "cared for" these members of the court and therefore became their *hānai.* Even today, descendants of those who served Queen Liliuokalani may refer to "our *hānai,* Queen Liliuokalani."

If *hānai* as a word seems confusing, remember that the Hawaiian language was happily unconcerned with nouns, verbs and such word labeling. *Hānai* as a cultural practice was precise and clearly understood.

Hānai traditionally functioned within the Hawaiian *'ohana.** This was the "family clan" in which blood relationship was recognized and family loyalties and mutual responsibilities were extended even to what in modern terms could be called 13th or 14th cousins.

**hānai was
permanent**

Within the *'ohana,* authority, knowledge, privilege and clan responsibility were vested in senior members, usually those of the grandparent generation. Among the privileges of grandparents was that of taking as *hānai* the *hiapo* (first-born child) of one's children. The first-born girl was the *hānai* of the maternal grandparents. The child was given outright; the natural parents renounced all claims to the child. This became a binding agreement when the parents said in the hearing of others, *"Nāu ke keiki kūkae a na'au,"* I give this child, intestines, contents and all." (Emotions, intelligence and qualities of character were associated not with the brain or heart, but with *na'au,* the guts or intestines.)

In this traditional practice, there was no feeling of turning the child over to strangers as there is with present-day adoption. The whole feeling was that the first grandchild *belonged* to the grandparents. The natural mother had the baby on a kind of "loan" basis. The baby remained within the all-important unit—in which his own parents held only junior rank—the family clan or *'ohana.* However, the child knew and was usually visited by his natural parents. If the child was of the *ali'i,* his genealogy was known in detail for many

---

*It also means the nuclear family.

generations back. If he was a commoner, his blood lines were reasonably well known. The *hānai* child had his own sense of personal and family identity and learned to know who were the *aumākua* (ancestor gods) of his *'ohana*.

Often, natural parents and adoptive grandparents or other adoptive parents conferred over the child's welfare. Co-author Pukui, who was herself the *keiki hānai* of her maternal grandmother and later reared several *hānai* children, recalls:

"I knew, loved and respected my real parents. My parents and my *hānai* grandmother always talked over decisions that might be important to me."

However, parents could not reclaim their child except for death or serious incapacity of the adoptive parents. This total surrender of the child was planned so he would not become a pawn in later *hukihuki* (literally "pull pull"), the adult power struggle that, says Mrs. Pukui, "could make the child get sick or even die."

luhi was
foster care

A part-time or temporary system of child care or foster placement is described in the multi-purpose word, *luhi*. Literally *luhi* means "tiredness." It carries a connotation of "working or laboring in behalf of a child and thus becoming tired." There is no overtone of being "sick and tired." This is merely fatigue. *Luhi* does connote love, patience and concern.

Luhi can mean the child. An aunt, older sister or housekeeper-baby-sitter may say, "this child is my *luhi.*" A child may be both *hānai* and *luhi*. He is the *hānai* of his permanent, adoptive parents; he is the *luhi* of the temporary helper who cares for him. In the present day, *luhi* may describe a child placed temporarily in a foster home or child care facility.

The significance of *luhi* is its non-binding, temporary quality. Natural parents may reclaim the child in any *luhi* arrangement.

Hānai is a nearly equivalent term for legal adoption or *ho'ohiki*. (*Ho'ohiki* literally means to vow, promise or take a binding oath.) *Lawe hānai* and *ho'ohiki* are actually the same only in their permanency. Where feelings are concerned, the two practices are quite different. For the *hānai* system continued the link between mother and child, functioned within the family clan, and retained for the child knowledge of his heredity. Legal adoption outside the family breaks all ties with *'ohana*. The differences mean emotional conflicts for many of today's clients.

An almost typical case is that of the unmarried mother who is willing to have her baby adopted but whose own parents insist on keeping the baby. If the coming child is a *hiapo* (first-born) the grandparents-to-be stress "this is our flesh and blood . . . this baby *belongs* to us."

At its best, this strong traditional feeling means family support for the unwed mother and full acceptance of the child; at its worst, it views the child as a possession rather than a person.

Hawaiian grandparents and other relatives feel strongly that even the child of unwed parents should know his family background, and object to legal adoption because it blots out the past. The Hawaiian couple who want to adopt a child feel much the same. They are not at all concerned if the child is illegitimate. What they are worried about is taking a child whose parentage is concealed.

"A child has a right to know his genealogy," is a frequent comment.

aia ma kāhi hāiki
not yet born

Families often put off deciding what to do about the baby until after it is born. More than one worker has discovered that this frustrating "indecision" is really a deliberate decision not to plan. It comes from the Hawaiian traditional belief that it is unwise to make plans and talk about the baby while it is yet *"aia ma kāhi hāiki,"* literally "in a place narrow," or not yet born!

When plans are made, grandparents, in many cases, do "want to keep the baby no matter what." The wish comes from deeply ingrained traditions and deeply felt emotions. Dr. Haertig comments:

"Keeping the baby may have been workable in the old milieu, but completely unworkable in the new. However, the feelings that prompt this wish to keep the *hānai* can be respected. On this basis of respect and recognition of feelings, discussion is possible, and the realization that situations have changed may emerge."

He tells of a case that is almost a composite of many cases in which relatives cite the importance of keeping the baby "within the *'ohana.*"

"This was an unmarried mother, a young Hawaiian girl living at home with her parents. The parents insisted on keeping the baby. The girl was leaning very much toward giving the baby out for adoption. The parents outlined the *'ohana* system to me with all its advantages. Very real advantages in the right *'ohana* in the right era! Yet this family was poorly functioning, and badly disrupted—and had been for many years.

"I put it squarely to the girl and her family. 'If you can and will create a real *'ohana,* one in the old, traditional sense, then it will make sense to follow the old, traditional customs and keep the baby.

"'Now . . . can you create a real *'ohana?'*

"They all said they'd think it over. So they went home . . . thought a few minutes . . . and had a real knock-down, drag-out fight! After they simmered down—it took a while—they reached their decision: To give the baby up for adoption."

The example holds good for more than baby placement decisions. The traditional Hawaiian solution does not always solve the modern Hawaiians' problems. But knowing the Hawaiian traditions, and recognizing and respecting the emotional influences of the past make it easier for client and professional worker to arrive at the best, most realistic solution.

hiapo—first-born child.

Deriv: unknown.

In the Hawaiian *'ohana* (family clan) the *hiapo* or first-born child had his future clearly outlined even before birth. Traditionally, the *hiapo* was given outright to grandparents as their *hānai* or foster child.

Occasionally, the *hiapo* was given to some other senior member of the *'ohana.* Rarely, if ever, was the first-born kept and reared by his natural parents. If the child's mother felt any pangs of parting, it is not known. Members of the *'ohana* lived close to each other, and the natural mother did not lose contact with her child. But perhaps the real reason Hawaiian mothers suffered no real emotional crises in giving up the first-born child was that they never considered the *hiapo* as totally their own child. Says Mrs. Pukui, "the first born son belonged to the paternal grandparents. The first-born daughter belonged to the maternal grandparents."

The system of giving the *hiapo* to senior relatives filled many of the needs of the society it existed in. Hawaiians placed great value on traditional ways and in knowing family genealogy and the family ancestor gods *(aumākua)*. Yet there was no written language to record this history. The *hiapo* was the "living history book." While other children of the *'ohana* learned to fish and tend taro, the *hiapo* memorized the family genealogical chants, social and religious customs, *kapus* (taboos) and specialized skills and knowledge. To do this he became the constant companion of the grandparents, listening, learning, rehearsing, so even the tempo and cadence of each *pule* (prayer) and *oli* (chant) would be traditionally correct.

The *hiapo's* training was not all memory work. He was also taught to assume responsibilities. Eventually, the *hiapo* would become the one to advise in family illness, dispute or other crises.

As the repository of responsibility, the *hiapo* was usually the *punahele* or favored child in the grandparents' home.* As such he might be served the most tempting bits of food, given massages *(lomi lomi)* or excused from manual labor. The other children were expected to obey him. The privileges were balanced with duties. Says Mrs. Pukui, "the *punahele* was at the beck and call of the grandparents. He had little time for play. He was 'on call' all the time."

Today, many of the traditions—and certainly the emotions—associated with the *hiapo* still exist. The first-born child is no longer routinely given to grandparents, yet Hawaiian grandparents feel strongly possessive of *hiapo* grandchildren.

The prospective grandparents in unmarried mother cases seem to suffer as much if not more than the mother when the child is given out for adoption. One caseworker estimates that in about nine out of ten unwed mother cases, the grandparents want desperately to keep the child, but realize that adopting out is better for the baby. Here the worker must help grandparents as well as mother work through the grief and deep regret *(minamina)* of giving up the baby.

In about ten percent of unwed mother cases, the grandparents still feel the *hiapo* "belongs" to them and resist offering the baby for adoption. Often this emotional decision puts the child into an already disturbed home. (See discussion under *hānai.*)

One rather extreme example is a current case in which a mother took her son's pregnant girl friend into the home. The woman so pampers the pregnant girl that her own children feel rejected and jealous. The son and prospective father is a school dropout, unemployed and already involved in car stealing. The son's mother is frequently ill and works to the limit of her strength at a low paying job. Yet, so far, her strong desire for the *hiapo* yet to be born has

---

Punahele status was not limited to the *hiapo*. Another child with evidence of special talents might be chosen as *punahele*.

blinded her to any objective view of what is best for the coming child or for her own children.

Another example involved a rare brother-and-sister incest which resulted in the girl's pregnancy. The mother of the two siblings, both minors, was torn between giving the baby out for adoption and keeping her *hiapo*. She felt because of its in-the-family parentage the child was doubly her own "flesh and blood."

Even in families with no such grave problems, the Hawaiian grandparent is apt to feel possessive of the *hiapo*. For example, one young Caucasian mother's rebuke, "you raised your children your way, now let me raise mine my way," resulted in an estrangement of several years with her Hawaiian mother-in-law. The baby involved was the first-born.

The *hiapo* in his adult status as senior member of a family or family branch is still an influence in Hawaiian family life.* The senior is arbitrator, counselor and comforter in domestic difficulties. This is discussed under listing, *kupuna* and *hānau mua*.

hō'ailona and hō'ike—sign and revelation.

hō'ailona—a sign, omen or portent; to make a sign.
> Deriv: *ho'o,* causative prefix.
> *'ai,* unknown.
> *lona,* the log on which a canoe rested. This took on the meaning of a marker or sign, showing the proper place for a specific, beached boat. Inspection of the log and surrounding sand also provided signs showing whether the canoe was taken out before or after a rain, how heavily it was loaded, etc.

hō'ike—a revelation. The knowing. To see, know or receive knowledge. Many other meanings. Among Center clients, most commonly used to mean a supernatural revelation.
> Deriv: *ho'o,* causative prefix.
> *'ike,* to know, understand. To receive a message from the gods.

Two Hawaiian women, let's call them Nalani and Noni, sat on the *lānai* (porch) one afternoon, enjoying a cooling summer shower. Then the rain ceased. A rainbow appeared, an opalescent arch, vaulting into the sky from the sea, and, so it seemed, descending at the very gate of the house where the women sat.

"What a beautiful *ānuenue* [rainbow]! It's a sign of something," said Nalani.

But Noni gasped and began to cry,

"My mother! It's my mother! She just passed away!"

Before long the message came. Noni's mother had died at that very moment.

---

*If the *hiapo* dies or is not competent to fill the senior role, another family member may become the senior.

The incident is a true one.

We use it here merely to illustrate two Hawaiian terms.

Nalani knew the rainbow was a sign. She recognized it as a *hō'ailona.* However, the portent was impersonal. It carried no message for her.

Noni, however, perceived a *hō'ailona* which she instantly interpreted and accepted as a personalized message. Noni had a revelation. She experienced *hō'ike.*

Hō'ailona and *hō'ike* have always been a part of Hawaiian life. Centuries ago, a *kahuna lapa'au* ("family doctor" or medical *kahuna*) on his way to see a sick person would cancel his visit if he saw a man with his hands crossed behind his back. This was a *hō'ailona,* a sign he could not cure the patient.[1] When Queen Emma was visiting at Puna, she saw a strange, moving light far out to sea and exclaimed, "Oh, please, wait until I get home!" She left for Oahu the next morning. When she arrived, she found the *hō'ike* conveyed by the moving light had been true. Her sister-in-law, Princess Ruth, had died just as Queen Emma saw the *hō'ailona.* Mary Kawena Pukui relates the story.

**types of
portents**

In the past and the present, *hō'ailona* or mystic portents take the following forms:

Manifestations of nature. These may be a chill wind, whirlwind, sudden mist, rainbow, the flight pattern or cry of birds, cloud formations, unexpected ocean waves, strange behavior of fish or animals. Without mystic overtones, any natural manifestation may be a sign. For example, a dark cloud is a *hō'ailona* of rain.

Man-made rites of divination. These range from Hawaii's ancient *kuni* fires in which the apparition of a murderer's face could be seen, to the adopted Christian ritual of using the Bible to provide a sign (see *wehe i ka Paipala*).

Hō'ailonas of pregnancy that predict the sex and personal characteristics of the coming child. Many of these are similar to beliefs in other cultures. If a pregnant woman held out her right hand, advanced her right foot, etc., this meant the baby would be a boy. Some are old food-craving signs. If a mother longed for a squid, the child would be affectionate (clinging as a squid clings). If she craved the *hilu* fish, the child would be quiet and industrious.[2]

In one legendary instance, a mother-to-be craved an eye of the fierce tiger shark. In due time, her son did indeed grow up bravest and boldest of men. He was Kamehameha the Great.

Body sensations and manifestations. These include smelling flowers or other scents out of their normal setting, sudden chilling, goosebumps *('ōkaka-la),* a bite or bruise mark (see *nahu akua,* "spirit bite") and various skin sensations described under *'ili 'ōuli.*

Visions, supernatural voices, and *dreams.* To Center clients, dreams, visions and voices are the most portentous of all *hō'ailonas.* All three are reported constantly. Because of their importance in Hawaiian life and their psychological implications, they are discussed separately under the topic headings: *akakū, hihi'o,* and *ūlāleo,* (visions and voices) and, in Vol. 2, *moe'uhane* (dreams).

Ho'ailona and *hō'ike* are mystic-psychic-cultural companions. Each can be found alone. More often, both work together. Sign stimulates revelation, *Hō'ailona* brings about *hō'ike.*

In the traditional Hawaiian view, a *hō'ailona* (in the mystic sense discussed here) was always sent by a spirit. This might be a known, recently deceased relative, lover or friend, an *aumakua* (ancestor god), a destructive *akua* (god) sent by an enemy, or any ghost, giant or demi-god. Even a sign made by man, as in rites of divination, took on significance because of spirit influence. The *hō'ike,* the immediate, awesome, emotion-charged flash of knowledge, carried mystic overtones. When a *hō'ailona* was explained later by another person (as in dream interpretation) the understanding gained was not considered *hō'ike.*

When a *hō'ailona* is perceived, the *hō'ike* or revelation it conveys is, of course, shaped by many influences. Perhaps the most pervasive is knowledge of historical and legendary precedents and the associations each particular *'ohana* (family clan) attaches to a particular *hō'ailona.*

"Families hand down interpretations like heirlooms!" says Mrs. Pukui.

Hō'ike might be a blend of handed-down legend and subjective personal interpretation. An example is the rainbow *(ānuenue).* When and where it appeared, its size and appearance, plus associated past events and *hō'ikes* all might color personal interpretation. Says Mrs. Pukui:

"The rainbow right in front of one could mean 'Go back. There is danger ahead.' Or it might mean that somebody close and loved is going to die. Or that an *ali'i* (member of nobility) had died and is rejoining his *aumākua.* Or that some kind of separation is going to happen. Or, a rainbow appearing just as a baby is born could mean this is an especially blessed baby."

A rainbow can mean supernatural approval, as this incident in midsummer, 1970, indicates:

A Hawaiian woman from a neighbor island had a dream which she took as a sign that she should talk over certain personal matters with Mrs. Pukui. She obeyed the *hō'ailona,* took the next plane and called on Mrs. Pukui. As the women talked, a rainbow appeared.

"Look! They [the *aumākua*] are pleased that I came to see you," said the visitor. "This is a good sign. They are glad I am here."

Legendary meanings live on in the following *hō'ailonas:*

The dog digs a hole near the house. Any *lua* (pit) is a *hō'ailona* of death. Fill the hole immediately!

The dog howls. To this almost universal death portent, Hawaiian belief adds an explanation. The dog howls because he sees the spirit of the dead or dying person.

A hovering bird may convey a protective warning, especially if the bird, usually owl or mudhen, is one's *aumakua.* But birds that single out a person or house may also mean disaster. One client family moved out because a flock of birds perched habitually on the roof of their house. Perhaps this was *hō'ike* by precedent. Previously, birds had flocked over another home, and, so went the talk in the community, "the man who lived there died."

How much of a revelation comes from legendary precedent and how much comes from personal fears or wishes is hard to sort out, especially in the frequently experienced *hō'ailonas* associated with an *ālai* (obstacle or obstruction). Nearly any obstacle or even a delaying incident can be a *hō'ailona* that means "Go back. Give up the project, at least for today."

Consider the 1970 example of a stalwart Hawaiian who went fishing and was knocked over by a small wave.

"They don't want me to fish here. Better I go home," he explained.

Hō'ike, or the self-interpretation of a sign, may be a mystically-tinged experience that reinforces what one already believes or wants to believe. For example, this excerpt from a 1969 case report:

hō'ikes
of grief

"This couple lost their son some time ago, and they go regularly to his grave. The mother gets a lot of comfort out of talking to him . . . bringing him up to date on what is happening at home, telling him how she misses him. All the time they are at the grave, there is this nice, cold sort of wind that comes down from the valley . . . the mother says this is a caress from the son . . . from his presence. The mother feels the *makani* (cold breeze) is the son."

(Here a common manifestation of incomplete grief work is expressed Hawaiian-style. To the mother, the son continues to be a living presence, rather than an important memory.)

For another person, a *makani* might foretell a death, warn of danger, or convey a less-specific message of fear or anxiety. A whirlwind is traditionally a warning. All these *makani* messages are, even today, believed to be carried by a spirit. (In fact, *makani* has a second meaning, "a spirit".) The spirit is *there.* With one. Even sensations of chill without a breeze or obvious cause may mean a spirit is present. (See *hui'hu'i* in section, *'ili'ōuli.*)

Hō'ailonas that signify a visit from the dead are common. The following 1969 account is typical of many case reports:

"Some nights when _____ is sleeping, she will smell the medicinal odor that she relates to her husband when he was in the hospital. [He died a year ago.] . . . She knows that her husband is returning to the house."

Or,

"The lights go on in the middle of the night." . . . "footsteps go up the stairs to the boys' bedroom."

These, even the erratic electricity, have all been viewed as signs that the spirit of a dead family member has returned. And while the *reason* for the spirit-visit may cause worry, the presence of the dead ordinarily does not. Hawaiians were and are yet very close to life-after-death.

Such are Hawaii's *hō'ailonas* and *hō'ikes.* Signs and revelations. They range from manifestations of nature to mystic omens concerned with birth, death and the world of the supernatural. Mankind through the ages has observed and interpreted portents. Hawaii's vast lore of *hō'ailonas* has much in common with medieval European beliefs.

In present day Center experience, *hō'ailonas* are reported constantly. Clients who talk about a *hō'ailona* invariably have already interpreted it, usually in the instant, revelatory *hō'ike.* (Dreams are the exception.) The *hō'ike,* personal, subjective, free of deliberate marshalling of facts and conscious weighing of pros and cons, is often especially revealing of individual emotions, relationships and experiences.

Even the less subjective interpretation that comes from ethnic or family legend and precedent may provide information about, for example, an individual's self-image. Does he see the portent as coming from the *aumakua* or from a recently deceased person, from the Holy Ghost, the Virgin Mary, the Dancing Goddess* or a kind of mystic merger? This may be a clue, but not by itself a conclusion, that the person sees himself as Hawaiian, Filipino, Japanese, Portuguese or Haole or that his own self-identification is confused.

the logic
of portents

In any cultural setting, certain portentous experiences make excellent behavioral sense. The future is foreseen by reading, consciously or unconsciously, the logic in a chain of events. Premonitions are based on subliminal (below the threshold of consciousness) perceptions.

In other omens, the interaction of mind and body is generally acknowledged. We know that suggestion or auto-suggestion can stimulate sensory experiences. We know that physical sensations may be caused by discharges in the autonomic nervous system when it is stimulated by excitement or anxiety. And we also know that the bodily accompaniments of signs and revelations are "handed down" in families, just as the interpretations are. One family line may feel and express anxiety in cold chills, and another follow what amounts to a "tradition" of feeling faint, and yet another tend to have joint pains. These phenomena of "heirloom sensations" have been observed; they have not been explained.

Other revelatory occurrences cannot be explained. In any culture, this is often true of seeing visions. In Hawaiian life, the fact that a visionary experience may defy explanation does not lessen its significance to the visionary or the professional counselor. Here, especially, the *hō'ike* may carry more meaning than the occurrence of the *hō'ailona*.

REFERENCES

1. Fornander. *Collection of Hawaiian Antiquities,* Vol. 1, p. 92.
2. Pukui. "Beliefs on Birth, Infancy and Childhood," p. 2.

"ho'i no 'ai i kou kahu"—A phrase meaning "go back and destroy your keeper." Addressed to the spirit bringing evil, it sent the evil back to the original sender, the "keeper" or controller of the spirit.

Referred to in *'unihipili, akualele, ho'opi'opi'o.*

"ho'i no kau me 'oe"—Phrase meaning, "what you have just given me, return to you." Ritual used by an innocent person who had been cursed for supposed wrong-doing. This sent the curse back to the original curser. One of many phrases to refuse or send back harm or evil.

See *'ānai.*

---

*The *Tensho Kotai Jingu-kyo* or "Dancing Religion" sect begun fairly recently in Japan now has devout followers in some rural sections of Hawaii.

honi pāha'oha'o—mysterious smell; smell that causes wonder; smell that brings longing.

> Deriv: *pāha'oha'o.*
> *pā*, prefix, "having" or "quality of."
> *ha'oha'o*, mystery, wonder, strangeness; also longing, desire.
> *honi*, scent, smell; kiss (touching sides of noses together).

The phrase, *honi pāha'oha'o*, is really "shorthand Hawaiian" that takes liberties with Hawaiian speech patterns. A Hawaiian describing a smell, mysterious or not, would probably not say *honi*. Instead he might use any of some 55 terms that specify in one word just how sweet or unpleasant or obnoxious a scent is, whether it is "cool" or "hot," and whether it is of animal, plant or mineral origin. The Hawaiian nose was capable of subtle perception. So the language indicates.

But if what the nose and mind registered was out of its expected setting, then the odor became a mystic portent. The content of the message came in the *hō'ike* (revelatory knowledge) of the one who had sniffed the mysterious scent. For example:

"I smelled gardenias in the ocean. I got back to shore fast." The explanation given was: Gardenias don't belong in the ocean, therefore someone dead was sending a message. Who grew and loved gardenias? Grandmother. Therefore Grandmother was warning me to get out of the water before some harm might come to me.

This is a slowed-down explanation. *Hō'ike* more often comes almost instantly. As,

"Then I caught his body odor. He had come back." (The odor referred to was the frequently appealing scent of a man, not that of stale perspiration. The "longing" connotation of *pāha'oha'o* seems evident here.)

The cultural significance and possible psychiatric implications of *honi pāha'oha'o* are, in general, similar to those of visions or hearing mystic voices. These are discussed under listing, *akakū, hihi'o* and *'ūlāleo.*

ho'opi'opi'o—implanting distress, usually pain or illness, by the use of gesture and concentration. In its original meaning, *ho'opi'opi'o* was possible only between two persons who could see each other.

> Deriv: *ho'o*, causative prefix.
> *pi'o*, arch or arc. Literally "to cause or make an arch."
> The connotation is that a mystical-mental arch existed between two persons. Spirits carried the pain over this arch, from sender to receiver.

When sorcery flourished in Hawaii Nei, one person could give another a pain or even a fatal illness, with no words spoken between the two. The "sender," usually a sorcerer, could pass his hand over his own forehead, and so cause a headache in the unfortunate observer. The sender could grasp his own chest, thereby starting a pain in another's chest. Whatever gesture he used, the sender also concentrated intensely, sending over the *pi'o* discomfort and distress.

As Mary Kawena Pukui views it, concentration in *ho'opi'opi'o* was always accompanied by gestures. Gestures so subtle they were not observed may have led to reports of *ho'opi'opi'o* by concentration alone.

For the victim who saw the sorcerer's gesture, quick action meant a quick cure. To quote Mrs. Pukui:

"If a person caught another in *ho'opi'opi'o,* he was supposed to repeat the gesture. He rubbed his own forehead, or clutched his own chest or stomach. This was counter-sorcery. This sent the pain back to the one who started the *pi'opi'o.*"

If the victim did not see and imitate a significant gesture, hope lay in two types of ritual counter-sorcery. Both were based on the belief that evil spirits carried the discomfort from sender to receiver. In one, *kauila* wood, closely associated with sorcery, was placed over the doorway. In the other, *ti* leaves, always a protective-purifying agent, were brought into the house.[1] With either,* prayers were said, and spirit and distress were told to "go back and destroy your sender" *(ho'i no 'ai i kou kahu),* or "what you have given me, return to you" *(ho'i no kau me 'oe).*

As a rule, says Mrs. Pukui, the victim of unobserved *ho'opi'opi'o* did not know what happened to him. He usually died of a "mystery disease," one that could not be diagnosed by *hāhā* (palpation) or traced to a psychic-mystic cause during *ho'oponopono.*†

Ho'opi'opi'o seems to be forgotten today, though Hawaii's laws still specify penalties for practicing it.[2] Memories of *ho'opi'opi'o* may be part of current reports of being "hexed" or the victim of the "evil eye." Here everything from Portuguese to Puerto Rican to Pennsylvania Dutch beliefs and vocabulary are often scrambled together.

We mention Hawaii's old, silent sorcery for two reasons:

It is one of the few exceptions (*mana'o'ino,* continuing hostile thought, is another) to the belief that thought did not harm until it was put into speech or action. (See *hua 'ōlelo,* broken promise or prophetic threat, and *'ānai,* curse.)

Ho'opi'opi'o is a most specific example of suggestion and counter-suggestion enacted in an atmosphere of susceptibility. The sender was already known to be a sorcerer with awesome powers. His victim was psychologically ready to accept his gesture-borne suggestion, or to take it seriously enough to return it. Returning it, he used counter-suggestion. This, too, was apt to be effective because of the sorcerer's guilt at starting the whole pain-inflicting process.

Kauila wood from trees on Molokai was used to send spirits on destructive errands. See *akualele.* In the above remedial use, the rationale was that the wood helped send the spirit forth again— this time to destroy the sorcerer. *Ti* leaves were used to keep the spirit from re-entering a house. They were not a "vehicle" for sending spirits.

†Literally, "to set right." The family council to find the cause of trouble and disturbed relationships and correct them.

The specific suggestibility in *ho'opi'opi'o* functioned among people generally sensitive to the feelings and moods of others. Tears, laughter and shivers of excitement spread contagiously. Psychosomatic suggestibility is often observed today; it seems to have been especially strong in the past. Old accounts tell of deliberate transfer of pain from a woman in labor to another person, often a man.[3]

For the sensitive, susceptible Hawaiians, belief in *ho'opi'opi'o* does not seem remarkable. For in any culture, if one person holds an intensely negative mental "set" or attitude against another, he sets in motion a chain of damaging responses and counter-responses, actions and counter-actions. These may be direct or indirect, conscious or unconscious, touched off by words, or without speech. In old Hawaii, this sequence was ritualized and invested with mystic significance as *ho'opi'opi'o*.

REFERENCES

1. Kamakau. *Ka Po'e Kahiko: The People of Old,* p. 138.
2. Section 772-1 current Hawaii Revised Statutes. Quoted in Honolulu Star-Bulletin, June 25, 1970.
3. Pukui. "Beliefs on Birth, Infancy and Childhood," p. 6.

ho'oponopono and related concepts.

ho'oponopono—setting to right; to make right; to correct; to restore and maintain good relationships among family, and family-and-supernatural powers. The specific family conference in which relationships were "set right" through prayer, discussion, confession, repentance, and mutual restitution and forgiveness. This specific practice is discussed here.

> Deriv: *ho'o,* to make, cause or bring about.
> *pono,* correct, right, in perfect order; approximately 20 other closely related meanings.
> *ponopono,* (reduplicate), in order, cared for, attended to. Both forms connote what is socially-morally approved and desirable.

The cassette of the 1971 model tape recorder turned as Mrs. S＿＿＿＿ told this incident of 15 years ago:

"My *hānai* [adoptive] Mom called from the Big Island and said she had a dream that bothered her. She said she had a problem, so better I come home already.

"I said, 'Why don't we talk about it now, over the phone? Maybe I can help you.'

"But Mom said, 'No, better you come home. We need *ho'oponopono.'* So early next day, I flew home for *ho'oponopono."*

What is this *ho'oponopono?* Why is it important enough to cause phone calls and plane trips between islands?

As Mary Kawena Pukui describes it:

"Ho'oponopono is getting the family together to find out what is wrong. Maybe to find out why someone is sick, or the cause of a family quarrel. Then, with discussion and repentance and restitution and forgiveness—and always with prayer—to set right what was wrong.

"to set right" with each other and God

"Ho'oponopono is to set things right with each other and with the Almighty. I took part in *ho'oponopono* myself for 47 years, from semi-Christian to Christian times. And whether my *'ohana* [family] prayed to *aumākua* [ancestor gods] or to God, the whole idea of *ho'oponopono* was the same. Everyone of us searched his heart for hard feelings against one another. Before God and with His help, we forgave and were forgiven, thrashing out every grudge, peeve or resentment among us."

who took part: a family matter

Ho'oponopono was essentially a family matter, involving all the nuclear or immediate family, or only those most concerned with the problem. Some leeway was possible. A non-relative living with the family might take part if he was involved with the *pilikia* (trouble). Children could be excused. And if an involved family member was absent, *ho'oponopono* might be held as a "second best" alternative to full family participation.[1] Though the entire extended family could hold *ho'oponopono,* this was usually impractical. Mrs. Pukui points out that with too many present, the whole person-to-person interchange of confession-discussion-forgiveness became impossible. Thus *ho'oponopono* was not a community-wide therapy. Only the title in its broadest meaning, and parts of *ho'oponopono,* such as prayer and periods of silence, apply to a large gathering.

"The ideal," says Mrs. Pukui, "is to keep it in the family and have all the immediate family taking part."

kahuna or family senior could lead

Either a helping-healing *kahuna* (but not the *kahuna 'anā'anā* or sorcerer) or a family senior could conduct *ho'oponopono.* In the closely knit community life of early Hawaii, the *kahuna* usually had a kind of "family doctor" knowledge of a family. This would allow him to lead *ho'oponopono* with real insight into the problems.

From Mrs. Pukui's memories and personal experience, and the shared views and experiences of Hawaiian staff members and associates, we have outlined an "ideal" or "standard" *ho'oponopono.* Basic procedures and therapeutic dynamics are the same, whether the *ho'oponopono* also included traditional-pre-Christian rituals or modern additions.

essentials of ho'oponopono

This *ho'oponopono* has certain specific requirements. Some concern procedure; others attitudes.

Always included in complete *ho'oponopono* are:

61

Opening *pule* (prayer) and prayers any time they seem necessary.

A statement of the obvious problem to be solved or prevented from growing worse. This is sometimes called *kūkulu kumuhana* in its secondary meaning.

The "setting to rights" of each successive problem that becomes apparent during the course of *ho'oponopono,* even though this might make a series of *ho'oponoponos* necessary. (This is *mahiki*).

Self-scrutiny and discussion of individual conduct, attitudes and emotions.

A quality of absolute truthfulness and sincerity. Hawaii called this *'oia'i'o,* the "very spirit of truth."

Control of disruptive emotions by channeling discussion through the leader.

Questioning of involved participants by the leader.

Honest confession to the gods (or God) and to each other of wrong-doing, grievances, grudges and resentments.

Immediate restitution or arrangements to make restitution as soon as possible.

Mutual forgiveness and releasing from the guilts, grudges, and tensions occasioned by the wrong-doing *(hala).* This repenting-forgiving-releasing is embodied in the twin terms, *mihi* and *kala.*

Closing prayer.

Nearly always, the leader called for the periods of silence called *ho'omalu. Ho'omalu* was invoked to calm tempers, encourage self-inquiry into actions, motives and feelings, or simply for rest during an all-day *ho'oponopono.* And once a dispute was settled, the leader decreed *ho'omalu* for the whole subject, both immediately and long after *ho'oponopono* ended.

pre-Christian
closing rites

In pre-Christian times, *ho'oponopono* was followed by *pani* (closing) rituals. These were usually chicken or pig offerings to the gods. Sometimes *pani* included the ceremonial ocean bath, *kapu kai.* Then followed the *'aha 'aina* (feast).

Today, post-*ho'oponopono* rites are virtually unknown. An ordinary meal or a snack usually follows *ho'oponopono.*

attitudes needed
in ho'oponopono

To bring about a true "righting of wrongs," certain attitudes were required. Some concerned the very decision to hold *ho'oponopono.* For this decision rested on the basic relief that problems *could* be resolved definitely if they were approached properly. They must be approached with a true intention to correct wrongs. Confession of error must be full and honest. Nothing could be withheld. Prayers, contrition and the forgiving-freeing of *kala* must come from the heart. Without these, *ho'oponopono* was form without substance.

Mrs. Pukui has written a hypothetical *ho'oponopono* to illustrate basic procedures. In this first quoted excerpt, she combines the opening prayer with statement of the problem.

"I have called you, Pukana, you, Heana, and you, Kahana [all children] to come here and look into this problem with me. Your brother, Kipi, is losing the sight of one eye . . . we want to save the other eye, so that is why we called you together. We will all pray together, and then we'll discuss things.

"Oh, Jehovah God, Creator of heaven and earth, and His Son, Jesus Christ, we ask Your help. To our *aumākua** from the East and from the West, from the North and from the South, from zenith to horizon, from the upper strata and the lower strata, hearken. Come. We want to discuss together and get your guidance and help, so we can know what is wrong with this boy."

Mrs. Pukui then questioned each child. What came to light first was that Kahana was angry with Kipi over some mischievous prank he had played. This brother-sister disharmony was settled promptly, before any further questioning. Kipi admitted his misbehavior. Then followed the conceptual ritual of *kala*. This, again geared to the young, went as follows:

Mrs. Pukui: "Kahana, are you willing to *kala* your brother?"

Kahana: "Yes."

Mrs. Pukui: "Free him entirely of this entanglement of your anger?"

Kahana: "Yes."

Mrs. Pukui: "Remember, Kahana, as you loosen your brother from his trespasses, you loosen yourself, too. As you forgive, you are forgiven. Now, who do you want to forgive you?"

Kahana: "Please, God forgive me."

Mrs. Pukui: "Yes, we will ask that now. You gods, hear now that Kahana is to free her brother of his trespasses, and to free him from the crown of his head to the soles of his feet, to the four corners of his body. May he be happy later.

"And you, Kipi, are you willing to *kala* your sister for being angry with you?"

Kipi: "Yes, I am willing."

Nearly identical phrases of *kala* were addressed to Kipi. (The significant use of "free" and loosen" rather than "forget" is discussed under *kala*). Then Kipi was questioned more intensively. The boy confessed to stealing some money. He also owned up to an "Hawaiian offense". He had thrown stones at an *'elepaio*, a bird form of a family *aumakua*. For both, he expressed contrition and asked for forgiveness. Then Mrs. Pukui again prayed.

"To You, O God, and Your sacred Son, and all the *aumākua* everywhere, hearken to this prayer. This boy is sorry for what he has done. I am sorry he has done such things. So, please free him of his trespasses."

Then followed arrangements for restitution. Kipi was to work at small jobs and earn enough to return the money. His sisters agreed to help him. And to make amends with offended *aumakua*, he was to offer and burn a food sacrifice *(mōhai 'ai)* of an egg and *ti* leaf. This symbolized the traditional

---

*in an actual pre-Christian *ho'oponopono*, the *aumākua* would be called on by name—M.K.P.

chicken and pig used in *pani* (closing) rites. This settled, Mrs. Pukui concluded:

"Now we dismiss our *ho'oponopono* and we pray that all this trouble be taken away and laid away.

"O, great eyeball of the sun, please take all this bundle of wrong-doing. Take it out to the West with you. And, as you go down again, to your rest, please take all the faults and trespasses that were committed. Lay all of this in the depth of the sea, never more to come back."

Mrs. Pukui's account is an example of *ho'oponopono* in a transition period from Hawaiian to Christian religion. God and the *aumākua* are invoked impartially. It is rich in Hawaiian concepts: that misconduct was punished by physical illness (the eye ailment); that the body was visualized as having four corners; that the "great eyeball" of the sun held mystic powers, and that mistakes and offenses could be taken away forever in mystic ways. It also illustrates the basic Hawaiian precept that when forgiveness is sincerely asked, it must be granted.

Because this *ho'oponopono* concerned children, it did not include the emotional depth, self-scrutiny of motives, guilts and aggressions, and the periods of silence *(ho'omalu)* of an adult session. In fact, Mrs. Pukui says that,

"In my grandmother's home, small children always sat in on *ho'oponopono* even if they didn't take part. Many times I was even bored, until I grew to understand better . . ."[2]

ho'oponopono
for Mrs. S——

The adult subtleties of guilt and remorse were very much present in the *ho'oponopono* mentioned in the beginning of this discussion. This is the one so urgently requested by the *hānai* mother of Mrs. S———. Mrs. S——— continues with her recorded account:

"So I took my baby with me, and went home to Kona the next day. All the family were there. My *hānai* cousin's Mom—she is a lady minister—was there to lead *ho'oponopono*.

(From here on, the minister is referred to as "This Lady" or *"ho'ōla"* literally "healer," but more generally used to mean a minister, often believed to have gifts of healing or prophecy.)

"My *hānai* Mom was in bed. They told me Mom had felt very sick and had gone to the doctor. She was 69. And she felt that some of her sickness was really physical. But some of it—well, maybe not. Then she had this dream. And then she knew I should come home and all of us should *ho'oponopono*.

"So we all got together in the living room. No, not kneeling down. Just comfortable. Not a real circle, but so we could see each other.

wehe i ka
Paipala

"First This Lady prayed, all in Hawaiian* . . . asking Jehovah God to show us His word and how to find out what was wrong. How to help Mom get well. And while This Lady prayed, Mom opened the Bible for guidance. (This was *wehe i ka Paipala*. See separate listing.)

---

*Everyone present understood Hawaiian. Intelligibility throughout is a requirement of effective *ho'oponopono*.

"Then Mom told her dream. She dreamed that I was alongside a high cliff and I was about to fall in the ocean. So Mom yelled. But when she yelled out at me, I said, 'Oh, I'm going.' And the second and the third time, she called me, and I said, 'I'm going.' And Mom said she thought this dream meant that because I was living in Honolulu I was *ho'okano* [conceited] and I didn't take any interest in her or her welfare. I thought, because of Mom's age and all, she just wanted attention.

"But This Lady, the *ho'ōla,* she thought the dream and my Mom's sickness meant that Mom was holding something back.* Something that she had not let me know.

**old wrong &
guilt emerge**

"So This Lady prayed again. And we all kept quiet for a while . . . trying to help Mom. And then Mom told us more . . . She said that before my grandmother died, she gave her [Mom] a Hawaiian quilt. Mom was supposed to give it to me when I grew up. It was really my quilt, meant for me.

"But my *hānai* Mom kept it. And when I grew up and got married, she never gave me that quilt. Others, but not this one. What happened was that Mom sold the quilt for $300. And she had been living with all this *'ike hewa* [guilt] all this time. This Lady said part of Mom's sickness was because of this guilt. She told Mom she would never get well until she got my forgiveness. And Mom cried. She really cried! She felt so guilty.

**confession &
forgiveness**

"Then the *ho'ōla* said Mom should confess to me and before God Jehovah. She did. She asked me to forgive her, and I did. I wasn't angry . . . And later Mom's sickness left her. Of course, she still had diabetes, but the rest—being so confused and miserable—all that left her."

Interviewer: "But what about your quilt? Did she arrange for any restitution?"

**restitution
was made**

Mrs. S: "Oh, yes. During *ho'oponopono* she said she would quilt another one for me. The others helped her. She got the quilt finished and gave it to me before she died."

Interviewer: "How did you end *ho'oponopono?"*

**next problem
is dealt with**

Mrs. S: "We didn't end it right away. We had to work more on the dream. You know, the dream where Mom saw me on the *pali* not paying any attention to her calls. Well, This Lady, she interpreted this to mean that because my *hānai* Mom had done this thing about the quilt and kept it a secret, this was really why I would not answer. And why I ignore Mom in real life. But I said, 'No, I am not ignoring Mom. It is just that I am married now

---

*Dreams are commonly prompted by something repressed, comments the Center's psychiatrist. The *ho'ōla,* also a relative, was able to draw on long knowledge of family affairs.

65

and have a baby and I am busy.' But Mom said that I did neglect her. That I did not write home, sometimes for a long time. And the *ho'ōla,* told me, 'After this, you should write often. Your mother is old, and she needs your letters. She looks forward to hearing from you.' And Mom cried again. And I felt, oh, so much love for her.

"And we talked about, oh, lots of little misunderstandings. And we forgave each other for so many things. The *ho'oponopono* brought us so close together. It did. It really did! And we stayed close to each other until the very day Mom died.

closing
prayer

"Then the Lady prayed again to Jehovah God, thanking Him for opening up the way and giving us an answer. And she thanked Jehovah for bringing things out in the clear. She prayed to Jehovah to close the doors, so no evil in the family or from outside would harm us . . . she asked the angels of Jehovah God to guard the four posts of the house. Then she *amen'd** all in Hawaiian.

"And after *ho'oponopono,* it was so peaceful-like, There was love—oh, so much love!"

Interviewer: "How long was this last prayer?"

Mrs. S: "About half an hour."

Interviewer: "How long was the *ho'oponopono?*"

Mrs. S: "Oh, all day. One person took care of the phone so we wouldn't be interrupted."

Interviewer: "After it ended, what did you do?"

Mrs. S: "We were hungry. We ate. Just supper—not a special meal."

alcohol is
not allowed

Interviewer: "I know that you, personally, do not drink. But could anyone else have had a highball or a beer during the day?"

Mrs. S: "Oh, No! Nobody ever drinks in *ho'oponopono.* Because when people drink they let their feelings, their temper run away from them. In our *ho'oponopono,* we cried a lot when we forgave and made up, but we had to stay in control. I mean over really strong feelings like anger."

Mrs. S_____'s account and Mrs. Pukui's earlier example show some interesting similarities and differences. Both point out one of the common traditional reasons for *ho'oponopono,* that of finding the cause of a puzzling illness. Said Mrs. S_____, "A part of Mom's illness was physical . . . but part of it, well maybe not." A century ago, *kahunas* often asked "has the *ho'oponopono* been held?" before they would proceed with treatment. And on Niihau today, families hold *ho'oponopono* first, then call Kauai for medical help if the illness persists.

---

*In this case, the Christian "Amen" has been used as a verb. In pre-Christian Hawaii, prayers and chants were concluded with phrases using *'āmama,* meaning "the prayer is free" or "flown" or "finished."

Both examples demonstrate *mahiki,* the dealing with each successive "layer" of trouble, one at a time. In the *ho'oponopono* for childhood transgression, these layers were of easily recognized conduct and emotion. First, childish misbehavior and the anger it caused, then the theft, then throwing stones at the *'elepaio* bird—all were brought out in turn. In the adult *ho'oponopono,* the layers were made also of emotion-underlying-emotion. Let's trace the structure of this disturbed relationship.

To borrow medical terms, the "presenting complaints" were a dream and an illness. At first, only the "top layer" of dream significance was discussed. It, said the *ho'ōla,* like the illness, meant "Mom is holding something back."

What was she holding back?

A hostile act, that of selling the quilt. This caused long-standing guilt. And this guilt was a factor causing Mom to accompany and complicate organic disorders with functional or psychosomatic illness.

How were these revealed layers "disposed of?"

For Mom, confession, discussion, restitution and expressed contrition. For mother and daughter, mutual forgiving and releasing *(mihi* and *kala).* All in the presence of God.

But was *mahiki* complete? All layers stripped away?

Not yet, There was more to the dream. As the *ho'ōla* interpreted it, the mother's hostile action (in dream form, placing daughter on the dangerous cliff) led to lack of communication between mother and daughter (daughter-in-dream refused to answer mother's calls). As Mom saw it, daughter ignored her from general selfishness and haughtiness exemplified in the move to Honolulu.

And, on the conscious level were actual instances of daughter's neglect and the mother's resentment of this neglect. These layers also must be taken care of. And yet more "layers" were peeled off and dissolved in discussion, in *mihi* and *kala*—and in tears and embraces.

("And we talked about so many little misunderstandings. And we forgave each other for so many things.")

Or, as Mrs. Pukui describes the abstract in terms of the tangible, "Think of peeling an onion. You peel off one layer and throw it aside, so you can go on and peel off the next layer. That's *mahiki."*

ho'omalu and
kūkulu kumuhana

In Mrs. S_____'s experience, two more components of *ho'oponopono* seem to have come into being spontaneously and simultaneously.

"Then we all kept quiet awhile ... trying to help Mom," Mrs. S_____ relates.

We could rephrase it as:

"We all kept quiet awhile." Or, "We all had *ho'omalu"* (a period of silence for thought and reflection).

"... trying to help Mom." Or, "... and we joined in *kūkulu kumuhana"* (the pooling of emotional-spiritual forces for a common purpose).*

---

*Both *ho'omalu* and *kūkulu kumuhana* are discussed at end of *ho'oponopono* listing.

The *ho'ōla* in this *ho'oponopono* did not need to control temper outbursts. ("I wasn't angry," said Mrs. S_____.)

the leader
intervenes

In a more recent *ho'oponopono,* the leader did intervene frequently. This *ho'oponopono* concerned primarily "Dan," his *hapa-haole** wife, "Relana," and Dan's mother. Mother and daughter-in-law had been increasingly hostile ever since the young couple married. As time went on, in-laws on both sides were drawn into the family *hihia* (entanglement of ill-feeling). Finally, after eight years, Dan persuaded his wife and mother to join him in *ho'oponopono.* Dan's great-aunt conducted it. As resentments and bitterness were brought out, open accusations were made.

"You never made me welcome at your house," charged mother-in-law.

"You never came to visit. Just to interfere," said daughter-in-law.

"I wanted to show you how to cook right. But would you let me teach you anything? Not you! *Ho'okano!*"

As voices rose, *Tūtū* ("Auntie") called for *ho'omalu.* Then after a minute or two of silence, she insisted each one must talk in turn, to her, not to each other.

"She laid down the law several times," Dan reports, "but in the end the two got down to talking about *why* they were angry, instead of just yelling at each other."

What gradually emerged then was a young, mainland-educated wife's attempts to be independent and to fashion her household along "modern" lines, and a Hawaiian mother-in-law's clinging both to her son and to Hawaiian traditions of close-knit family relationships and living patterns.

"It was a long, long *ho'oponopono.* Relana and Mom must have *mihi'd* and *kala'd* a dozen times. They never will see eye-to-eye. But we do visit back and forth now and we all get along pretty well," states Dan.

"Now we're trying to get all the others—all the in-laws—to *ho'oponopono* to straighten out the rest of the *hihia.*"

Intervention by the leader anytime it was needed was traditional, says Mrs. Pukui.

"The leader had complete authority. When he said *'Pau.* Enough of this.' everybody got quiet. Sometimes the leader would stop the talk because of hot tempers. Sometimes, if he thought someone was not being honest, or holding things back, or making up excuses instead of facing up to his own *hala* [fault]. Then the leader would ask the person, *'Heaha kau i hana ai?* What did you really do? *Ho'o mao popo.* Think about it.' And there would be *ho'omalu* for a little while."

emotions kept
under control

Obviously, a successful *ho'oponopono* was not mere emotional catharsis. Hawaiians seemed to know that neither crying jag nor shouting match solves a problem.

In fact, the Center's psychiatric consultant believes the emotional controls of *ho'oponopono* provide one of its great therapeutic strengths. To quote:

---

*half-Hawaiian; half-Caucasian.

68

"In *ho'oponopono,* one talked openly *about* one's feelings, particularly one's angers and resentments. This is good. For when you suppress and re-press hostilities, pretend they do not exist, then sooner or later they are going to burst out of containment, often in destructive, damaging ways. *Ho'opono-pono* used the 'safety valve' of discussion as one step towards handling old quarrels or grudges, and even more importantly, as prevention, so minor dis-putes would not grow into big grievances.

"But 'talking things out' is not enough. Something constructive must be done about the cause of the grudge, the reasons behind the quarrel. And to get this done, talking about anger must be kept under control. Let the anger itself erupt anew, and more causes for more resentments build up. 'Setting things to rights' requires all the maturity one can muster. When run-away emo-tions take over, so do child-like attitudes and behavior. The *ho'oponopono* provision that participants talk about anger to the leader, rather than hurling maledictions at each other was a wise one.

"Only when people control their hostile emotions, can satisfactory means of restitution be worked out. And usually, it's pretty hard to forgive fully and freely until, for example, property has been returned or damage repaired or one's good name has been cleared.

"Ho'oponopono seems to be a supreme effort at self-help on a responsi-ble, adult level. It also has the spiritual dimension so vital to the Hawaiian people. And even here, prayers, to *aumakua* in the past or God in the present, are responsible, adult prayers. The appeal is not the child-like, 'Rescue me! Get me out of this scrape.' Rather it is, 'Please provide the spiritual strength we need to work out this problem. Help us to help ourselves.'"

ho'oponopono defined in 1971

Unfortunately, very few Hawaiians practice this "supreme effort at self-help" in 1971. For when Christianity came in, more than a century ago, *ho'opo-nopono* went out. Because *ho'oponopono* prayers and rituals were addressed to "pagan gods," the *akua* and *aumākua,* the total *ho'oponopono* was labeled "pagan." Many Hawaiians came to believe their time honored method of family therapy was "a stupid, heathen thing." Some practiced *ho'oponopono* secretly. As time went on, Hawaiians remembered, not *ho'oponopono* but only bits and pieces of it. Or grafted-on innovations. Or mutations. Or complete distortions of concept, procedure and vocabulary.

In the past five years, Center staff members have compiled an almost un-believable list of incomplete or distorted explanations of what *ho'oponopono* is. Most—but not all—come from clients. Here are the most typical examples:

Fortune-telling was called *ho'oponopono.* So were unintelligible rituals: "This lady prayed over me—I think in Portuguese." "The *kahuna* prayed in Hawaiian, so low I didn't know what he was saying." "I went to this man and he chanted something."

A self-styled *"kahuna"* offered to kill by sorcery (evidently *ho'opi'opi'o)* and this was called *ho'oponopono.*

The Mormon Family Circle, and any family discussion were termed *ho'oponopono.*

Many Hawaiians called family prayers *(pule 'ohana) ho'oponopono.*

One client said *ho'oponopono* was "fasting and praying three days;" another said it meant "blessing the house" and "casting out demons;" others said it meant "reading the Bible" and "forgiving each other."

A non-client viewed *ho'oponopono* as "arbitration by a senior."

By far the most common comment was that *wehe i ka Paipala,* often a modern prelude, was in itself *ho'oponopono.*

Probably the most widespread departure from the "classic" or "model" is using *ho'oponopono* concepts and procedures in a church group with a minister as leader. In this, the family participation restriction is extended to take in "spiritual family."

true ho'oponopono:
the sum of its parts

Many of these fragments, innovations, additions or departures are themselves desirable. The point is they are not *ho'oponopono* in its entirety. For Hawaii's family therapy is the sum total of many parts: prayer, discussion, arbitration, contrition, restitution, forgiveness and releasing, and the thorough looking into layers of action and feeling called *mahiki.* It is this sum total of its many beneficial parts that makes *ho'oponopono* a useful, effective method to remedy and even prevent family discord.

Or, as Dr. Haertig states:

"*Ho'oponopono* may well be one of the soundest methods to restore and maintain good family relationships that any society has ever devised."

NOTES

1. *Ho'oponopono* with involved member absent. Shortly before this went to press, the following account was received: John H. of Oahu, was seriously ill and his own family planned *ho'oponopono* to find the cause. His estranged wife, Melea, on Maui, flatly refused to attend and said she would "never forgive John for cheating on me." John's family went ahead with a kind of "second best" *ho'oponopono.* Mutual forgiving-releasing was obviously impossible. However, John did confess and talk about his past infidelities and present hostilities. His family told him these were at the root of his illness. Whether or not this was a case of simply treating psychosomatic symptoms, we don't know. However, the report says John then recovered. Almost a year later, the same family members—but not John—went to Maui. There they held a long-delayed *ho'oponopono* with Melea to "cleanse her heart of all her hates." In this *ho'oponopono* a decision was reached. Reconciliation would never work. Melea should, with full family approval, divorce John. She did this.

   This is an interesting example of two *ho'oponopono*s (or one *ho'oponopono* in a delayed series) to deal with the total John-Melea problem. The decision for divorce when John and Melea could and would not sincerely forgive and release each other of guilts and resentments has interesting traditional precedent. In Hawaii of old, couples could *'oki* (sever) marriage arrangements. When any family discord was clearly irreparable, the family tie could be formally broken. This was expressed in the ritual term, *mō ka piko, mōku ka piko* ("The umbilical cord is cut.")

2. Children present at *ho'oponopono.* This was in keeping with Hawaiian involvement of children in nearly every aspect of family life. Little effort was made to shield children from the "realities of life" as Western society, for example, does this today. In old Hawaii, children learned skills by watching their elders; grew to know about death and sorrow by attending wakes and funerals and touching the corpse. Sexual information was not withheld; though women went into isolation during menstruation, even little boys knew why their mother was isolated. Childhood attendance at *ho'oponopono* not only gave lessons in how to conduct one in future adult life, it accomplished a more immediate purpose: that of letting children know that adults had problems, lost their tempers, and committed wrongs—and were willing to talk about them and find ways to resolve conflicts and improve conduct.

hala—fault, transgression, error; to transgress. After Christianity was introduced, also "sin" and "to sin." Also *pandanus* (screw pine) tree. Legend connected the *hala* lei with death, or gone forever.* This also took the opposite connotation of being gone or finished in a beneficial sense, as cleansed or purified. In *ho'oponopono* the meaning is wrong or transgression.

> Deriv: unknown.
> Variations: *ho'ohalahala* (to make fault) or to complain; find fault.
> *ho'omauhala* (hold fast the fault). To continue to think about the offense; to hold a grudge.

In the traditional understanding of *hala* as a transgression or offense, is a subtle but significant axiom of human relationships: that the wrong-doer and the wronged are linked together by the very existence of the transgression and its chain of after-effects.

Mary Kawena Pukui suggests we visualize *hala* as a cord. "It binds the offender to his deed and to his victim. The victim holds on to this cord and becomes equally bound."

To carry Mrs. Pukui's imagery still further, this cord has many other entanglements that bind together culprit, offense and victim. Anger, the wish for revenge, the time-strengthened knots of old grudges, the newly-tied knots of guilt for the deed, the fear of discovery, the dread of confrontation—all these are part of the cord that binds and constricts. There are lesser entanglements as well, such as social embarrassment and the inability to communicate. These, too, join offender and offended in a mutually distressing relationship. As others are inevitably drawn into the conflict, the cord of *hala* is visualized as a network of ever-spreading unpleasantness called *hihia*.

hihia—entangled or entanglement; snarl or snarled; enmeshed.

> Deriv: *hihi,* to entangle, intertwine; a fish net.
> *a,* passive suffix.

Hihia is that rare verbal gem, one word that carries whole pages of meaning. As *hala* is visualized as a cord that binds culprit, offense and victim, so *hihia* is viewed as a larger, yet tighter network of many cords tied in numerous stubborn knots.

Hihia is an entanglement of emotions, actions and reactions, all with negative, troublesome connotations. *Hihia* may begin with two persons as, for example, when one wrongs another. Both react emotionally, directing feelings

---

*The goddess Hi'iaka was wearing a *hala* lei when a medical *kahuna* asked her to help save a very sick patient. Hi'iaka replied that it was too late; the patient was already *hala* or gone. Therefore, wearing a *hala* lei became unlucky. However, a *hala* lei worn at the early *makahiki* (harvest festival, now New Year) meant that old grudges and troubles were gone. Thus a *hala* lei worn on New Year's Day meant good luck.

at each other and absorbing feelings inwardly. Action follows, whether it be tangible lawsuit, divorce, physical violence, or erecting a barrier of silence. Emotions, actions and counter-emotions and counter-actions spread to the family or close associates. Soon everyone concerned is entangled in a network of resentment, hostility, guilt, depression, or vague discomfort. Cause sparks effect; effect brings about cause. The net tightens, yet expands at the same time.

Even the "innocent bystander" is part of *hihia*. A child witnessing a parental quarrel is involved in *hihia* though he may not have caused the quarrel. Yet he senses anger, feels insecurity, and sooner or later will feed back into the entanglement his own reactions and responses.

Hawaiians sensed that in *hihia* one who inflicted a wrong on another suffers and is harmed by his own hostile feelings. The one who is wronged also suffers and is harmed by the grudge cherished, the self-pity nursed, as much as by the original wrong. Therefore both (and usually an entire group) must find ways to *kala* (free) themselves from this thicket of tangled emotions. The way was the *ho'oponopono,* a family conclave for the "setting to rights." In this is both concept and ritual of *mihi* or mutual forgiveness and restitution.

To cite any special *hihia* case reference is unnecessary. *Hihia* is part of all cases, yet it often goes unrecognized by clients. For example, a Hawaiian-oriented mother may say her child misbehaves because he is *noho* (possessed). A non-Hawaiian mother may say Johnny wets his bed to be naughty or, if she is a bit more psychiatrically sophisticated, because the new baby was born. Both try to isolate specifics; both have forgotten the interplay of people, emotions and events that form a negative "emotional climate" or *hihia*.

'oiā'i'o—absolute truth; sincere, sincerity; spirit of truth.

>   Deriv: *'oia,* truth.
>   *'i'o,* substance, flesh, meat, muscle.
>   Literally, *'oia'i'o,* is the "flesh, meat or muscle of truth." Figuratively, the "spirit of truth" or the "essence of truth."

Truth-telling, old Hawaii knew, had many dimensions.

It still has.

In the past or present, one might tell *'oia,* the simple statement of deed, event, generally acknowledged fact or honest personal conclusion.

"My canoes are sturdy; perhaps others made faster ones," said the builder of old. "I type 70 words a minute," said the job-seeking secretary of today. "Two and two are four" the teacher told the children. "I have studied the clouds carefully. They show this is not a good day for fishing," advised the *kahuna kilo.** You need new brake linings and a tune-up; otherwise the car is in pretty good shape," reported the mechanic.

All of these statements, given honestly and with every effort towards accuracy, are *'oia.* Plain truth. Unvarnished truth. Facts or conclusions told without embellishment, innuendo or emotional involvement in the telling.

---

*priest who studied natural phenomena.

72

One may also tell partial truths or slanted truths. Exaggerations of truth. Truths so emphasized that conflicting facts, opinions or arguments are minimized or omitted. The law, politics, advertising and public relations know this truth-telling well. So does irresponsible journalism. And, often to balance a patient's despair with hope, so do physicians.

This truth-telling is *'ohaohala*. The word comes from *'oha*, "spreading, as vines," and *hala*, "fault, wrong, error." *'Ohaohala*, then, is, more literally, "spreading error"—under the guise of truth.

Or, one may tell what is absolute and complete truth. One may speak the very "essence of truth": *'oia'i'o*.

'Oia'i'o has many characteristics. It is total truth told without innuendo, intentional omission, or slanting of facts and presentation. It is a "let the chips fall where they may" statement of facts; yet it is truth that goes beyond intellectual openness.

"*Oia'i'o*," says Mrs. Pukui, "is truth in the feeling sense. You **feel** whether what you are saying is *'oia'i'o* or not. Hawaiians believed the intellect and emotions both came from the *na'au* [viscera or gut]. Real truth—real sincerity—comes from *na'au 'oia'i'o*. From 'truthful guts'".

This is the spirit of truth specified in *ho'oponopono*. It must pervade the relating of facts or deeds. To quote Dr. Haertig:

"*Ho'oponopono* requires the telling of all the essential material, no matter how painful this may be. No matter if what is told pains others. The point is that the telling must not be done in vindictive ways or with any desire to hurt. Nothing essential must be held back. Actions and errors of omission or commission pertinent to the problem must be totally revealed.

"This absolute truth-telling often entails some introspective awareness— perhaps even real insight—but, as I see it, this is not a requirement. Nor is any great emotional effort. For one person in one situation, truth-telling may be the most painful process. For another, it may be easy, perhaps longed-for confession and catharsis. The essential requirement in *ho'oponopono* is the total revealing of what really happened. For until everyone involved knows clearly who did what to whom and why, no remedy for the situation can be reached.

"That, of course, is only one aspect of *'oia'i'o* or 'absolute truth.' It seems especially applicable—but not limited—to the relating of events.

"But *'oia'i'o* also means sincerity of feeling. Outside *ho'oponopono*, this sincerity was a basic requirement in all of Hawaii's forgiving, freeing, releasing practices. A curse might be removed by various means, if the one cursed was truly repentant. Prayer—sincere prayer, Mrs. Pukui stresses—could avert disaster, cancel punishment, restore health or happiness.

"If we take the *'oia'i'o* concept out of its *ho'oponopono*—or even its wider Hawaiian setting—the requirement of sincerity remains a sound basis for successful human relationships."

mihi—repentance, confession, apology; to repent, confess, apologize.

Deriv: unknown.

Mihi, repentance, confession and apology, was always a part of *ho'oponopono*. This does not mean it was limited to the prayerful family conferences designed to "set things to rights." Saying "I committed this wrong. I am sorry. Please forgive me" was a common, often-used way to keep harmony in the 'ohana (family).

As a family practice, *mihi* had its own rules—and reasons for the rules. The most important was the obligation to forgive the penitent. Mrs. Pukui gives the traditional explanation:

"When someone came to you and asked for forgiveness, you could not *huli kua* [turn the back] on him. You had to forgive fully and completely. If you did not, then the *aumākua* [ancestor gods] would *huli kua* on you."

Also, the sincerity of the errant one was not to be questioned. If his *mihi* was false, his contrition mere pretense, then the *aumākua* would punish him. A lying apology to a family senior was equally a lie to the *aumākua*. So went the reasoning.

Custom decreed as well that the person asking forgiveness must not become angry, even if forgiveness was delayed or withheld. He must remain humble throughout.

One who had committed an error so grave that he consulted a *kahuna* might be told to accompany *mihi* with gifts to the gods. "These gifts might be fish or a pig or whatever the *kahuna* advised," Mrs. Pukui says.

To the Western mind, restitution to the gods seems to leave the wronged person pretty much uncompensated for his injuries. But if we try to "think early Hawaiian," it becomes easier to understand that these food offerings were reparation to man as well as god. For living relatives and ancestors-become-gods were very much members of the same 'ohana. Offend one and you offend all. Make peace with one and you make peace with all. Confession, forgiveness and restitution were a three-way process among the culprit, those he wronged on earth, and the also-wronged gods.

(And, from a strictly practical viewpoint, the living family feasted on the offerings after the spiritual essence [*aka*] of the food had been ritually given to the gods.)

Today, reparation is usually a direct replacement or repair of property, or correction and apology for harmful statements. Forgiveness may be an interchange among wrong-doer, the wronged and God, as in *ho'oponopono*. It may be a human-with-God confession and absolution. Or it may be a social and emotional communication between persons.

However, the tradition that a penitent must be forgiven seems to remain unchanged and well-remembered, even though it is not always followed. The obligation to forgive is consistent with the special closeness and interdependence of the Hawaiian family. A rift among even grown and separated family members is a serious thing. It must be healed quickly or it will grow wider and deeper. For no one remains uninvolved in the Hawaiian 'ohana.

Which may have been the very reason for the provision that with *mihi* there must also be that forgiving-releasing called *kala*.

kala—to release, untie, unbind, let go.
    Deriv: unknown.
    Hawaiians recognized that the figurative cord linking sinner and sinned-against in mutual unpleasantness must be "untied," not by one but both. This

was done in *ho'oponopono* and in other practices. The culprit must confess, repent and make restitution. The one who was wronged must forgive. The requirement of reparation is especially wise. For until stolen property, for example, is restored or replaced, the thief remains burdened with guilt and social discomfort. The victim, though he forgives, continues to feel the loss of possessions. Neither is free of the *hala* or wrong, and the attitudes and emotions the wrong engendered.

Hawaiian mores specified both must forgive—and go beyond forgiving. Both must *kala.* Each must release himself and the other of the deed, and the recriminations, remorse, grudges, guilts and embarrassments the deed caused. Both must "let go of the cord," freeing each other completely, mutually and permanently.

This was *kala,* a concept and an ideal. Like most ideals, *kala* was not easy to attain. And so, the Hawaiian culture reinforced the subtleties of *kala* with prayers and rituals of release and freeing. In *ho'oponopono, kala* is expressed in the phrase, *"Ke kala aku nei 'au ia 'oe a pela noho'i 'au e kala ia mai ai,"* or, "I unbind you from the fault, and thus may I also be unbound from it."

With or without *ho'oponopono, kala* was sought in numerous *pules* (prayers) and ceremonies. Family members could be forever released from curses and their associated anxieties when a *pule kala* (prayer to release) was said directly to the corpse of a relative. (See *'ānai*). Or by prayer, and sometimes ritual, all faults, angers and guilts, could, as Mrs. Pukui's *ho'oponopono* example says, be taken up by "the great eyeball of the sun . . . and laid in the depths of the sea."

(In early days, *kala* in the broad sense might mean the release or freeing from physical, spiritual or emotional ills. It was sometimes dramatized by symbolism. A plant that was "slippery" rather than "binding" might be eaten or worn. *Limu kala* is an example.)

Today, *kala* is a mutual process in which both the instigator and recipient of an offense are released from the emotional bondage Hawaiians call *hala.* This forgiving, freeing and releasing concept of Hawaii's expressive culture is quite different from the "forgive and forget" ideal of a repressive society. For what is "forgotten" is actually repressed. Repressed material may reemerge into conscious thought. When a painful, "forgotten" incident so emerges, it may be doubly painful. *Kala* seeks to strip the incident of its pain-causing attributes. An insult or injustice may be remembered—but if *mihi* and *kala* have been sincere, it is remembered as "no big thing anymore."

mahiki—to peel off; to pry; as to peel the bark of a tree to judge the wood beneath; to scrape at the skin to remove a tiny insect burrowed beneath the epidermis. Also, to cast out, as of a spirit.

Deriv: *ma,* unknown.
hiki, to reach; get to.
Related words: *'ohiki,* to clean out; *'ohikihiki,* to pry into the past, especially an unsavory past.

"Think of peeling an onion," explained Mrs. Pukui in the previous *ho'oponopono* discussion. "You peel off one layer and throw it away, so you can go on and peel off the next layer. That's *mahiki*."

The "onion skins" are figurative ones. *Mahiki*, in its behavioral context, is the disposing of one "layer" of action, motivation or emotion to reveal and dispose of yet another layer of acts, feelings and causes. *Mahiki*, implicitly understood or also ritually stated, is a way of "getting to the source of trouble and resolving it."

In *ho'oponopono*, *mahiki* may be tracing the components of one problem and "setting it to rights" so that another problem can be considered. For example, the "top layer," a husband-and-wife dispute, is settled, so *ho'oponopono* proceeds to the next family worry, the whining or misbehaving child. What usually happens is that *mahiki* reveals a connection between what first seemed to be separate problems. The disturbing effects of quarreling parents on the consequently disturbed child become clear.

Or, *mahiki* in *ho'oponopono* may be investigation in depth of a specific incident or emotion. Revealing the unacknowledged anger and the more-or-less suppressed guilts involved in grief is one example. Disclosing the jealousy underlying a "personality clash," and the low self-image that feeds the jealousy—this "burrowing down" is also *mahiki*. In its disclosure of new problems and new aspects of old problems, *mahiki* may be both diagnostic and remedial. And when it reveals and resolves a minor trouble source before it becomes a major one, *mahiki* is also preventive.

Mahiki also connotes eradication of the ills disclosed through intensive questioning. This is especially clear in the *mahiki* rites to exorcise a possessing spirit *(noho)*. The procedure, in Hawaii's past and present, is almost identical with exorcism rites in medieval Europe. The spirit is first identified and then banished. In Hawaii, whether the *kahuna* of old or the churchman of the 20th Century took charge, inquiries directed to the possessing spirit went something like,

Who are you? Where are you from? Who sent you? Why?

Traditionally, this questioning might conclude with the following statement:

"Ke kala ka mahiki nei au i ke ia mau mea ho'opilikia."

("I am peeling off and removing the causes of this trouble.")

"Ho'i no ai i kou kahu."

("Go back and destroy your keeper.")

The Hawaiian clergyman of today would conclude with,

"Ke kauoha nei ou ia 'oe, ma ka inoa o Iesus Kristo e puka mai 'oe i waho."

("In the name of Jesus Christ, I order you to come out!")

In its most complete sense, *mahiki* is the total questioning plus self-probing plus ventilation plus some remedial action for each aspect or layer of troublesome behavior or emotion. The processes of analytic psychotherapy and particularly of psychoanalysis are *mahiki*. In fact, Dr. Haertig recalls that the psychiatric literature beginning with Freud uses the onion and tree bark analogies to describe peeling away of layer after layer of the unconscious. Reach the core as Freud pointed out, and you near the end of the psychoanalysis.

In a more limited meaning, detailed questioning for any helpful purpose is *mahiki*. Taking a medical or psychiatric history or a social case history is *mahiki*.

This serious questioning with intent to help is the exact opposite of the purposeless "nosey" inquisitiveness called *niele*.

Knowing and discussing this difference with the Hawaiian patient or client may help change resistance to rapport.

ho'omalu—to shelter, protect, make peace, keep quiet, control, suspend. A period of peace and quiet. Silent period.

> Deriv: *ho'o,* to cause; to make.
> *malu,* shelter, protection, peace, quiet, control.

Tempers might flare. Serious conversation might be turning into noisy prattle. A fisherman might need to screen family worries from his mind. The worried or sick might benefit from a quiet household.

There was a way to prevent quarrels and stop noise and confusion. Someone in authority could decree *ho'omalu.* He could "Make a shelter" for mind and sensibilities. A moratorium on disturbances.

Ho'omalu was invoked in *ho'oponopono* and on many other occasions. In Hawaii's early days, *ho'omalu* was decreed to insure quiet during important religious rituals.

Before Kamehameha's time, when the *kapu* (taboo) days of Kāne and Lono were observed, "no fires were made nor tapa beaters sounded, and all other sounds were silenced. Neither chickens nor owls must make a sound, lest the success of the ritual be destroyed."[1] Other accounts tell of ritual periods during which dogs were taken from the village lest they bark and children were anxiously hushed lest they cry.[2] Here *ho'omalu* was an absolute *kapu,* decreed by chief and priest.

Ho'omalu also allowed the Hawaiian fisherman to keep his mind on his precarious, deep-sea job. In his absence, women of the household were to remain quietly at home. They should pray, and wives should remain faithful to their husbands. There must be no drinking, no parties, no quarreling. They must not gossip, tell funny stories or be loud and boisterous. They must not talk about the dead, for this brings bad luck to the fisherman.[3] Or, in other words, the head of the household must feel sure that all is peaceful at home.

Ho'omalu is a safety precaution in the admonition not to talk to anyone gathering *'opihi.* It takes full concentration to avoid being washed out to sea.

During *ho'oponopono,* the leader may declare a *ho'omalu,* or family members may spontaneously fall into silent thought. *Ho'omalu* may last a few minutes or a few hours. *Ho'omalu* may be placed on the intervals between repeated *ho'oponopono* sessions. For example, if a family holds *ho'oponopono* on weekends to get to deeply-rooted causes of a problem, *ho'omalu* may be invoked during the week. This can mean that family members may not talk about the problem at all. Or that they may talk about it, but only with those immediately involved. The "no drinking, no partying" provision is usually a part of this *ho'omalu.*

While *ho'oponopono* is actually going on, *ho'omalu* is usually a time of complete quiet. Here, like the Quaker silences, the Catholic retreat, and the periods for meditation of Oriental sects, *ho'omalu* recognizes man's need for calm and prayerful contemplation.

REFERENCES

1. Kamakau. *Ka Po'e Kahiko: The People of Old,* p. 21.
2. Fornander. Collection of Hawaiian Antiquities. Vol. 6, p. 418.
3. Ibid., p. 118.

kūkulu kumuhana—the pooling of strengths, emotional, psychological and spiritual, for a shared purpose. Group dynamics characterized by spiritual elements and directed to a positive goal. A unified, unifying force. In broad context, a group, national, or worldwide spiritual force, constructive and helpful in nature. In *ho'oponopono,* the uniting of family members in a spiritual force to help an ill or troubled member.

Secondary meaning: statement of problem and procedures for seeking a solution, as in opening explanations of *ho'oponopono.*

Deriv: *kūkulu,* to build; pile up; a pillar.
      kumu, source; basis; main stalk or root of plant.
      hana, work; activity.

"When we knew a man was going off on a sea voyage, then all the family would get together and pray for his safety."—Mary Kawena Pukui, 1941.

"After Duke Kahanamoku had his brain operation, his family had a prayer session. It went on a long time. And when it was over, we went to our own homes and continued to pray for him."—Family friend, 1968.

"... And we all kept quiet for a while ... trying to help Mom."—*Ho'oponopono* account, 1971.

The three quotations refer to an identical process. In different words, each person expressed something like:

"We joined in creating, responding to, and thus re-creating a unifying force. We brought into being, shared, and sent to one in need a kind of powerhouse of spiritual-emotional energies. But as we contributed, we strengthened rather than diminished our individual resources of mind and soul.

"We took part in *kūkulu kumuhana.* "

Some aspects of *kūkulu kumuhana* are described less formally: "We're pulling for you." ... "We're with you all the way." ... "You were in our thoughts all the time you were in labor." ... "We'll be thinking of you when you take the final examinations." The phrases describe part, but not the whole. To be *kūkulu kumuhana,* "thinking of you" must include "praying for you"—whether in words or silent thought. For originally, *kūkulu kumuhana* was a pooling of *mana,* the special power each person possessed as an *akua* (god)-given attribute. The spiritual-religious element was, and is today, an integral part of the group dynamics.

Says Mrs. Pukui, "We concentrate our thoughts on one person or one problem, so that, with God, we get the help we need."

Kūkulu kumuhana is always present in a successful *ho'oponopono*. However, it is not limited to this occasion. Anytime family, friends, congregation or larger community pray or aspire together, becoming emotionally-spiritually involved in a common purpose, then this quality of solidarity may come into being. Mutual concern, sincerity, sensitivity, and responsiveness to others' feelings—all these intangibles help bring about *kūkulu kumuhana*. Conversely, boredom, calculated indifference, emotional coldness, disagreement with group needs or purpose—all these can keep an individual from becoming a part of *kūkulu kumuhana*.

However, Mrs. Pukui stresses the Hawaiian belief that being physically absent or unconscious does not prevent one from receiving the supporting strength of the group.

"The *pule* [prayers] send the *mana* [power] to the person who needs help," she says.

The Hawaiian view picks no quarrel with the probability that a member of a loving family knows he is going to be prayed for while he is away and in possible danger. Nor does it discard medical speculation that an unconscious person may hear and understand much of what is said. How the communication channel is cleared may be less important than the fact that the message does seem to get through.

It seems evident that Hawaiians also sensed the counter-balance of what we now call "the will to live" versus the exhausted "desire to give up" or the stronger "wish to die." Certainly, when there is any physical potential for recovery, the knowledge that one is loved, wanted, and is being urged to live can swing the delicate balance over to life.

Kūkulu kumuhana for a seriously ill member can bring benefits for the rest of the family. Disputes may be resolved in the greater shared concern and positive, constructive goal of the gathering. Lacking this purpose, the family may hold only a "weep and wail" session. At best, this brings the healthy ones only a temporary emotional catharsis. At worst, it convinces the sick one that he is indeed beyond hope.

The fusing of emotional-spiritual efforts in a common cause seems to operate in most societies and outside the family context. For example, four dramatic episodes from 20th Century Western culture:

• The Lusitania sinks, and passengers, joined in singing "Nearer, My God, to Thee," go to their doom in shared dignity and strength.

• "Let us so bear ourselves, that, if the British Empire and its Commonwealth last for a thousand years, men will still say, 'This was their finest hour.'" Winston Churchill speaks, and all England responds with renewed courage. Churchill senses the solidarity of the nation and is, in turn, infused with fresh reserves of leadership and endurance.

• In the cathedral and at television sets throughout the world, men and women watch funeral services for President Kennedy. A massed and universal feeling of sympathy, support and pride goes out to his widow. Mrs. Kennedy senses this and is helped to sustain her role of national heroine.*

• And, more recently, as men in space encounter peril, peoples of diverging faiths and dissident nations unite in a mighty supplication for the

---

*Such postponement of personal grieving may not be emotionally healthy. See listing *make, kanu* and *kaumaha*.

Astronauts' safety. Later, one comment summarized it, "The whole world prayed Apollo XIII back to earth."

If you believe religion and prayer also include man's shared though silently expressed feelings, then these four examples are indeed *kūkulu kumuhana*. Mary Kawena Pukui believes they are.

ho'oūlu ia—mild, helpful possession; enabling concept such as inspiration in an artistic endeavor.

 Deriv: *ho'o*, causative prefix.
    ulu, to grow.
    ia, carries the idea of intensifying, not the mild possession, but the achievement or inspiration resulting from the possession.

Literally the "making to grow." Inspiration given by one's *aumakua* (ancestor god) so that a mediocre performance or endeavor becomes a superior one. The extra bit of strength to finish work or artistic project. Thought of as a gift of the *aumakua*, this inspiration was evidence of mild possession *(noho)* of one's *aumakua*. One of several enabling concepts. See *aumakua*.

hō'upu'upu—implantation of thought into another's mind. Term applies to the process of implantation and the thought so implanted.

 Deriv: *hō*, transfer; give.
    'upu, recurring thought.
    Literally, "transfer thought."

A physician gives his patient a sugar-pill placebo, and the patient feels better. An old man in Polynesia or the West Indies or Africa literally "lies down and dies" because a sorcerer has placed a death spell on him. TV commercials whisper that Perfume X is a veritable man trap; an impressionable girl sprays on X and feels more alluring. A disc jockey of some experience suddenly finds himself dry-mouthed and panicky before the familiar microphone. The night before, he heard a symptom-by-symptom description of mike-fright.

**hō'upu'upu is
suggestion**

The Hawaiians had a word for it. *Hō'upu'upu*. Thought implantation. The Western world has a term for it. The power of suggestion.

In Hawaii's pre-history era, *hō'upu'upu* functioned in many ritualized practices, both punitive and curative. Some of these rituals yet exist. Even today, *pī kai* (sprinkling with sea water) for purification, and the use of *ti* leaves for protection combine religious and psychological elements to bring peace of mind.

Other rituals are lost or shorn of their mysticism, but their underlying power of suggestion lives on in a new setting. In Hawaii's healing art, *lā'au kāhea* (the "calling medicine"), *hō'upu'upu* was "positive thinking." In this, the *kahuna lapa'au* (a kind of "family doctor") first asked, "Do you believe this medicine will help you?" The answer had to be "Yes" before the *kahuna* would proceed with treatment. Today, even with miracle drugs and surgical advances, confidence in one's physician, surgeon or therapist facilitates recovery.

Hawaiians recognized the "power of suggestion" in three forms. Mary Kawena Pukui defines them:

"*Hō'upu'upu* is thought implantation from somebody else. Somebody else sends the thought by words or unmistakable signals.* The thought is usually implanted directly. One person says to another, 'You're going to grow up as worthless as your father.' Or, 'You're going to get sick.' Or 'You will get well.' Sometimes *hō'upu'upu* is sent indirectly. A neighbor says, 'Nolea looks awful! You know, her mother died when she was just about Nolea's age. Yes, the two are a lot alike. Both so frail.' Pretty soon, this is going to get back to Nolea, and she will start worrying.

ho'opi'opi'o by gesture

"*Ho'opi'opi'o* is intentional implantation of a thought or sensation without saying any words. It's very subtle. One person can pass his hand over his forehead and give a person watching a headache. *Ho'opi'opi'o* is always done to hurt. Never to soothe or heal.

hā'upu in own mind

"*Hā'upu* is having a thought come to one's mind. Maybe it just comes spontaneously. Maybe it's recalled from memory. But nobody else put it there."

In Hawaii's past, *hō'upu'upu* and *ho'opi'opi'o* functioned to harm when a man felt himself under the spell of evil sorcery. *Hō'upu'upu* marshalled religious-psychological forces to help as the counter-spell was chanted to overcome the sorcery.

"You will die! I send you death," went the incantation of doom.

"Live! You will live! Death returns to its sender," said the counter-prayer.

Hō'upu'upu was anxiety-fraught when a Hawaiian believed his *inoa* (name) was causing him trouble. *Hō'upu'upu* was remedial when name and/or unhappy associations were *'oki'd* (removed) by sincere prayer and a confident declaration of severance.

hō'upu'upu, hā'upu work together

In the past and today, *hō'upu'upu,* the implanted thought, works closely with *hā'upu,* the thought already in the mind. For what is in the conscious or

---

*A sorcerer might arrange rocks in a definite pattern that signified a death spell, and place them directly in the pathway of the person destined to be "prayed to death." When the chosen victim saw the rock formation he "read" the message.

unconscious mind helps determine whether suggestions are shrugged off, accepted or rejected. Hawaiians made this clear in the traditional provision that curses or threatening words were harmless unless the intended recipient had a guilty realization of wrong-doing. Hawaiians limited this to guilt for a specific wrong. Western psychiatry extends this to include specific, realized guilts and diffused, accumulated or irrelevant guilt feelings.

auto-suggestion
reinforces thought

When a suggestion is neither shrugged off nor decisively rejected, it sets in motion a process of self-reiteration or auto-suggestion. Either consciously or unconsciously, the one who accepted a suggestion repeats it many times, and thereby reinforces it. It is this self-repetition that makes a suggestion effective. Here again, *hā'upu,* or what is already in the mind, allows the self-reiteration-self-reinforcement of the suggestion to function. The suggestibility of the person increases. Or, to put it Hawaiian-style, "The *hō'upu'upu* starts working on him."

hō'upu'upu
& hypnosis

The greatest suggestibility occurs in the hypnotic state. Hawaiians of old evidently knew this. Mrs. Pukui believes *hō'upu'upu* was directed to and accepted by persons in the trance-like or hypnotic states common to certain ritual practices. See *haka* (medium), *noho* (possession by a spirit) and *'anā'anā* (sorcery).

hō'upu'upu
& projection

Early Hawaiians also understood that *hō'upu'upu* was often used as a denial or defense-and-projection mechanism. This is evident in what we might call the "boomerang belief." This maintained that injurious effects of words or actions directed to another could not only be refused, but returned to the sender. (See *"ho'i no kau me 'oe."*)

To put this denial-projection process in a universal and current example: Mary begins worrying that her husband John is going to have a heart attack. She puts John on all the special diets she has read about. She nags him about not enough or too much exercise. But John is young and healthy. He has no history or signs of heart trouble, John, depending on his own susceptibilities, can "catch" the anxiety directed at him and become a heart hypochondriac. Or, he can continue to be unconcerned about his nice, steady "ticker." If Mary cannot make her anxieties "stick" to John, they return, sooner or later, to their denied, more-or-less hidden origin. Mary is worried about her *own* heart.

For a specific, Hawaiian example, let's consider the 1969 case of Mrs. N_____:

Mrs. N_____ is the woman who felt *'ōkakala* (goose bumps) on her skin while she was talking with a Hawaiian staff aide. Immediately, she told the aide, "This is a *hō'ailona* [sign or portent] for you. This is a sign that harm will come to you."

Later, Mrs. N_____ smelled *mokihana** in church. Hawaiians often believe smelling a plant or flower not actually present is a death portent. Soon after this, the husband of a church member died. Mrs. N_____ told others,

"This man died because he strayed from the church. He died because he gave up the word of God."

Another time she said of her deceased husband,

"He died because his forebears did not do right by this church."

(Later, it was found that Mrs._____ translated *mokihana* as "work of Moses." With her, interpretation of the scent was a mixture of Hawaiian beliefs and Biblical accounts of Moses acting as messenger of God's wrath.)

Within the same week of the *mokihana* sign, the woman minister of the church came to read the Bible at Mrs. N_____'s home.

"While she was reading, I saw a vision of a dark pit," Mrs. N_____ related. "I told Reverend _____ and she gave a prayer to close the pit. The pit was death."

Late that night, the minister's "boyfriend" was seriously hurt in an accident. The two women agreed he had been spared death because of Mrs. N_____'s vision with its timely warning for the minister to "close the dark pit."

The signs, visions, mingling of Hawaiian and Christian religious mysticism, and the linking of conduct to death, and the escape from death by vision-directed prayer are all usual and normal in isolated, tradition-imbued Hawaiians, even in 1970. It is Mrs. N_____'s interpretation and utilization of portents that invite scrutiny.

Directly and indirectly, Mrs. N_____ attempted to implant *hō'upu-'upu*. In her interpretation of *hō'ailona* or signs, she applied harm, death warnings and death cause to others. Never to herself.

Mrs. N_____ herself is dangerously overweight. She had a hernia, but the surgeon did not want to operate until she had lost about 120 pounds. Yet she disregarded diet restrictions. She kept appointments with her physician only when the case worker sent for or personally escorted her. The same inertia or reluctance was shown in keeping appointments with the case worker.

Ten days after the "dark pit" vision, she was rushed to the hospital for emergency surgery. The hernia had strangulated, and one segment of intestine was extremely gangrenous.

Psychosomatic factors could have contributed to the muscle spasm that entrapped and cut off the blood supply to the loop of bowel.

A fairly clear picture emerges of a woman who tends to operate on denial and projection. And so operating, she fails to come to grips with her own problems. The psychological process functions in any culture. With Mrs. N_____, it functioned as *hō'upu'upu*. Coincidence made it easier for her to project. A strayed-from-the-flock member *did* die. Yet the consistency of Mrs. N_____'s thought implantation efforts invokes three questions:

Is she actually concerned about the dubious church status of her late husband and of the man who died after she smelled *mokihana*?

Or is she really anxious about her own spiritual and religious welfare? *And,*

How great are her own fears of the imminent death which she invites?

---

*A variety of citrus tree that grows only on Kauai. Both fruit and leaves are extremely fragrant.

**projection
in disguise**

Hō'upu'upu may be used to project feelings in fairly direct fashion, as Mrs. N_____ did. It may also take many disguises. A depressed person may deny depression and project it as anger. Miserable himself, he picks a quarrel with somebody else. Or, "I'm *afraid* you will fail" may be the first layer of disguise for the thought, "I *wish* you would fail." Still further concealed may be the unconscious desire, "I hope *I* flunk this test or flub this job so I can go home and stop all this competing and trying so hard." Or, shorn of yet more disguises, "If I don't really study for this test or don't really try to make good on this job, then I can keep on thinking that I failed because I simply did not make an effort. Not because I'm really not smart and capable. Why, I can make good any old time I really want to!"

One who projects *hō'upu'upu* denies his own distress and blocks off insight into its causes. The receiver of *hō'upu'upu* admits distress, but also may lack insight into its cause. For example, take the case of George.

**hō'upu'upu
plants fear**

George is 20, part-Hawaiian, and a resident of an isolated, still very much Hawaiian, community. Bright and ambitious, George won a scholarship to go to college. Soon after he won this, a member of the family warned, him that "you'd better get yourself blessed and you'd better watch your step, or something's going to happen to you in college."

The *hō'upu'upu* "stuck." George got himself blessed. To many Hawaiians, prayer *(pule)* and blessing *(pōmaika'i)* can remove or lessen the effects of such prophetic warning. (See *'oki.*)

**need for
objectivity**

With George, the blessing did not remove the implanted fear. For him, therapy depends pretty much on helping him to view *objectively* the processes of thought implantation; the motives, perhaps jealousy, that inspired the warning; and George's own private fears of failure at college or feelings that he did not deserve the scholarship.

Other examples of received and accepted *hō'upu'upu* are found in sections on: *'ānai* (curse), *hua 'ōlelo* in its meaning of prophetic statement or threat; *'anā'anā* (sorcery), *waha 'awa* ("bittermouth"), and *mana* (supernatural power).

**susceptibility
of Hawaiians**

A study of Center cases over six years makes possible a few generalizations about *hō'upu'upu*. Hawaiian clients seem most susceptible to:

Hō'upu'upu that carries a threat or warning or some connotation of death.

Hō'upu'upu connected with religion, mysticism, the supernatural or occult. Traditional Hawaiian, Christian or Oriental faiths singly, blended, or garbled, are found in mystic beliefs and experiences.

Hō'upu'upu that has built up gradually from repeated suggestions by others.

84

The saddest example of negative *hō'upu'upu* is that of Hawaiians who are ashamed of or deny their own uniquely Hawaiian qualities. This seems to be the internalized acceptance of repeated, handed-down opinions first expressed some 150 years ago. Told their gods were false, their rituals foolish, their dress, dances and manners unacceptable, their skills and talents unimportant, the Hawaiians as a people knew an "identity crisis" long before the phrase was coined. Today, this may show up in self-images molded into the "happy beachboy" stereotype. Or shaped to conform to a "super-Western, super-Christian" pattern. Here a kind of "double *hō'upu'upu*" seems to have instilled the conviction that everything Hawaiian is undesirable and everything of the Christian West is ideal.

It is not uncommon to hear a client say,

"Oh, no, I'm not at all Hawaiian!" (Meanwhile following many basically Hawaiian practices.)

Or, at the other extreme,

"I'm no good. I'm Hawaiian, so I'll never amount to anything. It's all bad, bad, bad—the Hawaiian part of me."

Here person-to-person and mass media communication and educational means can all help build a better self-image. Today's apologetic Hawaiians need to know what was beautiful in their old beliefs, wise and beneficial in their rituals. Or as Mrs. Pukui sums it up:

"You [Hawaiians] don't need to follow the old ways. You do need to know them and their true meaning and purpose. Then you can look back on your past with understanding and pride."

hua 'ōlelo—limited to a behavioral context it carries the idea that speech causes consequences. Specifically, this idea is present in two meanings: 1. a broken promise; 2. a rash, vindictive and somewhat prophetic statement.

Deriv: *hua*, fruit, egg, ovum.
'ōlelo, speech; language. Literally, "fruit of word or speech."

The interview had reached an impasse. Patiently the social worker, a non-Hawaiian in a public agency, repeated the condition on which the client's assistance depended.

"All we ask is that you promise to find a house within this rental allowance, in 90 days. You have three whole months. But you must give us your word *now* that you will do this."

Across the desk sat the client, Hawaiian mother of six. She looked sullen —or was it merely thoughtful? Her face was heavy, her eyes blank with the inward struggle to reach a decision. At last she made up her mind.

"No, I won't. No promise. Cannot."

hua 'ōlelo
broken promise

Such is the 1966 example of avoidance of a *hua 'ōlelo* as "broken promise." The example has a happy ending. The caseworker, sensing something more than mere stubbornness in her client's attitude, consulted the Center and learned about *hua 'ōlelo*. She found that through uncounted centuries of Hawaiian tradition a *ho'ohiki* (promise) is a binding pledge not to be taken unless it can be kept. Break a promise and you are guilty of *hua 'ōlelo*. You have called down on yourself disaster, illness or even death. Originally and indigenously, this was believed to be punishment sent by the *aumakua* (ancestor god). Today the "hand of God" is usually seen chastising the "sinner."

And so client and worker reached a mutually agreeable solution. The client promised to make every reasonable effort to find housing within cost and time stipulations, for this was a promise she could keep. It was understood she was not promising house-hunting success within the deadline.

hua 'ōlelo, the
rash statement

Hua 'ōlelo as the threatening, malicious statement, is found in the following examples:

A woman, jealous of her neighbor's success, exploded, "You don't need to act so *ho'okano* (conceited). Mark my words, some day you'll come down in the world!"

And:

A child, physically mistreated by her *hānai* (adoptive) mother, muttered between clenched teeth, "I hate you. I wish you were dead!"

And:

A mother, furious because her daughter married a man she did not approve of, shouted, "As long as I live I never want to see any children born of this union!"

What do *hua 'ōlelo,* the broken promise, and *hua 'ōlelo,* the impulsive, vindictive statement, have in common?

Stated briefly, a sense of consequences resulting from words. Hawaiian tradition holds that a spoken word becomes an actual entity, an operative agent that can bring about events.

Thus, *hua 'ōlelo,* broken promise or malicious statement, becomes a psychological vehicle, heavily loaded with all the basic components of mental agony and unhappiness.

The difference between promise not kept and vengeful statement comes in how this vehicle is unloaded.

In the broken promise type of *hua 'ōlelo,* the victim feels purely human disappointment or deprivation. He fails to receive, for example, the food, the property, or the affection promised him. This breach of trust invariably leads to ill-feeling on both sides. It may even involve entire families in the tangled snarl of animosity called *hihia* (see listing). But in Hawaiian belief, the one who made and broke the promise receives the full, load of supernaturally sent punishment.

Apparently, it is this fear of punishment that makes Hawaiians often reluctant to promise to keep a definite appointment, finish a job by a certain date, or, in general, pin themselves down to specific pledges. This fear may be clearly known in its framework of tradition, or it may be little more than a half-understood, handed-down feeling. Either way it signals: "Don't make a promise. Don't risk a *hua 'ōlelo.*"

One way to prevent a *hua 'ōlelo,* is to use an evasive phrase. "Maybe I'll come Wednesday." "I'll try to finish the planting this week." "I'll see about it."

The vindictive statement *hua 'ōlelo* functions like the traditional *'ānai* (curse). The target of an angry, threatening statement could accept it, thereby accepting the attached disaster. To use the three earlier examples, with acceptance the successful neighbor would "come down in the world." The *hānai* mother whose death was openly wished would die. And, as it actually happened, the woman who married against her mother's wishes did not have children during her mother's lifetime. After her mother died, she had eight.

On the other hand, if the intended target was innocent of wrong-doing, he could refuse to accept the *hua 'ōlelo* and send it back to the speaker. This was easily done. Says Mary Kawena Pukui, "Right away say *'ho'i no kau me 'oe.'* That means 'what you have just given me, return to you.' Or just say 'Keep yours. I won't accept it.' Then ignore the whole thing. Forget about it!"*

With this ritual, the punishment is reversed. The one who said "drop dead" would die; the one who threatened "you'll come down in the world" would meet failure. In fact, the whole load of recrimination, hostility and misfortune would dump itself right back on the person who started the whole destructive process.

Use of the identical rituals employed to return a curse makes it clear that in Hawaiian traditional thought the *hua 'ōlelo* can become the most doom-dealing *'ānai,* even though "I curse you" or "Be accursed" was never said. This is hard for the Western mind to grasp. The *hua 'ōlelo* phrases, "I wish you'd die," "I hope you fail," seem so innocuous.

Here the thin line between an unpleasant remark and a curse is in the receiver's perception and interpretation. How does he view the speaker? How does he interpret the *hua 'ōlelo,* the utterance itself?

waha 'awa, the "Bitter Mouth"

Traditionally (and this is true today) anyone who customarily has made vindictive statements with overtones of wish or prophecy and then had a few of these "wishes" come true was called a *waha 'awa* or "Bitter Mouth." How each target of a Bitter Mouth's wrath interpreted these words depended, among other things, on how seriously he took the *waha 'awa.* To one individual, a *waha 'awa* might be merely a cantankerous character whose words were shrugged off. This individual was not too susceptible to suggestion or the "thought implantation" called *hō'upu'upu.* But to another, the *waha 'awa* might be viewed as a dangerous person with the *mana* (special power) to destroy another's health or happiness. As such, the *waha 'awa's* words were indeed an *'ānai* or curse.

(See listings, *waha 'awa, hō'upu'upu* and *mana* for discussion of these important and inter-woven concepts.)

---

*The sending back of undeserved penalties and misfortunes is a major principle of Hawaiian beliefs.

Having interpreted the words of a *waha 'awa* as *'ānai,* the recipient either accepts or rejects the curse. (He may return the curse by Hawaiian ritual described previously.) Fundamentally, Hawaiian concept and Western psychiatric tenets now travel parallel pathways. For accepting the curse stems from feelings of *'ike hewa* (guilt). Refusing the curse comes from a consciousness of *hewa 'ole* (freedom from guilt; innocence).

And so, for the one who accepts *'ānai* or *hua 'ōlelo*—or accusation, blame or punishment—remedial therapy is frequently based on an exploration of and insight into guilts.

Is the guilt reasonable and the accusation or punishment just?

Or is the guilt irrational, irrelevant to the subject of curse or accusation? If so, why and from what formative origins did this guilt take form?

hu'ihu'i—a physical sensation of coldness; a cold sensation interpreted as a portent; numb or tingling feeling as in physical passion.

Deriv: *hu'i,* ache.

The sensations of cold, all involving a measure of tension, were evidently associated with a slight feeling of aching. This association is similar to the Western expression "aching with love" and "aching with cold." See discussion under *'ili'ōuli.*

hukihuki—the constant, opposing emotional pull two or more persons in conflict may exert on a third person, ostensibly to win his love, loyalty or influence but actually to gain supremacy in the two-way power struggle.

Deriv: *huki,* to pull.

Pull anything in opposite directions long enough and something has to give. Usually what's in the middle. The toy two youngsters claim. The fabric two women clutch in a bargain basement sale. Or in human relationships, a person.

For *hukihuki* describes a total, damaging situation that exists when opposing individuals or groups tug, pull and pressure to gain emotional ascendancy over another individual or group. Often it affects children. Mother and father are rivals for their child's affection. Divorced parents battle for child custody. Parents and grandparents shuttle a child from one home to another in disputed *hānai* (adoption-like) arrangements.

Hukihuki also affects adults. Wife and mother-in-law struggle for first place in the affections of husband-and-son. Competing office subordinates woo supervisor with special attentions to gain promotion. Lobbyists for conflicting causes try to manipulate politician to win his support.

When the one-in-the-middle becomes involved in the struggle, *hukihuki* becomes harmful. Adults who are forewarned, experienced or naturally wise can escape such involvement. Others cannot. Children are almost always caught. Children are almost always hurt.

Hukihuki, concept and occurrence, is universal. Only the term is Hawaiian. However, there are traditionally Hawaiian situations in which *hukihuki* is found. One, typical of many case examples, may be summed up in the troubled-loaded inquiry,

"Is Keone—or Mary or Leilani or Pili—*hānai* or *luhi?*"

An old Hawaiian belief was that the first-born child belonged permanently to the grandparents. The first girl went to the maternal grandparents; the first boy to the paternal grandparents. The term *hānai* is used loosely to mean the child, the grandparents and the adoption-like arrangement itself. In contrast, *luhi* describes the child or even the arrangement in which a foster-parent cares for a child on a non-permanent basis. Here parents could reclaim their child. Legal adoption has generally replaced *hānai* child-giving. However, Hawaiian grandparents still show extremely possessive feelings toward grandchildren, especially the first-born (*hiapo*) child. This can provide a ready-made foundation for *hukihuki,* especially when a foster-parent status is not initially made clear.

Hukihuki certainly exists in the current case of 16-year-old Leilani. Natural daughter of a wed but separated mother, she has been living with her paternal grandmother since early childhood. When Leilani was about seven, the mother and her second husband moved to the mainland. Leilani remained with the grandmother. The gap between mother and daughter widened; the bond between grandmother and girl strengthened. Now the mother has returned to Hawaii and wants to take Leilani back. The mother claims that Leilani was left in the grandmother's care as a temporary foster-child or *luhi.* The grandmother, though she realizes there was no traditional pledge of permanency (see *hānai*), feels that Leilani is her *hānai keiki* and utilizes the very lack of a previous clear understanding as a means to keep the child.

And so *hukihuki,* its seed planted 16 years ago, comes to full fruition. Leilani is caught between the possessive claims of parent and grandparent. Personally she vacillates, reaching out to her mother; returning to grandmother. Caught in conflict, Leilani acts out her emotional confusion in, for example, open, public "I want to be caught" glue-sniffing. Perhaps partly in response to Grandmother's refusal to let Leilani date, she also takes the part of the "Butch" in Lesbian relationships. This is not yet thought to be a permanent behavior pattern. Other causative factors are known to be operative.

Leilani acts out her reaction to the push-pull-tug of *hukihuki.* A different child might "tune out" the struggle and become apathetic. Another might counter-manipulate, playing one adult against the other so that each provides more treats, favors and privileges in the competition for power over the child. Yet another might internalize his conflicts. Or, as Mary Kawena Pukui outlines the traditional Hawaiian view:

"When there is *hukihuki,* the child can get sick or even die."

The statement is fairly close to modern psychiatric views that the unhappy, anxious person is apt to have lower resistance to physical ills, including the bacteria-borne diseases of childhood.

Hukihuki can also be an agitating element for adults. It is for Keaka, chronologically 31, but emotionally a teen-ager. Keaka's life is certainly unhappy; it is also predictably short. For Keaka is apparently skidding swiftly downward on his own path to self-destruction. He has sniffed paint and solvents for years. Recently his weight dropped drastically, he began vomiting, having diarrhea and became impotent. He refuses to see a doctor. He continues his sniffing, fully aware of its harmful effects. Without medical check-up, we can only speculate on his physical condition and its causes. Of Keaka's tangled personal and family relationships, we do know these facts:

He was the first-born son, the child traditionally given to the paternal grandparents. (Concern over a dream about his grandfather brought him to the Center.) However, his mother first had promised to give Keaka as an infant to an aunt, then changed her mind and kept him. The words "promised" and "kept" are significant. Even today his whole family contests proprietary claims to Keaka. Mother and aunt still continue their struggle to dominate him. Sisters and brothers unite to tug Keaka emotionally away from his wife and his marriage. His wife's family when sober disapproves of Keaka; when drunk, the family thinks "he's a great guy." One sister-in-law issues unmistakable sexual invitations to him. As the case-worker outlines the situation:

"There's *hukihuki* over Keaka between his aunt and his mother. There's *hukihuki* over him between his mother and his wife. There's *hukihuki* over him between his family and his wife's family."

All this *hukihuki*, the caseworker points out, is known on a conscious level. Yet Keaka is now too ill—and perhaps has always been too infantile—to break out of the struggle himself. The various family members are unable or unwilling to put an end to it.

Obviously, Keaka, the emotional child, and Leilani, the chronological child, are pawns in the power-play that is *hukihuki*. And here emerges the true nature of this tug-of-war. Psychiatrist Dr. E. W. Haertig, delineates it:

"Nominally, *hukihuki* is a struggle between two persons for the possession of another—let's say—of a child. Possession, perhaps, of his physical presence in the home. Possession of his love and loyalties. On the surface, the concern is for the child. The struggle may be sugar-coated with sentiment; masked as love. But actually this is a struggle for the ascendancy of power, for dominance of one adult over the other. The true motivation is not love of a child. The true motivation is love of power."

Once adults gain enough insight into their power struggle to realize they are harming, not loving a child, they face a kind of prove-your-sincerity, show-down situation. If they genuinely love the child, one or both will take definite, positive steps to resolve the *hukihuki*. This may be the surrender of a child to a parent most able to provide wise and loving care. It may be acceptance of marriage counseling or family-centered therapy. It may be, in the case of an "adult child," a moratorium on or outright end to wife and mother-in-law visiting. Whatever the concrete action, it is arrived at by seeing the child and his needs as more important than the adult desire to dominate.

As Mrs. Pukui puts it in the Hawaiian tradition, "when *hukihuki* hurts a child, somebody has to give up."

Give up the child? Sometimes.

Give up the lust for power? Always.

'ili kapu—taboo against wearing another's clothing.

Deriv: *'ili*, skin.
kapu, taboo or absolute prohibition.

Clothing, because it touched the body, contained some of the wearer's *mana* (personal, somewhat mystical power) Hawaiians believed. A garment in close body contact contained more *mana* than an outer wrap. In fact, enough *mana* permeated a garment worn next to the skin that it, like hair or fingernails, could even become bait (*maunu*) for sorcery. Clothing was a completely individual possession. Therefore, no one must wear another's garment. The sole exception, and only with permission, was a close family member of the same sex.

'Ili kapu, as an ingrained revulsion against wearing other's clothing is encountered today among hospitalized patients·who rebel·at wearing hospital gowns. The resistance goes far beyond the fact that the gowns are neither becoming nor comfortable. It is summed up in the phrase, "*A'ohe i like ka 'ili*," "the skin is not the same," or "they are not of the same skin."

Older patients explain, "Somebody else...many others...wore this. ...I know people have die in it. No make difference how many times wash..." or, "Hawaiians do not wear other people's clothing. Especially right against the skin!"

The objection is more common among older patients who may have always observed the old *kapu*, or in illness return to the beliefs and emotions of childhood.

A second cause for resistance comes from the Hawaiian tradition that exposing the buttocks (*ho'opohopoho*) was a gesture of complete contempt (*ho'onā 'aikola*) and a grave insult to the beholder. The slit-in-the-back hospital gown thus becomes a threat to ordinary courtesy.*

In 1971, a pre-natal clinic on a neighbor island found that young Hawaiian women were not keeping their appointments because they had to wear hospital type gowns for physical examinations.

In ordinary living, older clients often insist on doing their own personal laundry, especially their underthings. "The garments of the aged should be washed alone," is one account. Belief that men's and women's garments should be handled separately has also been noted.

Carry-over of feelings about *'ili kapu* still exists among a few young people reared by or in close contact with Hawaiian grandparents or older relatives. Usually this applies to undergarments only. Among Center staff members are young women who, as teen-agers, never traded clothing. On the other hand, Kamehameha School male students wear rented uniforms for graduation, many Hawaiian bridegrooms rent dinner jackets, and many Hawaiians join their multi-racial friends in today's fad of finding thrift-shop clothing. In most cases, only outer garments are rented, borrowed or bought second-hand.

Case records show *'ili kapu* is sometimes involved in conflict between generations. One grandmother insists her teen-age granddaughter wash her underthings separately the minute she takes them off. This could reflect some belief in *mana* clinging to the garments or, says Mrs. Pukui, "it could be just

---

*When wearing the hospital gown is unavoidable, harmful, unpleasant effects may be traditionally averted through *'oki'ing*. See listing, *'oki*.

Hawaiian fussiness or fastidiousness." Wearing the clothing of a family member who died is properly done only if the relative gave specific permission before death. In one case, a Hawaiian woman tried wearing a deceased aunt's clothing without permission and had to stop. "I felt funny . . . uncomfortable. It just was not right," she related.

'ili 'ōuli—disturbed skin sensations interpreted as signs or portents. Literally "skin sign."

Deriv: *'ili*, skin.
'ōuli, portent, omen, sign.

On a hot July morning, a Hawaiian staff aide of the Center called on a Hawaiian client at her home. The client broke out in *'ōkakala* or "goose bumps."

'ōkakala,
goose bumps

"*Ke pi'i mai nei ka lī*, [The chill is coming]" said the client, showing her her arms. "*'Ōkakala* has come on me. This is *hō'ailona* [a sign]." And then, projecting her own unexplored feelings, she told the aide, "My *'ōkakala* is for you. Something is going to happen to you."

Such immediate, obvious projection onto another person is not too common—and is not the subject of this section. What is frequently encountered is the Hawaiian belief that a tingling, or prickling, or creepy-crawly or chill or numb feeling of the skin is an omen of misfortune or a sign that a supernatural spirit is present.

wela

Not all skin sensations were, or are now, given this significance. The sudden chill felt when ocean breezes fan a wet body is recognized as a natural reaction, but a cold shiver without apparent cause is a kind of psychic "calling card" presented by a spirit. *Wela*, a sudden hot feeling, is not considered an omen, nor was it traditionally associated with menopause. It is recognized as a normal reaction sensation, whether the cause is fever, sudden external temperature change or the heat of physical passion.

The deviations from normal skin feelings that are most often considered psychic premonitions are: *'aki'aki*, a feeling of little pinches, nibbles or prickles; *'e'eu*, formication, the "ants crawling on or under the skin" feeling; *hu'ihu'i*, sudden chill *(lī)*, numbness or tingling; *mā'e'ele*, the "foot gone to sleep" sensation, and *'ōkakala*, the "goose bumps."

These are defined more fully under separate listings. Discussed here is their common denominator: the mystic-psychic portents ascribed to the sensations.

'aki'aki

'Aki'aki is thought to be an omen whether its "nibbles and prickles" are felt in a waking state or dreamed. The message may be a warning of harm or unhappiness to come. Or, by a symbolic play on words, *'aki'aki* may signify that someone is spreading lies or gossip about one. The word *'aki* means to

"nibble or bite as a fish does," or, by extension of meaning, the taking of constant, malicious "bites" out of the precious fabric that is personal reputation.

In both interpretations, significance is given to which side of the body feels 'aki'aki. On the right side, a man is somehow involved; on the left, a woman. This "right is masculine; left is feminine" concept is consistent in Hawaii's traditions and rituals.

'e'eu
formication

'E'eu, the "creepy-crawly" formication, brings the following comments from Mary Kawena Pukui:

"Sometimes Hawaiians go somewhere and pretty soon they have the 'e'eu sensation. They look around and say "e'eu.' They feel 'there's something around here that doesn't accept me. Something around that's disturbing.'"

Or as another present-day Hawaiian puts it, "You sense, not so much danger, but supernatural things. There's a presence that you can't see, but you can feel."

Again quoting Mrs. Pukui: "Your skin—maybe even your scalp—is crawly, and inside you feel the creepy sensation."

hu'ihu'i

Hu'ihu'i is thought of both as the pleasant "tingling with love" and the less pleasant numb, cold or tingling feeling of vague foreboding usually conveyed by a spirit presence.

"Some part of your body feels cold all of a sudden—and something around you is causing this." "An icy wind seems to be blowing on you." So hu'ihu'i is described.

In the traditional view, a spirit sends the icy wind as a warning, Mrs. Pukui explains. (An actual whirlwind carries the same significance.)

mā'e'ele

Mā'e'ele carries no ominous overtones. It means merely a cold, numb foot or leg "gone to sleep" from sitting on it, from pressure of the fetus in pregnancy, or as a reaction in making love. If the foot felt numb from any less obvious cause, this was thought to mean "you are going somewhere" or "you are going to have a visitor." No fear or supernatural influence was involved. However, the foot that really "goes to sleep" is also going to "wake up" with all the uncomfortable sensations of 'e'eu. And so the spirits and portents of 'e'eu are often verbally attached to mā'e'ele.

When the possible neurological and circulatory causes for any of these disturbed skin sensations are investigated and ruled out, it seems likely that what remains is a universal cause: anxiety. Anxiety expressed in Hawaiian ways.

However, diagnosing anxiety is not a matter of ruling out the body. The various skin sensations neatly packaged in the medical term, paresthesias, are the end results of a chain reaction. Anxiety may bring about over-breathing. Over-breathing produces changes in the blood chemistry. This changed blood chemistry produces the distressed—and distressing—sensations of the skin.

Dr. Haertig speculates that skin manifestations as anxiety symptoms were probably much less frequent in the indigenous culture of Hawaii than they are now.

"In the less repressive era of Hawaii, thought was closer to action. There was less need to 'store up' anxiety. In today's more repressive society, all of us are often anxious, even though we may not quite know what we are anxious about. This anxiety, denied the direct and cathartic exit of consciousness and action-taking, produces symptoms."

How these symptoms are interpreted subjectively is basically much the same, whether the anxious person is Hawaiian or non-Hawaiian. For anxiety, already present for some time, is in one way or another forecast into the future. "Something is *going to* happen." "Some misfortune or trick of fate *awaits* me." The message is one of premonitory anxiety, whether the message is routed via supernatural spirit and traditional *ho'ailona* or more directly by feeling "upset and nervous."

Similarly, when anxiety is further denied and projected, only the pattern of projection is really different in differing cultures. The Hawaiian client, in our example, projected the ominous content of *'ōkakala* onto the Hawaiian aide. (This is mysterious only to those who do not know Hawaiian traditions and subjectively *feel* Hawaiian.) The *haole* (Caucasian) housewife may project, in her cultural context, anxieties onto husband or child. A mother, for example, may fuss and stew over her child's health and safety, as a projection of her own anxiety about herself.

In these cases a messenger named "symptom" knocked on the door marked "consciousness" to deliver a message that read "you are anxious and fearful." However, the messenger met closed doors and obeyed the instructions, "deliver message somewhere else," as in a bodily symptom, or "to somebody else."

inoa—personal name; in pre-missionary times no distinction was made between first name or names and family name.

Deriv:　unknown.

In the early days of Hawaii, personal possessions were few, but highly valued. *Poi* pounders, woven mats, a man's *malo* or loin cloth, the stone adze of a canoe maker, the bone hooks of a fisherman, the spear of a warrior—all these were prized. But even more precious was each man's most personal possession, his name.

One's *inoa* was both owned property and a kind of force in its own right. Once spoken, an *inoa* took on an existence, invisible, intangible, but real. An *inoa* could be a causative agent, capable of marshalling mystic elements to help or hurt the bearer of the name. And, so went the belief, the more an *inoa* was spoken, the stronger became this name-force and its potential to benefit or harm.*

---

*This is consistent with the belief that certain words, once spoken, existed, and might even set in motion events of consequence. This was an essential concept in *'ānai* (curse) and *hua 'ōlelo* (rash statement or threat).

Obviously, the *inoa* for a new child must be chosen only after careful thought, family consultations, and, ideally, with the supernatural advice of a family *aumakua* (ancestor god). Depending on its connotations and method of selection, the *inoa* usually belonged to one or more of the following classifications:

Names given or suggested by supernatural means, such as: *inoa pō*, name in the night; *inoa hō'ailona*, name in a sign; and *inoa 'ūlāleo*, name spoken, voiced name.

Or —

Names not mystically suggested, such as: *inoa ho'omanao*, a commemorative name given to honor a person or record an event; *inoa kupuna*, the handed-down name of an ancestor; *inoa kūamuamu*, a "reviling name."

At the bottom of the list were the simple names that meant a rock, tree, stream or any natural object. These names, devoid of *aumakua* influence, scrupulously free from reference to god, to *ali'i* (royalty) or famous event, were taken by the *kauwā*, Hawaii's despised slave class.

Name classifications often merged. For example, a name that in one generation was coined to commemorate an event might be handed down to a descendant, thus becoming both a commemorative and an ancestral name. And because an individual could have one or several names, a single person might bear an ancestral name, a commemorative name and a newly coined name.

inoa pō, inoa hō'ailona, inoa 'ūlāleo

Three types of names carried the awesome seal of the spirit world. All were chosen by a god, usually a family *aumakua*. In an *'ohana* (family clan) that awaited a baby's birth, someone would have a name indicated or pronounced in a dream. This was the *inoa pō*, literally "night name" or "name in darkness." Or a family member might have a vision, or see a mystic sign in the clouds, the flight of birds, or other phenomenon, that clearly indicated a name. This was the *inoa hō'ailona* or "name in sign or vision." Or someone might hear a mystical voice speaking a name directly or in an oblique message. This was the *inoa 'ūlāleo*, the "voice name." Seen, heard or dreamed, such a name was both a gift and a command from the *aumakua*. This name must be given the child. Says Mary Kawena Pukui:

"The name given by the *aumakua* shows a relationship between the god and the person named. The name need not contain the name of the god, but Hawaiians know who is referred to. A name that includes phrases that mean 'mountain dweller' or 'earth devourer' refers to Pele, for example.

"Such a name absolutely must be used. To refuse to give the name will result in either a crippled body or death for the child. The crippling of the body is a warning. If it is not heeded, death follows."

This belief carried over to post-missionary times. Some 78 years ago, a baby girl was born on the island of Hawaii. Shortly after the birth, an aunt was given an *inoa pō* for the child. But because she had become a Christian, the aunt kept the name a secret and the child was not given the mystically-indicated *inoa*. The little girl soon became ill. The family held a *ho'oponopono**

---

*The formal gathering of all family members for mutual confession of wrongs, forgiveness and restoration of good relationships.

during which the aunt told about the *inoa pō*. Clearly, the family agreed, an offended *aumakua* was making the child sick. And so after a *mōhai* (sacrificial offering, in this case, food), a feast, and many prayers, the old name was *'oki'd* (severed or removed) and the child was given the *inoa pō*.

And forthwith *Kawena-'ula-o-kalani-a-Hi'iaka-i-ka-poli-o-Pele-ka-wa-hine-'ai-honua* ("The rosy glow in the sky made by Hi'iaka, reared in the bosom of Pele, the earth-consuming woman")* recovered and grew up to be Mary Kawena Pukui, co-author of this book.

Once a person is given an *inoa pō*, the name becomes that individual's exclusive possession. No one else should use it without permission of the original bearer of the name. To do so incites illness or bad fortune. As Mrs. Pukui explains the tradition, "there is a *kapu* (taboo) attached to the name. The *kapu* exists equally for the *inoa* given in a dream, a sign or vision, or by hearing a supernatural voice."

inoa kupuna

When a person hands his name down to a family descendant, the name becomes an *inoa kupuna* or ancestral name. The name so handed down might have been originally an *inoa pō* or other mystically suggested name. It might have been a commemorative name, or simply a coined name. It was up to the owner of the name to make sure he did not hand down any *kapu* or harmful influences attached to the name. In the genealogy conscious society of old Hawaii, this may not have posed a problem; the history of a name was clearly known.

inoa ho'omanao

In a society without a written language, history was a matter of human memory and human voice. Long *olis* (chants) told of great events and heroic sagas. But for a "verbal shorthand" reminder, the nimble-tongued Hawaiians used the *inoa ho'omanao*. Let a grandmother call out to a child, "Come here, *Ke-li'i-paahana*" ("the industrious chiefess") and everyone within hearing remembered Po'oloku, the beloved chiefess who kept her people busy and prosperous, and even personally dug holes for planting bananas.

Giving names to commemorate events in the lives of *ali'i* could have been a risky business. Nobody took another's name without permission, and names of royalty were especially *kapu*. The danger was nicely evaded by placing the emphasis on event and merely incorporating an *ali'i's* name as one part of a many-syllabled phrase. And so when Dr. Gerrit Judd performed his historic operation on the breast of Kapiolani, a child born to a relative about then was given the name *Ke-'oki-waiū-o-Kapi'ōlani,* meaning "the cutting of the breast of Kapiolani." Queen Emma's name was not even used when her trip to Europe was noted by naming a child *Ke-li'i-holo-i-ka-hiki,* "the ali'i who went to foreign lands." On the other hand, royalty might personally bestow a commemorative name. King Kalakaua, playing billiards at Waiohinu, Ka'u, named a baby born then *Ke-li'i-pahupahu-o-Kalakaua,* "Kalakaua is a billiard-playing chief." Christian events also inspired commemorative names. When the first Communion service was held in Kona, a baby was named *Ka'aha-'āina'a-ka-Haku,* or "the Lord's supper."[1]

---

*Refers to an old—very long—legend concerning Hi'iaka, Pele's mystically born sister.

Less than a century ago, Hawaiian youngsters were still occasionally being named *Maka-piapa, Kūkae* or similar names. The fact that *Maka-piapa* means "sticky eyes" and *Kūkae* is the word for "excrement" bothered no one, least of all the child so named. A frail, sickly youngster was often thought to be bothered or even possessed by a harmful spirit. To make the spirit disgusted and stay away, the child was given a name that connoted something loathsome.

Mrs. Pukui says the child was not disturbed by such a name:

"As soon as the child was old enough to understand, he was told the reason for his name and assured that he would have a new name in a few years. Later, the reviling name was *'oki'd* and a dignified new name was given."

Also an *inoa kūamuamu,* but for quite different reasons, was the reviling name given to perpetuate harm or insult directed at *ali'i* or family. This had the quality of a commemorative name, but in a negative context. The ideal situation for such naming came when someone living close by had hurt or insulted another family. Then when the insulted family had a baby by birth or *hānai* (adoption-like practice), the child was named with a phrase that referred to the offense. Each time the youngster was called, the neighbor heard a reminder of her misdeed. Again, Mrs. Pukui provides an example:

"A snobbish, ill-tempered woman made an unkind remark about her neighbor. The bad-tempered woman lived in a nearby plantation house. So the target of the remark named her foster child, *Wahine ho'okano'noho'i-ka-ina-hui,* which means 'the haughty woman who lives in the plantation house.' The hope was that the woman would hear this phrase many times and feel humiliated."

A child with a resentment-perpetuating *inoa* was told why he had the name, and, says Mrs. Pukui, was "proud of the name or else thought it was a good joke." One woman of the present day who has a "reviling name" of this type, says a happy compromise was achieved early in her childhood. The old *inoa kūamuamu* was known to only a few; her Christian name was generally used.

Occasionally, Hawaiians selected names in other, traditional ways.

A name might show family descent in straightforward fashion. Liloa, 50th king in succession after Wakea, the traditional founder of the Hawaiian people* named his son Umi a Liloa, meaning "Umi, descendant of Liloa."

One's *inoa* could show rank and predestined role in life. The name, *Kahoali'i-kumai'-eiwa-ka-moku,* meant its bearer was "To Be The Chief of the Nine Districts" (Hilo, Puna, Ka'u, S. Kona, N. Kona, S. Kohala, N. Kohala, Hamakua and Mokuola).[2]

An *inoa* could inform the knowledgeable of family line and family migration from one island to another. And, especially in the chiefly ranks, one could start out life with one name and have others bestowed as verbal trophies of accomplishment. Defeated enemies gave Kamehameha I the name *Pai'ea* (hard-shelled crab) as a tribute to their conqueror's impenetrable courage and endurance.[3]

---

*Wakea is said to have come from Tahiti and sired the Hawaiian people here. More mythological accounts tell that Wakea and his wife, Papa, gave mystical birth to the islands and human birth to descendants.

Two children in the same family might bear the same name. For example, one child on the island of Hawaii was named *Puuheana makua* ("older Puuheana") and a younger sister was called *Puuheana li'ili'i* ("little Puuheana").

The name of a recently deceased relative could be taken in a name-exchange held over the corpse. Mrs. Pukui describes the simple ceremony: "When my grandfather's oldest brother died, before they took him to the burial cave, my grandfather placed his hands on his dead brother's chest and said to him, 'May my name rest with you and your name be borne by me. I will take your name so it will be heard and live.'"

In Hawaii's pre-history, pre-Christian era, naming precepts and practices showed many similarities to beliefs held by primitive people in distant parts of the world.

name influence
on bearer

What was basically most alike was the conviction that a name became a living entity and that these syllables which identified a person could influence health, happiness and even life span.

This belief and the tenet that a name is a personal possession have lived on through the changes brought to Hawaii by other cultures.

These changes began in the 1820's when adults who were converted took a Christian first name and began using their Hawaiian name as a last name. Some sects required that an *inoa pō* or other mystically-inspired name be *'oki'd* (severed) because it was connected with belief in the *aumākua*. As *ali'i* began to write, their signatures became a mixture of Hawaiian-English, in name and spelling. An 1831 public proclamation shows the transition period. Signatures read *Elizabeta Kaahumanu, John Adams Kuakini* and *Aberahama Kaikioewa*, and, for two staunch single name individualists, *Naihe* and *Hoapili*.[4]

As immigrants from the Orient settled in Hawaii, they began to add Christian names to their original names.

first act to
regulate names

What began as religious custom later became law. In 1860, Kamehameha IV signed the Act to Regulate Names. This specified that a married woman should take her husband's name as a family name, and that:

"All children born in wedlock shall have their father's name as a family name. They shall, besides, have a Christian name suitable to their sex ... All illegitimate* children shall have their mother's name as a family name. They shall, besides, have a Christian name suitable to their sex."[5]

"Christian name" was usually interpreted to mean "Biblical name." Before long, newly literate Hawaiians were inscribing pristine family Bibles with such names as *Kakelaka* (Shadrack), *Iopa* or *Ioba* (Job), or *Bateseba* (Bathsheba). After the Catholic missionaries became established, converts to Rome began taking the names of saints. Given the chilliest of non-welcomes in 1827,

---

*Both the term and the concept of illegitimacy were introduced with Christianity.

the Catholic missionaries scorned (or were not given access to) the Hawaiian alphabet developed by the Protestants, and devised their own. Name spelling could then show a man's religion. As *Iokepa,* Joseph was clearly a Protestant; as Ioseve, Joseph was unmistakably Catholic.

(One hundred and seven years passed before the Act to Regulate Names recognized the cosmopolitan nature of Hawaii. A 1967 amendment changed "Christian name" to "given name."[6])

Meanwhile, an 1872 addition to the Act made it unlawful to change any name, except upon decree of His Majesty the King.[7] *'Oki'ing* (removing or severing) an old name that harmed its bearer and taking a new one, ceased to be a simple matter of prayer and spoken declaration. Instead it became a legal process.

inoa in the present day

Today most Hawaiians and part-Hawaiians have both English and Hawaiian given names. The special potential to cause trouble or anxiety—or less frequently, inspire happiness—is invariably attached to the Hawaiian name.

What are these worries and woes?

The experiences of social agency clients and staff members chronicle them in this often-overlapping list: fear of revealing damaging family history through meaning of a name; fear of a possible *kapu* attached to a name; naming without permission of the original bearer of the name; pre-conceived role-casting reinforced by naming; less specific feelings that a name is unsuitable or has unpleasant associations; and simple concern to find out what a name means.

In all current casework examples, Hawaiian names are not used. Rough translations of name meanings are substituted when possible. English names are fictitious.

inoa can reveal family history

One client had his name legally changed some years ago as a kindly protection to his family. His Hawaiian name, originally a given name that had become the family name, indicated that an ancestor had been a *kahuna 'ana'ana,* a sorcerer who could "pray people to death." Changing the name kept Hawaiian-speaking people from knowing the family background and treating current family members with dislike or even fear.

kith, kin and kapus

The following case involves husband and wife, non-clients who told Committee members their story for teaching purposes. James is Hawaiian; Carol, his wife, is a Caucasian from the U.S. mainland. Both are under 40, college educated, professional persons. James tells this account of 1969 events:

"When our baby was born, we had my mother's permission to give her my mother's name. But what we didn't realize was that my mother had been given her name by my great-grandmother who also bore the name."

Here James recounted the recent illness and nightmares of his wife, a death in the family, a feeling that "something was wrong in the house" and episodes of sudden, frightened screaming by the baby. He continued:

"After the baby was so frightened, we called in Reverend _____.

He said that when you have been given a name by the old folks, there are *kapus* around the name. This *kapu* must be *'oki'd* or be severed by blessing."

Earlier, an aunt had *pī kai'd* part of the house (given it ceremonial purification with sea-water sprinkling and prayer). Now the minister, a Congregationalist, blessed the little girl and the house.

"Since then, we've been living a fairly calm life. The baby has slept well and has not had any episodes of startled screaming."

Both James and Carol recognized that tension in the home existed and that it was caused primarily through strained in-law relationships not described here. They were both aware that Carol's illness could have been physiological reactions to emotional stress. James first viewed the baby's screaming as caused by "seeing something." This is in the Hawaiian tradition of *hō'ike* or "revelations." Later he accepted Dr. Haertig's explanation that even very young babies sense tension around them and respond in physical ways. (Discussed under *hō'ike*.) Yet both James and his non-Hawaiian wife felt emotionally a kind of occult presence in the house. Both realized an immediate easing of tensions after Christian prayers had removed a Hawaiian *kapu*.

In a separate but similar case, a Center client concluded an account of complicated family troubles with this incident. It centers around M————, aged two-and-a-half:

"M———— woke up screaming. Her eyes were real big and she wouldn't stop crying. I think this was *hō'ike*. I called my mother, and she told me to call the church people. I did, and Elder ———— came over. He blessed the house. Then he said that M———— was a *kapu* name. So he *'oki'd* the name and blessed the baby."

how to
'oki names

Both cases show the alternate ways tradition provides for handling *kapu* names. Mrs. Pukui describes them:

"You can *'oki* the name and take a new one, or you can *'oki* the *kapu* and keep the name."

'Oki'ing was traditionally done with sacrificial food offerings and prayers to the gods and family *aumākua*. One Center staff member had her original name *'oki'd* when she was seven. Her grandmother did this with Hawaiian prayers to the *aumākua*. Today *'oki'ing* either name or *kapu* is usually done by prayers to the Christian God. Mrs. Pukui says:

"My name isn't supposed to be given away. My name is for me. But people are always naming babies after me, so I have many namesakes. I don't want any of them hurt if there's any *kapu* that goes with my name. So I pray, 'Since so-and-so named this child for me, then please do me the favor to *'oki* the *kapu* and bless the name. Whatever *kapu* there is, bring it back to me, but don't let it bother this child.'

"This prayer is called *pule ho'onoa*, 'prayer to free.'"

ancestral name needs
ancestral permission

In this *inoa kupuna* (ancestral name) case, the stage for trouble was set in a non-client family clan, marked by a high degree of financial solidity and, on the surface, almost complete adaptation to current, Western social-religious mores. On stage come:

Elizabeth and Frank, a middle-aged, caught-in-the-middle couple;

Mother K_____, Frank's 86-year-old mother;

Hilary, son of Elizabeth and Frank;

Marie, Hilary's wife;

A good dozen relatives by blood and marriage;

And the baby. Her English name is Jeanne. It was selection of her Hawaiian name that stirred the mighty tempest in the family teapot.

Hilary and Marie live on the mainland. In Hawaii, Mother K_____ gave verbal permission through Elizabeth and Frank that the coming baby, if a girl, could bear her name, K_____. Elizabeth relayed this permission in a letter to Hilary and then-pregnant Marie. The baby was a girl and was promptly named Jeanne K_____.

In Hawaii, the teapot began to boil and sputter. Mother K_____ became incommunicative or openly rude to Elizabeth and Frank. She exhibited little interest in her great granddaughter's birth. Finally the reason came out.

"You had no right to tell Hilary and Marie they could give the baby my name. I never gave permission for my name to be used!"

Soon family members were taking sides. Half the clan stopped speaking to each other. Everyone became entangled in the network of angry actions-and-counter-reactions Hawaiians call *hihia*.

Phone calls and letters went to and from the mainland. Mother K_____ changed her mind and wrote Hilary and Marie they could use her name. This, traditionally, carries a sense of giving the name and an obligation to use it. In almost the same mail went a letter from Elizabeth and Frank telling the young couple not to use Grandma's name.

Here the tradition of "owning" one's own name precipitated the family quarrel. However, the real cause seems to be family inability to recognize and accept the varied mental changes of senility. Daughter-in-law Elizabeth has tried to convince the others that "Mother K_____ is old. She probably forgot she had given permission to use her name." To which others have responded, "Well, she's not too old to sit around and think and make trouble for other people, so she can't have forgotten she okayed use of her name."

The argument fails to take in the mental malfunctions of old age. As Dr. Haertig explains:

"In senility, there is usually more than just forgetfulness involved. Old people, especially when sufficient arteriosclerosis exists, often become temperamental. They fly off the handle about things which earlier would not have troubled them. They may become forgetful and change their minds impulsively. Their behavior may become inconsistent and their reactions exaggerated. These are the phenomena of senility, the mental consequences of organic deterioration. As such they should be overlooked."

To restore peace in this *inoa*-precipitated, senility-fed situation, a Hawaiian solution could go right along with efforts to build family understanding of senile changes. Mrs. Pukui suggests that the young parents give the child a second Hawaiian name, have the child blessed, and pray. The great-grandmother, as her moods and memory-recall change, could call the baby either name she wished. The parents, having satisfied the obligation of using the name, K_____, implied in the later written permission, could call the baby either name. Because they live on the mainland, the baby would probably never be confused by the different names. If Mother K_____ had not "given" her name in the letter, the traditional solution would have been to *'oki* the name and remove all the associated unpleasantness through prayer.

With the *inoa* troubles settled, a *ho'oponopono* (see listing) might be an ideal way to resolve all the secondary quarrels that have spread through the family. Certainly, this prayerful, conscience-searching family gathering of old would provide a situation for discussing and understanding senility. However, the ideal seems impossible. At present, icy refusal to talk on the part of various family members precludes any constructive, remedial discussion.

never take name
without permission

If taking a family ancestor's name without clear-cut permission leads to trouble within the family, taking anyone's Hawaiian name without permission can precipitate a more wide-spread quarrel. The non-relative, too, "owns" his name, and all its precious references to family events or *aumakua.*

"Even today, Hawaiians are mighty touchy about their names," Mrs. Pukui says. "Some are so touchy they don't even want their Hawaiian names printed in the newspaper. Someone might see the name and use it."

inoa and the
preconceived role

Inevitably, the *inoas* of Hawaii may carry role-casting significance just as certain English names do. The teased "Percival" of the West may indeed fill the "sissy" role his name connotes or, by rebelling, cast himself as Superman. And how much conforming or rebellion is due to the name itself, the teasing and isolation suffered by its bearer, or the reasons his parents chose the name is speculative. A name is probably never a cause; it is frequently an influence.

To put name role-casting back in its island setting, here are two case examples involving the same Hawaiian name, L_____. The name has several meanings, subject to even more connotations. At one end of the connotative pole, the name can mean "floating high" which can be interpreted as being "happily carefree," "freed from grief," or "completely irresponsible." At the opposite pole, the name can mean "victory" with all its attributes of courage, manliness, triumph in battle or achievement.

The Case of the First L_____:

To the Center came a mother, divorced, and in great distress about her teenage son, L_____. She described her son's behavior as:

"He won't get a job . . . I want him to do his chores right after school, but he stays late to practice with the ball team . . . I tell him exactly where to put the trash cans. He throws them down just anywhere . . .

"He's named after his father and his grandfather . . . he acts just like both of them . . . Grandpa never did pay his bills . . . threw it all away on women . . . he had plenty *wahines,* that's for sure . . . My husband—same thing. Run around. *Wahines.* Spend his pay before he got it.

"Grandpa got mad once and said L_____ [her husband] was just like him. He said all the sons in the family would turn out the same. And it's true. This was *'ānai* and it's true. I·know it because of the name . . . what it means. I can't do anything about L_____. It's because of his name."

Here a first essential is to correct the woman's misunderstanding of *'ānai* (curse). Apparently the grandfather merely made an angry prediction; the mother interpreted this as a curse. And even if he had placed a curse on his son, traditionally *'ānai* is not passed on down to innocent descendants. (See *'ānai* and *hua 'ōlelo*).

Where *inoa* is concerned, comes a quite obvious clue. The client herself choose the interpretation, "completely irresponsible." Which suggests she was casting both son and name into preconceived roles. (And possibly had previously shaped or reinforced her husband's role as a duplicate of the grandfather's.) Certainly she took a like-father-like-son view of everything her son did—or did not—do.

Dr. Haertig comments:

"There is undoubted *hō'upu'upu* (thought implantation) here. This is reiterated in words and non-verbal ways. But there is also—and this is more subtle—a selective perception and selective interpretation of the son's behavior. The mother concentrates on anything that at all resembles the misbehavior of the father. She stresses it, bears down on it, in order, she thinks, to eradicate it.

"What she is really seeing is kid behavior. Perfectly normal mischievousness or stubbornness or laziness or even rather desirable participation in activities that happen to keep him after school. This behavior doesn't mean a thing except that kids *are* kids.

"Yet his mother sees all this as the 'bad father coming out.' She battles this behavior so strenuously that the son is antagonized and feels, with some justice, that he is being treated unfairly. And so the boy rebels, often by 'acting out' in ways that bear some real resemblance to the feared, dreaded misbehavior of father or grandfather. The boy is to some extent pushed into the very mold fashioned for him.

"The father's irresponsible 'running around' behavior was often childish. A case of an adult keeping the prerogatives—impulsive grabbing at immediate pleasures, shrugging off duties or obligations—of childhood. This childish behavior of the father is unhealthy because the father is an adult. But the childish behavior of the son is healthy *because he is still a child*.

"However, the mother sees this behavior as identical. The handed down *inoa* and the significance she gave it was one factor that distorted her mental vision.

"Here the traditional Hawaiian remedy—to *'oki* the name and associations, or to just *'oki* the associated influences—are perfectly congruent with Western therapeutic approaches. For when you get rid of all the implications of the name, you can then see the *individual*, not a personality based on all the name conveys.

"What we see here is a nice kid, involved in sports and school affairs that are very appropriate for his age.

"Helping the mother to see this nice kid is another matter. We must help her recognize the *hō'upu'upu* or thought-implanting involved, help her realize there is no transmitted curse. And I suggest that the adverse influences of the *inoa* be *'oki'd* with enough ritual and ceremony to make a dramatic and convincing impression."

If a name can play a part in adverse role-casting, can it also be an influence for good?

Possibly. But, it carries its own dangers. In another case, a mother felt so strongly that her son was "no good" that she renamed the boy *L*_____ and interpreted the name to mean "victory." This is a fairly recent incident. We can't draw any real conclusions. However, while role-casting attached to a favorable name change may help counteract negative role-casting, it can back-fire. For again, connotations of a name are focused on, rather than character and personality. Again, it is all too easy to see a name rather than a person.

naming to
replace dead

Some distortion of reality may exist when a child is named after a well-remembered deceased relative. In any culture, the child may be an emotional replacement for the dead. This possibility is strong among Hawaiian families where ties between the living and the dead are enduring.* Traditionally, a child was often *hānai'd* (early adoptive practice) as a consciously recognized replacement. As Mrs. Pukui outlines this, "A *kupuna* [in this case, grandparent] would say 'the child I dearly loved is gone. This child will be a substitute.' And so the *hānai keiki* would represent to the grandmother all that the dead child used to be."

1970 case notes tell of a little girl born less than a year after her teenage uncle died and given his Hawaiian name. The young uncle was a carefree, mischievous, charming youth. As the family recalls fondly, "he was a real rascal . . . a regular devil." The little girl, now four years old, is a timid, quiet, sensitive child. Yet her parents describe her as "a little rascal" . . . "a mischief" . . . "full of the devil." The Center caseworker feels sure that "the parents have ascribed to the little girl a role that does not fit her."

Mental health intervention is indicated. And for these tradition-imbued parents, *'oki'ing* the Hawaiian name might well be the base on which insights are built.

The total Hawaiian doctrine of *inoa* has its own built-in remedy for assorted troubles: the provision that a name can be *'oki'd* if it proves incompatible with its bearer. The cause for *'oki'ing* need not be as portentous as a *kapu* or as quarrel-inspiring as naming without permission.

The "incompatible" name is often the name that does not agree with a wanted self-image. From earlier days comes one example: A boy was named Kaohe, meaning "bamboo." However, the boy knew that bamboo was Hawaii's knife, before metal was imported. In his own opinion, his name was symbolic of cutting, and therefore cruelty and unkindness. He asked for and was given a new name, Kanaiopuna, meaning "the Puna conqueror." "Then he got along fine with his new name," says Mrs. Pukui, for the example comes from her own large *'ohana* (extended family).

'Oki'ing and disuse, Hawaii's cultural ways to get rid of an unwanted name and take a new one, fail to satisfy Hawaii's legal requirements. Changing a name, deleting all or part of a name, taking a new name or even

---

*The spirit of a dead relative was deliberately recalled in the practice of *'unihipili*. Belief in communication between living and dead also permeates the concept of *noho* (possession) and the seeing of visions *(hihi'o)*. Spirits of long-dead ancestors, the *aumākua*, also spoke to descendants in dreams and in mystical experiences.

changing spelling all require a petition to the Lieutenant Governor, legal notices in newspapers, and, when the petition is granted, a new birth certificate. Which all means a fee to the attorney who draws up the petition, newspaper ad costs and the standard $2.00 for any copy of birth registration.* *'Oki'ing kapus* and unhappy associations of a name, but keeping the name itself is a highly economical problem-solver!

And, reminds George Tokuyama, State Registrar, parents have three months leeway to name and even rename a new baby. Within 90 days after the baby's birth, birth registration changes can be made on parent's petition or a notary public's affidavit alone. The only charge is $2.00 for a new copy of the birth certificate.

For the Hawaiian family, the 90 days can be used to clear an *inoa pō* of *kapus;* make sure permission is gained to use an *inoa kupuna;* check that the descendants of commoners are not taking an *ali'i* name, nor that of *kauwā;* that a member of the *'ohana* descended from Pele is not taking a name that belongs to the *'ohana* descended from Kamehameha; and that the *inoa* carries with it no aura of hostility, grief, death or doom!

Which rather intricate, preventive psychiatry can make 90 days all too short. Perhaps Mrs. Pukui offers the best advice-through-example for preventing Hawaiian woes that cluster around the ill-chosen *inoa:*

"When _____ [an adult] asked me for a Hawaiian name he could take, I didn't want to trespass on any family background. So I went to the Bible and read the First Psalm and made a name from it. I picked 'And he shall be like a tree planted by the rivers of waters. That bringeth forth his fruit in its season; And whatsoever he doeth shall prosper.' So I named him *Kekumu-i-ka-wai-o-ke-ola. Kekumu* for 'the tree'; *ikawaiokeola* for 'beside the living waters.'

"...for a baby boy born beneath Kilohana Peak, I made the name *Ka-ohu-kau-i-Kilohana.* Kilohana also means 'outstanding.' So you get the idea of beauty, seeing in all directions from Kilohana, and 'outstanding' in the sense of being distinguished. The whole name is translated 'the mist that adorns the summit of Kilohana.'

"...my two sons-in-law are like brothers, always ready to help each other. So when one of them had a son, I named him *Pili-aloha-o-na-makua,* 'the beloved companionship of uncle and father!'"

The Bible, a baby's birthplace, or fond family relationships—these are sources to inspire new Hawaiian names, full of beauty but free of trouble. They are today's creative answer to the often anxious question of the Hawaiian:

"He aka ko loko o ko'u inoa?"

"What's in *my* name?"

REFERENCES

1. All names in paragraph from "Beliefs on Birth, Infancy and Childhood."

2. Beckwith, *Kepelino's Traditions of Hawaii,* p. 4.

3. "Beliefs on Birth, Infancy and Childhood."

---

*When the mother of an illegitimate child marries, a new, replacement certificate is made which lists the child's last name as that of the mother's new, married name. This is done free.

4. Archives of Hawaii. Original, unbound material in vault.

5. *Laws of His Majesty Kamehameha IV, King of the Hawaiian Islands, Passed by the Nobles and Representatives at their Session, 1860.* Archives of Hawaii.

6. *Session Laws of Hawaii, 4th State Legislature, 1967.* Archives of Hawaii.

7. *Laws of His Majesty Kamehameha V, King of the Hawaiian Islands, Passed by the Legislative Assembly at its Session, 1872.* Archives of Hawaii.

iwi—bone or bones; where any interpersonal or person-with-deity relationship is concerned, the word means human bones.

Deriv: unknown.

On March 12, 1970, Kolokea C_____, a 43-year-old Hawaiian woman, not a Center client, related the following account to the Hawaiian Culture Committee. The events she described had taken place within the previous two weeks. As Kolokea spoke, Mary Kawena Pukui translated the older, often poetic Hawaiian phrases. Kolokea's narrative has been edited for brevity:

"When my brother died in California, I made the funeral arrangements because he had named me 'next of kin.' So I called the mortuary and told them to cremate his body and have the urn sent here. I felt this was the best way . . .

a kauoha (command)
forbade cremation

"Then I called my older sister [on Oahu]. As soon as she heard I was having the body cremated, all the *pilikia* [trouble] started. She got angry and nasty over the phone. She cursed me! She said she was given a *kauoha* [command] when she was very young . . . a *kauoha* that none of us in the family are to be cremated. She said this was handed down to her. I asked her what the reason was, but she was so angry by then she wouldn't even listen to me.

"She went on and said, 'You go ahead with this cremation and see what will happen to you from now on. You'd better heed this warning if you want your life to be pleasant! And then—BANG—she hung up the phone.

"I was so upset! I dropped tears. My tears fell for about two hours. At first I didn't know who to turn to. Then I called my great-great-grandaunt. She's 73. But before I could tell her everything that happened, she said in Hawaiian:

"'*Auwe, noho'i kaikamahine, honehone ke ala i ka moana.*'"

("'Alas, my child. The sounds of the sea have been heard faintly.'

In other words, 'Yes, I have already heard the news.'"—M.K. Pukui)

"Then I told her the whole conversation with my sister, and my grandaunt said, still in Hawaiian, 'Listen, and let me help you. Let me guide you before the trouble comes upon you. The first thing that has taken place between you and your sister—and it will entangle your other sisters and brothers—is *hihia* [a network of spreading, worsening anger and hurt feelings] and *kū'ē* [conflict].

"'As for this second thing your sister has said, about what will happen if you go ahead with cremation, this is *ha'awi' i ka aumakua.* * This is *'anai* [a curse].'

"And then Auntie said that cremation was *puhi i ka iwi* [bone burning] and my ancestors would not approve of this.

"Then she said, '*Aole maluhia ka mea make.*'
("The body will be without peace.)

"'*E pono no'oe e ho'oponopono i ko 'ouko noho ana.*'
("Better hold a *ho'oponopono.*)†

"'*Ho'oku'i kahi i loko o ka 'ohana.*'
("To make peace with the family.)

"'*Holopono kau lawe hana ana no keia kino make.*'"
("Then your work for his body will be successful.")

"Then Auntie explained that the command not to cremate had come down from my great-great-grandfather. She told me that my brother's body must be buried in the ground or in the deep ocean. She said the reason he could be laid with the sharks was because his *aumakua* [ancestor god] was the *manō* [shark]. She said to give him to the shark was *kākū'ai.*"**

After this conversation, Kolokea had called the California mortuary, cancelled the request for cremation, and arranged to have her brother's body flown here for funeral services. With this done, she had time for personal grief, for thought, for questioning. Why was cremation so terrible? Was this merely a family prejudice? Or had she violated some widely accepted belief of old Hawaii?

The answers center around a single word: *Iwi*. Bones.

bones, sign of immortality

In the pre-Christian creeds of Hawaii, man's immortality was manifest in his bones. Man's blood, even bright drops shed by the living, was *haumia* (defiled and defiling). Man's body, when death made flesh corrupt, was an abomination and *kapu* (taboo). The *iwi* survived decaying flesh. The bones remained, the cleanly, lasting portion of the man or woman who once lived.

Even the bones of the living became symbols of the link between man's progenitors and his own eventual immortality. This symbolism is found in many of Hawaii's figures of speech. These and other *iwi* phrases are listed at the close of this section.

respect shown bones of dead

The bones of the dead were guarded, respected, treasured, venerated, loved or even deified by relatives; coveted and despoiled by enemies.

---

*Literally, "to give you to the god" so that the god *(akua)* or ancestor god *(aumakua)* can punish you.

†*ho'oponopono,* a prayer-filled family gathering to restore harmonious relationships. Literally a "setting to rights." A major concept, discussed under *ho'oponopono.*

**Defined in a following paragraph.

Evidently, this respect was not limited to the bones of Hawaiians. When King Kamehameha II (Liholiho) was on his ill-fated trip to England* in 1824, he was taken on a tour of Westminster Abbey. There he refused to enter the chapel where the remains of Henry VII rested. Comments author Stanley Porteus, "... to a Hawaiian king used to the hiding of royal bones ... the tomb ... was not to be lightly profaned by the foot of a stranger."[1]

Reluctance to say final farewells to a beloved dead person often found expression in keeping the bones. At one extreme was 'unihipili, the deification of bones. In this, ritual practices kept the spirit of the dead alive in the bones. The 'unihipili spirit could be summoned to perform services for its kahu (master or keeper). This ritual and underlying concept are described under 'unihipili.

Verging on 'unihipili was the keeping of bones without deifying rites. David Malo provides the following account:

**bones of loved
secretly kept**

"Sometimes a person would secretly exhume the body of a beloved husband or wife and remove the four arm and leg bones and the skull, washing them in water until they are clean. They were then wrapped up and enclosed within the pillow, and the friend [spouse] took them to bed with him and slept with them every night ... These parts of the corpse were preserved by the fond lover until such time as the love came to an end ..."[2]

Relatives might keep cleaned bones or perhaps the skull in a calabash hanging from the rafters, Mrs. Pukui adds.

**bones emphasize
individuality**

This bone-keeping was one of several practices that indicate Hawaiian recognition of the uniqueness of the individual. Even bones of the dead retained individuality. The 'unihipili spirit was not an obscure, faceless mystical presence, but the spirit of a named and known person. To the bereaved lover, the bones in the pillow *were* the very personality of Aukele, she of the musical voice, or Kami, so stalwart and dignified. (Or, if one hated, he vented his spite-satisfaction by desecrating not merely "some bones" but the specific bones of Palakiko, sneering braggart, or of deceitful, wife-stealing Ahia.) Even in the role-conscious, family and group centered society of early Hawaii, individuality was strongly emphasized.

**kākū'ai sends
dead to aumakua**

In these bone-keeping, "I don't want to say Goodbye" practices, the living tried to prevent or delay the spirit's final entry into *Pō* (eternity). However, Hawaii also had a ritual to speed the spirit on its way. This was kākū'ai (transfiguration). This ceremony not only sent the spirit to join its *aumakua* in *Pō;* it changed bones or body parts into shark or lizard or volcano flame or whatever form the *aumakua* might have. The dramatic ritual is described in the section, kākū'ai.

---

*He died of measles during his visit.

108

With or without *'unihipili* rituals, there was a feeling that the spirit might yet be hovering near the *iwi.* If the bones were desecrated, the spirit was insulted. Even the living descendants of the profaned dead were shamed and humiliated. So the Hawaiians believed.

disposal rites
guard bones

These beliefs brought about body disposal practices designed to keep bones from falling into despoiling enemy hands. Relatives or a chief's most trusted followers often first stripped or steamed the *pela* (decomposing flesh) from the bones, and threw it into the sea. Or the well-guarded, well-concealed corpse might be exhumed after a time so the bones could be washed and kept or ceremoniously returned to the *aumakua.* Or body and bones might be left undisturbed in a secret cave or pit.

Infinite caution surrounded the bones of an *ali'i* (member of nobility). High rank brings powerful enemies, and a chief's bones were especially in danger of being profaned. The bones of Kamehameha The Great were so well hidden that, despite rumors to the contrary, they have never been found.

One powerful chief, Kaha-kaulia, was so afraid a rival chief might desecrate his bones that he planned the following ruse:

"When I die," he told his followers, "do not wail for me until you have hidden my bones. Then go to the middle of Kawainui (stream), dive about in the mud, raise lamentations for me, and tell the people that Kaha-kaulia fell into the stream and was carried down in the current."[3]

bone desecration
took many forms

The desecration feared might take many forms. Merely leaving bones uncovered and exposed to the sunlight was disrespectful if not an outright profanation. But according to historian Fornander, "To turn bones into fish hooks or [use them] for other practical uses [arrowheads or needles] was the most dreaded insult."[4]

Infinitely worse was obscene misuse of the skull, the very dwelling place of the spirit. "Using the skull as a spittoon or even a slop jar—this was terrible. A horrible, humiliating insult!" says Mrs. Pukui.

Bones, usually the leg bones, of a defeated enemy were sometimes put inside the supporting pole or standard of a *kāhili.** Though this began as an insult, it later took on the nature of a tribute. A *kāhili* containing a leg bone of the chief Kaneoneo stands today in Hawaiian Hall at the Bishop Museum.

The ultimate desecration was the complete destruction of bones. As Mrs. Pukui explains, "If the bones were destroyed, the spirit would never be able to join its *aumakua.*"

burning bones
worst insult

Burning the bones added ultimate insult to ultimate destruction. For by tradition, burning was reserved for the defeated enemy. The first man killed

---

*The feather-adorned standards that were both religious symbol, mark of high rank and sometimes the equivalent of a flag.

by victorious battle forces was burned on the sacrificial altar. Or a man might roast his most hated enemy, until all bones, especially the skull, were ashes.

cremation decisions
vary in present day

It was this entrenched sense of *kapu* that Kolokea had offended when she ordered her brother's body cremated. Not only had she violated traditional ethnic beliefs about *iwi;* she had also disobeyed the handed-down edict of a family ancestor. Not all Hawaiians of the present run into such trouble. Today, one family may yet obey the old edicts. Another may have discarded or forgotten *kapus* against bone burning. The ashes of one Hawaiian surfer or fisherman may be scattered at sea; another's corpse may be dropped deep in the water.

How do family members decide what to do?

Mrs. Pukui outlines the custom generally accepted today:

"If a person specifies before his death that he wants to be cremated, then the family should follow his instructions. The wishes of the person who died supersede the old *kapus*. But if the person did not clearly specify cremation, then don't cremate.

"One reason Kolokea had so much *pilikia* with her family was because her brother didn't leave any instructions."

In Kolokea's case, bone burning or *puhi i ka iwi* merely incited the family quarrel. The basic causes were long-existing. One question the Committee asked was why the elder sister cursed Kolokea for breaking a *kapu* she did not know existed. Why did the sister refuse to explain or even listen to Kolokea?

Later, Kolokea had a talk with her sister and asked her this.

punahele treatment
jealousy cause

This is what she learned:

Her immediate offense was failure to consult other family members, especially seniors, about funeral plans. This independent action flaunted the Hawaiian custom of family discussion and decision making. Also, said the elder sister, Kolokea had always been *hō'oio* ("stuck up"). This feeling went back to the fact that Kolokea had been *hānai'd* (given in the Hawaiian adoption practice) to her grandmother. Traditionally, the first born is *hānai'd*. So, in all innocence, Kolokea had supplanted her sister. As the *hānai keiki* ("adopted" child), Kolokea had, in many ways, been treated as the *punahele,* the "favored child" of Hawaiian tradition. And to top off a jealousy-producing situation, Kolokea had enjoyed educational and economic advantages her siblings were not given.

So what seemed to be family discord over a *concept* was really based on both concept and total family situation.

Does *hihia* yet ensnarl the family? Is Kolokea yet under the *'ānai* (curse) pronounced by her sister? How did this all end?

The ending is a happy one.

Kolokea's anxiety about being cursed was lifted when the Committee reminded her that, traditionally, anyone innocent of wrong-doing need not accept and could not be harmed by a curse. (See *'ānai.*)

The talks Kolokea had with her sister led to frank exploration of long-existing differences between the two. The *ho'oponopono* suggested by the great-great grandaunt was not held. However, the sisters' meetings incorporated some *ho'oponopono* remedial measures: scrutinizing one's own behavior and attitudes, forgiving and being forgiven, and making reparations for wrongs, or changing behavior. Kolokea is making an effort to be less impulsively independent and to become closer to her family. The sister and other siblings have indicated they will share the funeral expenses Kolokea had assumed. In Kolokea's opinion, "My sister and I are closer than we have been for 25 years."

Kolokea's persistence in arranging talks with her sister is interesting. At least three times the sister had refused to talk, even over the phone. Perhaps two other Hawaiian beliefs may have given Kolokea the impetus to mend this frayed relationship.

Kolokea tells of one such belief:

"When I was sitting there (by the corpse), my eyes went to my brother and I asked him to take everything away."

She was acting on the old belief that a recently deceased person can take away with him and, in effect, erase all family quarrels, curses, hurt feelings and even harmful *kapus*. This was called *lawe i ka wa make* ("take in time of death.")

The other traditional practice was for family members to make up their differences before the funeral of a relative. The request that grudges be taken into eternity was traditionally spoken aloud. This and family peace-making were done over the dead body, before burial.

Kolokea followed both traditions in modified form. Yet the fundamental benefit of both remedial measures seems to have operated in this *iwi*-caused dispute of 1970.

phrases using or referring to bones

holehole iwi—stripping the bones of flesh. Once actually done, this "bone stripping" is now a figure of speech meaning to speak unkindly of relatives.

(see page 1 of *niele*.)

iwi kanaka—human skeleton.

iwi koko—blooded bones; a living person.

iwi koko'ole—bones without blood; a dead person.

111

iwi kua mo'o—back bone or close relative; A chief's retainers were always relatives. Retainers guarded the chief from attempts on his life. Complete trustworthiness was required. Therefore, "back bone" took on the connotation of loyalty as well as kinship.

iwi loa—long bones; a tall person.

kaula'i na iwi i ka lā—bleaching the bones in the sun. Such bleaching, literally done by an enemy or through carelessness, was an insulting practice. Figuratively, "mental exposure" or talking unnecessarily about relatives to non-family members. (see page 1 of *niele*.)

kula iwi—literally, "land of bones." Used as birthplace, with the idea that "here my bones began."

"Na wai e ho'ola i na iwi?"—literally "who will make the bones live?" By extension, "Who will take care of a senior relative?"

'ōiwi—native son; native of the land. Very close to meaning of *kula iwi.*

"Ola na iwi"—"The bones live," or, figuratively, a senior relative is being given loving care by a family member. The phrase shows approval of the senior's condition or praise for the relative giving the care.

pela—the flesh and organs removed from a dead body and usually sunk in the ocean.

pūholoholo—in this context, steaming a corpse in a pit to facilitate removal of flesh from bones.

REFERENCES

1. Porteus. *A Century of Social Thinking in Hawaii,* p. 308.
2. Malo. *Hawaiian Antiquities,* pp. 98-99.
3. Kamakau. *Ruling Chiefs of Hawaii,* p. 217.
4. Fornander. *Collection of Hawaiian Antiquities,* Vol. 5, p. 212.
5. Pukui. "Featherwork."

kahu—attendant, guardian, keeper; one post-Christian meaning is pastor of a church.
Deriv: unknown.

The meanings of *kahu* range from that of owner-master of a pet dog or cat to attendant to royalty or, even more specifically, guardian of a high chief's garments or body products (so they could not be used for sorcery) to the guardian-keeper of supernatural beings. In general, no matter what or whom the *kahu* kept, watched over or directed, his duties were charged with a high degree of responsibility.

This responsibility was an awesome one for the *kahu* who kept or summoned and directed a spirit. The *kahu* as spirit-keeper might activate and send on errands an *'unihipili,* the deified spirit of a dead relative; an *akua* or god; an *aumakua,* family ancestor spirit; a *kupua,* demi-god; or a host of various mystical giants and beings from the unseen world.

When a *kahu* sent a spirit out to harm someone, he ran the risk that the spirit might be returned to harm him. This was done in the ritual phrase, "*ho'i i no 'ai i kou kahu,*" meaning "go back and destroy your keeper."

In the traditional seance that summoned a spirit to possess a chosen human called the *haka,* the *kahu* filled a formalized, permanent role. Each *'ohana* or family clan had a carefully selected *kahu* who was sometimes also a *kahuna* (priest).

In this seance-induced possession *(noho),* the *kahu* was master-of-ceremonies as well as master-of-the-spirit. He ritually laid out *ti* mats, offered the ceremonial drink, *'awa,* to the gods, and through prayers and chanting summoned the spirit (usually an *aumakua*) to come and possess the *haka.* The *kahu* then asked questions of the *aumakua* which were answered through the voice of the *haka* or possessed one. Psychological interpretation of this is discussed under *noho.* Other types of spirit directing by a *kahu* are discussed under *akualele* (flying poison god) and *'unihipili.* See *noho, akualale* and *'unihipili.* All three are major concepts which sometimes still influence beliefs and behavior in Hawaiian communities.

Kahu, in modern Hawaiian use, usually means a clergyman. The "spirit keeper" of old has become more the guide and guardian of the immortal soul. Hawaiians often now say *"Kahu"* for "Reverend," "Brother," "Father," "Pastor" or "Elder."

kā i mua—the practice of ritually and symbolically pushing a young boy out of the feminine setting of babyhood, and thrusting him into the world of his father and grandfather. This was done when a boy was about six years old.

Deriv: *kā,* to thrust, push or toss.
i, to, into, in.
mua, men's eating house.
Literally, "thrust into the men's eating house."

In old Hawaii, every man had his Men Only club-restaurant-chapel-lodge hall-locker room, and general refuge from the ladies. This was the *hale mua.*

The *hale mua* was both the men's eating house and the place where images of the household gods were kept. Here men ate their own meals and symbolically fed the gods, making formal daily offerings, and less formally communing with the gods over the eating mats, asking their help or intervention in affairs of the entire *'ohana* (family or extended family).

Here legends, bold and brave, were told; exploits of hunting and fishing related; the fine points of navigation discussed. Here, among *ali'i, 'awa** was drunk. This was a man's world. Women could not set foot in the *mua.*† Nor could a *keiki lewalewa.*

For the *keiki lewalewa*—usually shortened to *lewalewa*—was yet a "dangler." A small boy, so young his penis dangled. As a dangler, he wore no *malo* (loincloth) and he lived and ate with the women. For he was yet *poke'o,* too young to join the men.

When the little dangler became six or seven years old, his status changed in one decisive ceremony. This was the *kā i mua.* Mary Kawena Pukui relates: "There were prayers to *Lono,* the god who made things grow, and an offering of pork, because pork was *kapu* to women. Then more prayers and chants. The rituals might be more elaborate with families of high rank.[1] And then the little boy came out of the women's eating house *(hale 'aina)* for the last time.

"At this moment, he was symbolically 'pushed' or 'thrust' out entirely from babyhood and dependence on women and into the world of men.

"After that the boy spent most of his days with the men and boys. From then on he wore a *malo.* At night he returned to the *hale noa* (house free of taboos) because everybody slept there. Maybe he spent a little time during the day with his grandmother or mother. But he never again ate in the *hale 'aina* with the women. That was important. That meant he really was a man."

Hawaii's *kā i mua* gave ritual emphasis to a significant period in a boy's development. Somewhere between five and six, boys ordinarily began turning to their fathers—or substitute father-figures. In Freudian terms, the Oedipal stage of viewing the father as a rival and an obstacle to closeness to the mother is ending. The boy is now beginning to identify himself, to emotionally "line himself up" with the father, the father's maleness and his masculine interests and ways of living. The stage of "latency" is beginning.

England in its "old guard" days had a fairly analogous practice. Little boys were reared very much like little girls until, at around six or seven, they were packed off to the all-male boarding school.

Hawaii's old practice had in it a tacit understanding the British public (boarding) school system lacked. Male sex urges in the boarding school were subject to "cold-shower and athletics treatment" and exposed to homosexual experimentation. When the Hawaiian boy showed evidence of sexual awareness, he was allowed sex experiments and experience with girls and women. In fact, a youth from the *ali'i* was taught techniques of intercourse by an older chiefess.

Kā i mua, as far as we know, is an all-but-forgotten practice. Recalling it to a Hawaiian mother who "feels very much a Hawaiian" may be useful. For one thing, some Hawaiian mothers feel that the professional, perhaps *haole,* person knows everything about child care—and they know nothing. The under-

---

*the ceremonial drink which acted on the central nervous system. Only *ali'i* (aristocracy) and priests were allowed *'awa,* but there is evidence this prohibition was frequently disregarded.

†Because of menses, women were considered too defiled to eat with the gods, and therefore, to enter the men's eating house. When the eating *kapus* (taboos) were destroyed, men lost one of their most vital functions in Hawaiian society—that of eating with and communing with the gods.

lying wisdom, in their past setting, of such rituals as *kā i mua* might be discussed to help build a better self-image and to increase confidence in "mothering" ability.

More specifically, talking about *kā i mua* may help the overly possessive Hawaiian mother understand that she must loosen the apron strings that bind her son. For *kā i mua* carries a timeless and universal message: "Stop clinging. He can't remain a baby forever. Let him go. Let the boy learn from his father to be a man."

REFERENCES

1. Chants and ceremonies associated with *kā i mua* are given in detail in *The Polynesian Family System in Ka'u*, pp. 95, 6, 7.

kākū'ai—transfiguration: the ritual offering of the dead to the *aumākua* (ancestor gods) and the acceptance and change of spirit and body remains into the visible form or manifestation of the particular *aumakua*. An aborted fetus or malformed living infant might similarly be offered and transformed.

Deriv: *kākua*—to worship gods, especially with food offerings; appeal to gods.

'ai—food. The gods so worshiped were thought to eat the "spiritual essence" of the food and be strengthened by it. From being strengthened by food offerings, the belief extended to one of *creating* a god or spirit from another substance.

In the religion of old Hawaii, the compassionate, approachable gods were those who were once men. These were the *aumākua*,* now supernatural beings; once, long ago, progenitors of one's own mortal self. The *aumākua* dwelt in *Pō* (eternity). Yet at the same time they could assume the form of animals, plants—or even become flame or thunder and lightning.

For the living, there beckoned an eternal reward. Please the gods during life—and join the *aumākua* after death!

Only one thing about this belief seems to have worried the relatives of one who died. Could they be sure the deceased one was on his way to the *aumākua?* Or might he, even now, be miserable and hungry as one of the *ao kuewa*, the eternally homeless, hungry, wandering spirits? Was there no way to send a loved one speedily and surely to his ancestor gods?

There was. It was *kaku'ai*.

Here was the ritual that sent the dead one directly to the family *aumākua*, whether it be in the form of shark or lizard or Pele's flames or Kanehekili's thunder bolts.

---

*A major concept. See separate listing.

115

**reunion
with Pele**

From Hawaii's dim past, comes this elaborate ritual of offering the dead to Pele:

"For a dead beloved one whom they wished to become a volcanic manifestation . . . the Hawaiians . . . would take to the volcano the bones, hair, fingernails, or some other part of the dead body; sacrifices and offerings for the gods; gifts for the priests and prophets and guardians of the volcano; a pig, *'awa** and a *tapa* garment. . . . They would ascend to the pit of Pele. There they ritually killed the dedicatory pig . . . if the rituals went well, a pouring rain would pelt the uplands, and the sounds of thunder would reverberate to the sea as a sign of consent to the admission of the *malihini* [newcomer] spirit. In the morning the pig was roasted. The *'awa* was chewed, and all would feast. Then the prophet of Pele [*kāula* Pele] and the relatives of the dead, from 10 to 40 eyewitnesses, would throw the corpse and the offering, a live pig and some *'awa,* to the very center of the fire . . .

"The prophet stood and pleaded for the acceptance of the *malihini* and for his being united with the *kama'aina* [long established inhabitants] of the pit. He recited the ancestry of the dead one so that his ancestors in the crater would know him as one of them . . . "[1]

No one knows how far back these full ceremonials go. Mary Kawena Pukui recalls later, somewhat simplified transfiguration in her family.

"My great grandmother was taken to the volcano. This was after Christianity had come. But because we're related to the fire—the line of Pele—great grandmother's people took her secretly, after the flesh was removed from the bones. They wrapped the bones and took her [the bones] to the Halemaumau fire pit of Kilauea Crater and chanted and prayed and let her go happily to her people who were fire.

"Earlier, others in the family who were related to the sharks were given the *kākū'ai* ceremony and their bodies were placed into the sea."

For transfiguration to a shark, Mrs. Pukui explains:

"The bones were wrapped in *tapa* . . . then the family would go down to the sea and pray and give offerings (food and *'awa*). Then, it was believed, the shark would come and take this bundle of bones right under its pectoral fin. The shark would hold the bones there. Then for a while the family would keep coming back with offerings, until the bundle of bones took the form of a shark."

**transform
to shark**

Ka Po'e Kahiko ("The People of Old") gives this description of final stages of shark transfiguration:

"The *kahu manō* (shark keeper, either a relative or a *kahuna*) took *'awa* at dawn and at dusk for two or three days, until he saw clearly that the body had definitely assumed the form of a shark, and had changed into a little shark, with recognizable marks (of the deceased) on the cheeks or sides, like a tattoo or an earring mark. After two or three days more, when the *kahu manō* saw the strengthening of this new shark . . . he sent for the relatives who had

---

*The ritual drink made by chewing roots of the kava (Piper methysticum) shrub.

brought the body [so they could] go with him when he took the 'awa ... and when the relatives came they would see with their own eyes that it [the deceased] had become a shark, with all the signs by which they could not fail to recognize the loved one in a deep ocean. If the relatives should go bathing or fishing in the sea, it would come around and they would all recognize the markings of their own shark. It became their defender in the sea."[2]

An almost identical ritual was followed when a malformed living infant or an aborted fetus was offered for transfiguration. If child or fetus resembled a fish or lizard, it was offered to the *mo'o* (water *aumākua*) in ocean or fresh water stream, or to the *manō* (shark) if it looked like a shark. This was separate from *'umi keiki* (infanticide, literally "choke infant").[3]

Bones or bodies returned to Pele were usually wrapped in red or red and black *tapa*. Those returned to water creatures might be wrapped in predominantly yellow *tapas*. When the dead were sent back to thunder and lightning, dark colors symbolized Kanehekili. For Kanehekili once mortal, now chief of the thunder-lightning spirits, often manifested himself in a body that was black on one side. His touch, it was known, could char and blacken the living on earth.

**return to
thunder god**

Kamakau wrote and Mrs. Pukui translated the following description of this spine-tingling ceremony:

"On the night when a body was to be transfigured, strict regulations were imposed, and ... prescribed ritual prayers were offered continuously until day. Then there came black threatening storm clouds, and shining black storm clouds, and lightning ... The earth trembled, and like the rattling to and fro of a sheet of *tapa,* came the persistent rolling of thunder until one great bolt sounded that seemed to crush the earth with its force. A billow of smoke arose, and the sacrifices that had been offered mounted into the air upon the smoke, and the corpse that had been transfigured was carried into the firmament and vanished ...

"That is how a person became thunder and lightning in the old days."[4]

Behind the drama and the liturgy, what was *kākū'ai?*

A ceremony of consignment for the dead? Or a rite of realization for the living? Probably both.

Certainly, many aspects of *kākū'ai* helped the living relinquish the dead. The preliminary process of stripping flesh from bones, the wrapping and transporting bones or body, the all-night prayers, religious feast and processions— all these established and emphasized the reality of death. These preparations made by family members also renewed the bonds of kinship, both within the surviving *'ohana* (family) and of the living *'ohana* with the spiritual ancestor-gods, the *aumākua*.

Transfiguration itself was the acknowledgement that the familiar physical presence of a relative is gone forever. At the same time it was affirmation that the relative's spirit continued to exist, in changed but tangible, recognizable form. While the sombre preparations of *kākū'ai* were a kind of start on what Western psychiatry calls "grief work," transfiguration as a belief in survival after death may have eliminated the need to complete this grief work.

To the religious-mystical Hawaiian, transfiguration took place at ocean side, volcano site or mountain top. The drama-charged moment may have aided or even hastened an ultimate "transfiguration" experienced in the minds and emotions of the living. This transfiguration came when the still-hovering, almost living presence of the dead had changed imperceptibly to become merely an important memory.

kākū'ai and the case worker

Whether or not *kākū'ai* is openly mentioned today is anybody's guess. Center caseworkers have encountered it by implication when Hawaiian clients talk about their *aumakua* or say, "My grandmother was a shark." The old belief comes into an elder's objection to cremation. (See incident of Kolokea's great-great grandaunt in section on *'iwi.*)

Possibly, *kākū'ai,* like other long-discontinued rituals, has been emerging in the material of dreams, fantasies and visions, but has not been recognized by the non-Hawaiian therapist.

NOTES AND REFERENCES

1. Kamakau. *Ka Po'e Kahiko: The People of Old,* pp. 64-65.

2. Ibid. pp. 76, 77, 78.

3. Infanticide was practiced when a woman of the *ali'i* (nobility) had a child by a *kauwā,* or member of the despised slave class. Such *'umi keiki* or choking the child to death was an openly recognized act of killing. In giving a malformed infant back to shark or lizard, the rationale was that of returning the child to its own realm. In fact the malformed infant was thought to have been sired by a shark or other water creature *aumakua.*

4. *Ka Po'e Kahiko: The People of Old,* pp. 70, 77.

kanaka makua—a mentally and emotionally mature person; a person, even a child, who demonstrates mature behavior. The term can apply to both sexes.

Deriv: *kanaka,* person, man, human being.
makua, parent, member of the parent generation.

Ask a thoughtful Hawaiian what he hopes his children will be when they grow up, and he probably will *not* answer, "president of a company," or "first Hawaiian Astronaut" or "Miss America" or "successful doctor, lawyer, scholar or businessman" or "All-American halfback."

If he puts it in his ancestral language, chances are he will answer, *"Ke kanaka makua"*—"A mature person."

And, what are the qualities of this mature person? This *kanaka makua?*

Here we leave our hypothetical Hawaiian and turn to the answers of Mary Kawena Pukui:

"A *kanaka makua* thinks. He doesn't jump into things."... "He takes responsibility"... "Controls temper"... "Is not scatterbrained."... "Realizes that anger can cause *hihia"*... "Sensible."

But a "cool head" alone does not make a *kanaka makua*. There must be equally a "warm heart." For, as Mrs. Pukui explains,

"A *kanaka makua* is kind. He is thoughtful... senses the feelings of others."

Or, points out our psychiatric consultant, there is an absence of neurotic hostilities; a presence of good will.

So far, this could be a description of mental-emotional maturity in nearly any culture. However, the true *kanaka makua* also has the prized Hawaiian attribute—he must be hospitable.

In part, this is specific host-hostess hospitality. Mrs. Pukui points out that traditional *kanaka makua* behavior included, "Calling out to visitors when you saw them coming, '*Heahea! Kāhea 'ai.*' 'Welcome! Come on in. Come in and eat!'"

Less specifically, this hospitality connoted a warm and generous giving and sharing, whether of food or companionship or concern and comfort, always in a person-to-person way. (He has outgrown the infantile grasping to get all one can and keep all one has, comments our psychiatrist.)

'ōpu ali'i a
like concept

The *kanaka makua* concept, like that of *ōpū ali'i,* was used as a goal of development, and a measuring stick of behavior. An elder would tell a child to "learn to behave like a *kanaka makua.*" A rash, impulsive adult was counseled to emulate a person who was *kanaka makua.* A wise decision was credited to both supernatural inspiration and *"kanaka makua* thinking." Grandparents beamed at the compliment, "Your *mo'opuna* [grandchild] is only a *keiki* [child], but he acts like a *kanaka makua.*"

Listen to the opinions and judgments others make of one long enough, and they will be incorporated into one's own self-judgment or self-image. And, to an extent, one's behavior is shaped by this self-image.

So, if part of one's wanted or realized self-concept is *kanaka makua,* it is essential to know what *kanaka makua* means. Center clients have given indications they do not know this. For example:

"I am a *kanaka makua!*" one client insisted, during an interview in which he displayed marked aggressiveness, hostility and open rudeness. "That means I am all man!"

His Hawaiian vocabulary was a bit limited. He understood *kanaka* as meaning "man," and disregarded its more inclusive meanings of "person" and "human being."

His idea of "manhood" was also limited. To him, "man" connoted the super "he-man," not the balanced individual, capable of tenderness and compassion as well as masculine strengths.

His declared self-concept also seemed a rather shaky super-structure formed over his genuine feelings about himself. This is suggested in his repeated statements that "I can handle any woman"... "Any woman would be lucky to get me"... "I am all man!"

---

*An ever-widening, increasingly damaging network of ill-feeling that can turn a two-person quarrel into a family feud. See listing, *hihia.*

Here the client's own introduction of and repeated use of *kanaka makua* made the phrase a useful springboard to discussion.

Kanaka makua, the total concept of a mature, responsible Hawaiian, can also be discussed with the client or patient who equates "being Hawaiian" with being irresponsible and acting purely from impulse or emotions. "I am Hawaiian" or "It's because I'm a Hawaiian" is often given as the excuse for leaving school, job failure, temper display or impulsive, ill-advised sexual encounters. The image of "Myself, the Hawaiian" is a negative one.

Here—as antidote to the "lazy, impulsive, happy beachboy" stereotype that too many Hawaiians have incorporated within their self-concepts— *kanaka makua* may be the effective prescription.

NOTE

1. *'Ōpū ali'i. 'Ōpū,* belly. *Ali'i,* aristocracy, such as king or chief. Literally, "belly of a chief." Hawaiians believed that emotions and intelligence were both centered in the *na'au* (intestines), or, more generally, in any part of the *'ōpū* or belly. *Ali'i* were believed to have such fine qualities as wisdom, generosity, compassion. The *ali'i* in closest contact with the commoners were chiefs or chiefesses. A chief with the ideal qualities of his rank demonstrated concern for his subjects, helping them if food supply was scarce; blending clemency with punishment for transgression. Such a chief had an *'ōpū* filled with mercy, forbearance, sagacity and reasoning ability. Therefore, a commoner who acted with judgment, control and compassion was paid the tribute, "He has *'ōpū ali'i,* the belly of a chief."

kāne o ka pō or wahine o ka pō—spirit lover; dream husband or wife.

Deriv: *kāne,* man or husband.
wahine, woman or wife.
o, of.
ka, the.
pō, night, dark, obscurity; realm of the gods; eternity.

When a *wahine* of old retired for the night, she might have a highly romantic adventure before she woke. To her sleeping mat might come a spirit lover, perhaps an *akua* (god) in human form. There, in night's silence and the hidden world of dreams, the lover might comfort her with words of reassurance and advice. More often, words were dispensed with, and the solace given was that of love and sexual intercourse.

The nighttime adventures might come to men or women. A man visited by a female spirit had a *wahine o ka pō.* A woman so visited had a *kāne o ka pō.* So Hawaii once believed.

It was the dream-mating of a woman to spirit-husband that most often became known. For the woman, impregnated in sleep, might bear an *e'e'pa* (strange, unexplainable) baby. The child might resemble an eel, lizard, shark or bird, or be *'eho'eho,* hard like a rock.[1] Or he might look perfectly ordinary, but have unusual powers to prophesy or heal. The child (or fetus) who looked like fish or fowl or rock was taken to the river, sea or any place where *aumākua* (ancestor gods) of similar form were found. This was not considered infanticide. Mary Kawena Pukui explains the traditional rationale as "returning the child where he belonged."

For the child who looked like a shark belonged to his shark *aumakua*. His spirit-father had, in fact, been a shark god who turned into human form for the dream love affair. This ability to change from god to human, animal, plant or mineral substance was called *kino lau* (many forms). It was a basic Hawaiian belief.

Both men and women with spirit lovers were in danger of trading reality for their dream world. Or, as Mrs. Pukui explains:

"The human lover might become so enamoured with the spiritual one that he or she might be continuously sleepy and eventually die. When this sleepiness was noticed, a *kahuna* was consulted. He would try to make the spiritual lover go—and stay away."[2]

The lover-in-a-dream was known to numerous cultures. In medieval Europe, many a maiden was seduced by an *incubus;* many a sleeping knight or knave embraced his unearthly *succubus*. And if—in Europe or Hawaii—visits of a god-or-demon-or-spirit lover were used to cover up indiscretions—well, human nature proved itself ingenious as well as fallible!

Mrs. Pukui wrote in her *Polynesian Family System in Ka'u :*

"There was a woman in *Ka'u* said to have had a *kāne o ka pō* who was a *mo'o* [giant lizard/water spirit]. She had gone to visit relatives in Honolulu, and there she fell in love with a handsome person who came to her only at night. She did not know where he came from, but thought he was a human being like herself. It was not until she grew listless, lost her appetite, and longed continuously for the night, that her secret was discovered. Her right side, which came in contact with his body during the night, was said to have become slimy and pale like a fish's. The uncle with whom she was visiting undertook to exorcise the night visitor with incantations. Finally the woman was restored to health again, and returned to her native land [Ka'ū]."[3]

Or, describing another case:

". . . A man in Hilo was said to be unable to have children of his own. Whenever his wife dreamt of a man coming to her from the sea, who was the perfect image of her husband, she became pregnant. All of these children were said to be the offspring of her husband's brother, who was a shark *aumakua*. He was her *kāne o ka pō;* his brother, her husband, was called the *kāne i ka 'ili*, the husband for the skin. It is said there was no jealousy between the two brothers, and no harm ever came to their common wife."[4]

Here the *kāne o ka pō* tradition and the belief in *kino lau* seem to have operated in the interests of family solidarity.

In fact, visits of a dreamed or fantasied *kāne o ka pō* might have enabled a woman—the Hilo woman, for example—to become pregnant by her real husband. 20th Century medical and psychiatric observations point out that some women conceive more readily during intercourse with the husband when they are thinking about and responding to a fantasied lover. This "dream lover" may be an actual person, a composite of several men, or a creation of the imagination, with or without mystical attributes.

After birth, a child so conceived may develop a personality quite different from the rest of the family. The mother, if she remains caught up in her love-fantasy, may relate to the child as if the fantasy-sire were really the father. The mother may then tend to "mold" the child into the pattern her own wishful imagination has supplied. This "different" child might indeed be considered *e'epa* or remarkable.

Certainly, the spirit-lover concept could prevent or relieve guilt. This seems especially true for the woman who delivered a fish-like embryo, a rock-like calcified fetus, or any grossly malformed fetus or infant. The *aumākua* were responsible. Therefore the child represented an honor rather than anyone's genetic defect or the mother's "marking" of the coming baby.

In 1971, Hawaii's *kāne* or *wahine o ka pō* might be merely a cultural curio, except for one fact. A few women still tell Center social workers about having had *"mo'o* babies." One client said she had had an *"eho'eho* baby from a dream marriage with a rock spirit."

In such cases, rare though they are, the worker must have some background knowledge of *kāne o ka pō* and *kino lau* before he can really consider the client's sincerity or sanity.

NOTES AND REFERENCES

1. Miscarriages at different stages of fetal development may strongly resemble various lower animals. Somewhat the same resemblance may occur in children with certain congenital anomalies.

2. The love-sick person was also placed upon a layer of *'ape* leaves. The irritation-producing substance in the *'ape* was believed to keep the spirit away. Also, the flower sheath of the banana *(pola mai'a)* was laid between the legs.—M.K.P.

3. Pukui. *Polynesian Family System in Ka'u,* p. 121.

4. Ibid.

kapu kai—ceremonial bath in the sea, in sea water or in other salt water.

Deriv: *kapu,* taboo
kai, sea; sea water; sometimes any salt water.

Kapu kai is the ceremonial bath taken in the sea or in other sea or salt water. This was done to purify oneself after evil or defilement, physical or spiritual, and to remove the *kapu* (taboo) under which the person usually came because of his defilement. The *kapu kai* was done in privacy and with prayers. Women took this *kapu kai* after each menstrual period because menstrual blood was considered defiling *(haumia).* The bath might be taken after contact with a corpse, also considered a defiling object. Sometimes *kapu kai* was a precautionary measure to insure purification *if* evil or defilement existed. It marked the preparatory ceremonies of a hula dancer's *'ailolo* or "graduation" from training, and often came at the close of treatment by a medical *kahuna.* Many, but not all, illnesses were considered to be the result of some erroneous or wicked action by the sick person, or by some evil influence acting in him.

Kapu kai is different from *pī kai,* ceremonial sprinkling with sea or salt water. (See *pī kai).* It has no connection with *'au'au kai,*[1] bathing in the ocean for physical cleanliness alone.

An old chant *(oli)* tells that the volcano goddess, Pele, went into the sea for her *kapu kai* after erupting.

Individuals, even today, sometimes take *kapu kai.* The belief that the ceremonial bath is most beneficial when it is done for five consecutive days is still reported. *Kapu kai* is sometimes taken periodically for general improvement of physical or spiritual health, even if there is no feeling of having been defiled or made *kapu.*

Co-author Pukui tells:

"I went with an old lady out past the Blow Hole, right where the sandy stretch of beach begins. Out there is a stone where Hawaiians used to go. The name of the stone was *'ōku'u* which means "crouch." The old lady headed out there and sat beside *'ōku'u,* and had her ceremonial bath before we went on. She said that's where her people always went, with prayer. *'Ōku'u* was the healing stone."

A child or seriously ill person could be given the ceremonial bath by someone else. A present day example of this came to Center attention when a woman was hospitalized and her father came early every morning to bathe her. In this case the father not only believed his daughter's life was endangered by some evil that *kapu kai* could remove, but he invested the bath with a second significance. He felt that he might, at the same time, offer his life as a substitute for his daughter's.

In this case, awareness of the custom of *kapu kai* prevented misinterpretation of the father's pre-dawn bathing of an adult daughter. In the context of modern, Western culture, the ablutions could be viewed as anything from suspect to scandalous. Within the cultural traditions of Hawaii, a prayerful ceremony was being conducted.

NOTES

1. *'au'au* (bath; bathe) + *kai* (ocean).
2. So named because people crouched beside it while taking the *kapu kai.* Healing stones were found near the shoreline of each island. Each stone was given a name.

"kau ka lā i ka lolo, a ho'i ke aka i ke kino"—phrase designating high noon; the time when "the sun is directly overhead and the shadow retreats into the body," or, more literally, "rests the strong sun on the brain, and retreats the shadow into the body."

Key words: *kau,* rests, is placed; *lā,* sun; *i ka,* on the; *lolo;* brain; *ho'i,* return, retreat; *aka,* shadow; *kino,* body, form.

In the beliefs of old Hawaii, morning was masculine and afternoon was feminine. Once a day the two met in a brief union. Morning then retired, his day's work done; Afternoon took over. At the time of this meeting, no shadow could be seen. Man's own mysterious *aka* (shadow) neither followed nor preceded him nor paced at his side. Instead it retreated into the body, directly into the brain. Near the very region of the spirit pit (tear duct of the eye) through which one's own living spirit might exit and return in the wanderings of dreams! In the topmost part of the entire *po'o* (head), sacred to the *aumākua* (ancestor gods)! In view of all this, what we now call "high noon" was thought a time of great *mana* (spiritual power).

How could man benefit from this fleeting time of bounteous *mana?*

He could prepare sacrifices to the gods at this time. Or administer medicine, previously gathered with ritual and prayers addressed to Ku, the masculine, and Hina, the feminine, deities.

Another way was in the ceremony of *mānewanewa*. This was often done by families who thought they were under a sorcerer's spell.

Mary Kawena Pukui witnessed the old ceremony when she was a child. She relates:

"The family all stripped to the skin. One person stayed by the house doorway, praying. The others, also praying, walked completely around the house five times. Then, as each one went back into the house, the one at the doorway poured water over each person's head, I believe to cleanse away evil."

This and in the *mānewanewa** of extreme grief were probably the only times Hawaiians of both sexes were ever nude in public. Exposure of the genitals was not approved.

As far as we know, this *mānewanewa* has not been practiced for a half-century or more. However, the ritual contained some rather basic mystic components that are still known and sometimes practiced. These include ritual purification by water, significance of the number five, and the belief that the head was sacred to the *aumākua*.

kaukau—to present a problem or outline a situation for consideration. This is done in a calm, reasoning manner, though "please see it my way" is usually said or implied.

Deriv: *kau,* to place. Literally, "place-place."

Though *kaukau* has four quite different meanings, and its root, *kau,* has 14, none of these is "food." Such use of *kaukau* may be a corruption of the Chinese "chow," with perhaps, the added idea that food is "placed" before one.

As the Culture Committee has encountered the word, *kaukau* means a "here are the facts ... I've laid my cards on the table" appeal for reasonable consideration and cooperative response. This "placing the matter before one" can be addressed to a family elder, to a troublesome child—or to a landlord about to raise the rent! So far, *kaukau* under a different name could be part of any culture. What makes it Hawaiian is the fact that, as Mary Kawena Pukui explains, "you can *kaukau* to the living, or to the dead, or to the gods."

Mrs. Pukui provides these examples:

---

*the same word applies to eccentric behavior in extreme grief and the ritual done to dispel sorcery. Both excused genital exposure on similar grounds: being *pupule* from grief, or being extremely distraught because of sorcery fears.

A mother or grandmother might *kaukau* to a naughty child. She might say,
"You have a bad habit of interrupting while your elders are speaking. This is bad manners. It reflects on me—how I am bringing you up—and it shames the whole family. You don't want us to feel shame [*hila hila*], do you? Well then, next time just stop and think before you speak out."

Or, if a spirit of somebody keeps coming back after death, you can *kaukau* directly to the spirit. You can say,
"Now, I know you don't mean to harm us, or even to scare anybody. But, you see, the younger children are frightened. They can't go to sleep after you appear. So, please stop visiting us and let the children sleep at night. Please go to your rest and leave us alone."

In *ho'oponopono*, the family council to "set to rights" disputes, sickness and problems in the family, *kaukau* is used. A family senior might say,
"Almighty God (or *aumakua*), and all of you, our *'ohana* [family], we are here together because we are worried about Joe. We know he has sniffed glue. His schoolwork is not good. Today we got another note from his teacher. With God's help, we can talk this over, and hear Joe's side of the story too— and maybe we can find out why he misbehaves and how we can help him."

Kaukau as a truly Hawaiian practice is marked by courtesy and dignity. Reasons may be lined up with quiet determination—but the table is never pounded. One may request, or even appeal, for *kōkua* (help or cooperation) —but one does not implore or emotionally grovel. Even addressed to the supernatural, *kaukau* uses the "think it over" approach, rather than the "I bow before thee" entreaty. The Hawaiians did not behave like children before their gods.

kīheipua or ki he i pua—enabling concept; help given by one's *aumakua* or ancestor god.

Deriv: *kīhei*, shoulder cover (later meaning is shawl).
pua, flower.

Literally, *kīheipua* was a "shoulder covering of flowers." This was a poetic way of expressing the concept that the *aumakua* helped the ill, aged, or a helpless child by "placing over the shoulder a covering or mantle of comfort and aid." This, a mild possession *(noho)* by the *aumakua,* gave the helpless person the temporary ability to function.

One of several enabling concepts. See *aumakua.*

kino lau—many bodies; many forms.

Deriv: *kino*, body
lau, many, numerous.

Kino lau nearly always refers to the many forms or bodies both the *akuas* (impersonal gods) and the *aumākua* (personalized ancestor gods) were thought to take. These deities took animal, plant or mineral form, changing back and forth at will. Lesser god-like beings, the *kupuas,* also were thought to appear as, or to inhabit, rocks and plants. The mythology of virtually every culture has its equivalent of *kino lau.*

In the present day, Center clients sometimes extend the belief in *kino lau* of gods or *aumākua* to belief that the spirit of a recently deceased person appears in animal form. Sometimes the animal is an actual family pet; sometimes it is seen in a vision or dream. See *aumakua* and *akakū, hihi'o* and *'ūlāleo.*

kupua—demigod.

Deriv: possibly from *kupu* meaning grow, or to sprout, or one rising up suddenly; upstart. The *kupua* was a kind of "upstart god."

A *kupua* or demigod was a minor supernatural being, not as powerful as the *akua* (god) or as closely concerned with a mortal's welfare as the *aumakua* (ancestor god). *Kupuas* stayed within definite localities. Like *akua* they could change form, though the *kupua* most often took the form of a rock or stone. They were given male or female identities. These were benign deities unless they were mistreated. The stories told of a "stone becoming fond of a person" probably refer to *kupuas* in stone form.

Kupuas were among a host of supernatural entities, for early Hawaiians believed in demigods, ghosts, giants and wandering spirits as well as the *akua* and *aumakua.* This religious-mystic proclivity is apparent in most of the Hawaiian clients seen at the Center, whether or not old rituals are still pronounced and former gods yet remembered or invoked.

kupuna and hānau mua

kupuna, (pl. *kūpuna)*—grandparent; relative of the grandparent generation, such as grandaunt or granduncle, living or dead;

hānau mua—specifically, the eldest living member of the senior branch of the family clan or *'ohana;* the ranking senior.

Deriv: *hānau,* born; child; offspring.
mua, first.
Literally, "first born child."

"I didn't know who to turn to. Then I called my great-great-grandaunt," said Kolokea, whose family problem is discussed under *iwi.*

"Any time I need advice, I go to Kona to see my grandfather," an 18-year-old Oahu youth told me. "Grandpa and I have always been close. Besides, he is the family senior."

"... I was so worried. But that night Grandma came to me in a dream and told me what I must do."

Listen to these statements, and the importance of the senior relative in Hawaiian family life begins to be clear. All seniors or *kūpuna* were respected. Grandparents were especially loved. But the *hānau mua* was the acknowledged head of the clan. He—or she—was *the* senior. The *hānau mua* was the accepted source of wisdom, the arbitrator of family disputes, the troubleshooter in family problems, and the custodian of family history.

The *hānau mua* had an even greater power, one mystical and benevolent. He could *'oki* (remove) an *'ānai* (curse). With his death, the senior could take with him beyond the grave all family curses and associated ill-feelings. At any time during his life, perhaps decades before his death, he could inform the *'ohana* (family clan) that he was going to do this. This immediately made the curse inoperative. Anxiety and family tensions were thus immediately lessened. (Such curse removal was called *lawe i ka wa make,* "take in time of death.")

Genealogy rather than age or sex determined *hānau mua* status.[1] A 50-year-old, eldest in the senior branch of the total family clan, could be *hānau mua* to a 70-year-old cousin who was eldest in a junior branch. Senior responsibilities to one's blood relatives were not canceled by the responsibilities of marriage. A senior man with many children was not only head of his own household, but continued to be ranking senior to his own younger siblings and their children. His wife, if she were senior in her own blood line, continued to be senior to her siblings and their children. Fortunately, *hānau mua* responsibility did not include provision of "bed and board and bill-paying."

The exception to senior status by order of birth came when a child born to junior status was selected to be the future senior.

Whether birth or selection designated him—or her, the future *hānau mua* was trained for the job. Mary Kawena Pukui tells that,

"I was born a junior, but I was *hānai'd* (permanently given) to my grandmother. I was the *punahele* (favored or selected child), reared to be the senior."[2]

As her grandmother's tag-along companion, Mrs. Pukui stored up knowledge. What she learned spanned her grandmother's pre-missionary era past, and the turn-of-the-century years before her own birth. Sometimes she was given specific assignments:

"Grandmother made me memorize all the relatives, both the living ones and the family *aumākua* (ancestor gods).

"She taught me etiquette and family customs... the traditions of land ownership[3]... how to sit down quietly and talk to people in trouble... when I should call for *ho'oponopono.*"*

More often, she learned by watching and listening:

"I used to wake up at night, and hear Grandmother chanting. And so I memorized the chants." (Prayers, legends and genealogy were all handed down in *olis* or chants.)

---

*Hawaii's serious, prayerful family conference in which wrongs were made right and relationships among family members and the gods were restored to former harmony. A major diagnostic-remedial-preventive practice. See listing, *ho'oponopono.*

"When somebody did something wrong, Grandmother and the others would talk about it . . . why was it wrong? . . . What should be done now?" Little of total family life around her was held back from the young Kawena: How babies were born. What *inoas* (names) should or should not be given a child. What this portent meant, or that dream signified within its context of person and events. How to prepare a corpse for burial. What the family can do if somebody grieves too long. That one must always *kala* (forgive and release) when forgiveness is asked.

Mrs. Pukui's preparation to be *hānau mua* may have been more the ideal than the typical. However, the ideal illustrated the function of the ranking senior. Clearly, the *hānau mua* was intended to be a source of help and wisdom, rather than an authority figure. Being senior was indeed an honor—but the honor was earned by discharging responsibilities, not by wielding power.

how to depose
the erring senior

The possibility that the senior might fall short of the ideal was provided for. If a normally helpful senior made a serious error in judgment, the family could ask him to reverse his decision. This might be done informally or in *ho'oponopono*. And here, even the *hānau mua* enjoyed no diplomatic immunity. Mrs. Pukui says,

"Even if the *hānau mua* himself conducts *ho'oponopono,* the others can still use this occasion to point out his own mistakes and ask him to correct them."

The *hānau mua* who was consistently incompetent or even a source of family friction could traditionally be "removed from office."

"The family would get together and talk everything over and choose a new senior. Then anyone who needed advice would just quietly go to this new one."

The newly selected senior might or might not be next in line genealogically. Rank in the family line was balanced against ability, character and judgment.

seniority
in the 1970s

Center social caseworkers—at least those based on Oahu—report the term *hānau mua* is used only occasionally. It is the concept that continues to permeate family life and shape family decisions—and "family" in this case means the extended clan or *'ohana.* Most clients continue to recognize one specific senior who outranks other seniors or elders in the *'ohana.* However, when Hawaiian terms are used, all seniors are loosely classified as *kūpuna.*

A Hawaiian staff member describes the operation of senior rank in his extended family:

"My father is the senior. He lives here, on Oahu. But if anything happens to my uncle and his children on Kauai, they call my father, and my father goes to Kauai to help them. My uncle's own children, my cousins, may take a problem first to their own father. But if he can't solve it, then they call my father, their Uncle Eddie. And if there is a disagreement among my father's sisters and brothers, they call my father. In any case, after they talk it over, whatever my father decides—well, that settles it."

Senior responsibility and a corresponding respect for senior status continue down through the ranks of the modern Hawaiian family. Older children are usually charged with the care of younger ones, just as they traditionally were. A party or beach picnic may run smoothly because of this chain of responsibility. But, yesterday's tradition must be adapted to the 1970s' realities. Yesterday, the older sibling cared for youngsters who from babyhood, for example, could handle themselves in water. Today, the older child is too often made responsible for youngsters who have not learned to swim or to avoid the hazards of traffic and the home medicine chest. "Take care of your little brother" may set the stage for tragedy and life-long guilt.

close grandparent—
grandchild ties

The closest of emotional ties continue to exist between Hawaiian grandparent *(kupuna)* and *(mo'opuna* (grandchild). Probably no person appears more frequently in Hawaiians' dreams or waking visions than a loved and trusted grandparent. Often, of course, the grandparent may have reared the child, thus becoming a virtual parent. But even without such rearing or a *hānai* background, one's *tūtū-man* (grandfather) or *tūtū-lady** (grandmother) remains a *hulu kupuna* or "precious person" long after childhood days.[4] As one young woman expresses it,

"My *inoa* [name] sounds more beautiful when Grandmother says it. There is, oh, such tenderness in her voice."

This close grandparent-grandchild, elder-junior relationship may sound quite perfect. It is not always so. For the family senior may be a blessing—or a bottleneck.

the 20th Century senior:
blessing or bottleneck?

In the Center's experience, trouble with "bottleneck seniors" falls roughly into four typical situations:

Situation A: The ranking or *hānau mua* senior is asked to remove an *'ānai* (curse) from a member of the *'ohana*. The senior refuses, sometimes because he does not know the traditions of curse-removal (see *'oki;* also *lawe i ka wa make* on previous page). Or, he may not want to take any helpful steps and may even enjoy seeing the family squirm.

Situation B: The ranking or *hānau mua* senior has the family "buffaloed" in some other way. Often the senior claims special "powers" or *mana* and uses this claim to manipulate family members. Sometimes the senior refuses to let a handed down *inoa* (name) be changed, even though through the years the name has taken on a connotation that is highly embarrassing. (Actual—and vivid—examples cannot be given. This would identify individuals.)

Situation C: Grandma—or Grandpa or Great-aunt or other *kupuna*—may or may not be the ranking senior. This *kupuna*—let's say Grandma—refuses to give up the grandchild she is rearing, even though the child himself wants to return to the parents. Sometimes the child involved is a *hānai keiki* (perma-

---

*recent terms.

nently given child). Sometimes he is a *luhi* (temporarily cared for foster child). Often the status is not clear.

Situation D: The troublesome-triangle of grandmother, daughter and the daughter's child. Grandma wants the youngster reared her way. The child's mother *(makua)* seethes more or less quietly, or tells Grandma off in open quarrels. It is a standard conflict in nearly any culture. However, the conflict may be especially sharp when a Hawaiian grandmother has a Spock-quoting *Haole* (Caucasian) daughter-in-law.

Especially in Situations A and B, two specific facets of the *hānau mua* tradition may be useful. As Mrs. Pukui pointed out, the incompetent or deliberately perverse senior could be asked to correct judgmental errors, or could be replaced by another selected senior. Either action was arrived at through a family meeting, not through impulsive, individual decision. Ideally, this meeting was the *ho'oponopono* with its techniques to control anger and encourage sober thought.

Both corrective provisions were based on the open recognition that the senior was neither sacrosant nor infallible. Thus tradition gave permission to be objective—not only about the *hānau mua,* but any *kupuna.*

senior: the role
and the individual

And so, with complete respect, one could see Grandpa, The Individual, separate from Grandpa, Seniority Personified. And with this separation of person from role, it becomes possible to balance the person's performance against the intended function of the role. The intended function of the senior was to help family members. Is Grandpa so functioning? If he is not, then the family decision—he is no longer *hānau mua*—is made. This concensus guards against acting from personal hostility. Group decision to "retire" the senior is apt to be based on a fairly accurate appraisal of the senior's present judgment and behavior.

In this sober appraisal of performance of the *hānau mua* role comes a more objective look at Grandpa himself. The individual. Is he ill? Senile? Lonely? Does he hold a threat or a curse over the family because he really has powers to harm? Or because this is a way to gain family attention? Does he need diversion? Approval? Companionship in general, rather than the particular companionship of the clung-to grandchild? Is he no longer the fountainhead of wisdom—but only a senior in years? An old person, dignified by age—yet subject to the very incompetencies and idiosyncrasies age has brought.

Hawaii's family decision to "retire" a *hānau mua* was essentially a formalized expression of the same psychological process that leads one to change physicians or switch to a new music teacher. The expert can indeed help you more when you believe in his "expertise." Lose this belief and much of the helping-teaching ability is—to you—also lost.

hulu kupuna, the
"precious elder"

In the Hawaiian *'ohana,* the "retired" *hānau mua* was in no way cut off from family respect and affection. Only his official standing was removed. The senior himself remained very much a venerated and loved member of the family. To the end of his days, he was a *hulu kupuna*—a truly "precious elder."

130

In these last few pages, we have stressed Seniors, Family Bottlenecks, and apparently overlooked Seniors, Family Blessings. The reason is that our examples come from case histories. Case histories are concerned with problem families. Look at less troubled families and you will find the Hawaiian seniors who enrich family life. It is the *kupuna* who can convey a sense of continuity in family structure and a knowledge of and pride in the Hawaiian cultural heritage. It is the grandmother who can provide a stable maternal presence for the child of a working mother.

With the present, though overdue, revival of interest in Hawaii's past, the elder can make a great contribution to community as well as family. The old beliefs, arts and skills must be recorded and handed down. The *kupuna* is a needed *kumu* (source) of all this knowledge.

In fact, the senior whose unique abilities are being used is less apt to be a problem. Or, within the Senior Bottleneck may be the potential to be a Senior Blessing.

NOTES AND REFERENCES

1. Goldman. *The Ancient Polynesian Society,* pp. 212-214. Men were preferred as chiefs or family heads until somewhere between 1100-1450 A.D. Gradually, rights of primogeniture became more important than sex of the ranking senior.

2. In Mrs. Pukui's case, a cousin born to an elder aunt was genealogically destined to be the senior. However, the cousin's parents, enthusiastic converts to Christianity, believed the *hānau mua* system was tied too closely to "old"—therefore "pagan"—ways. They refused to let her become family senior and learn pre-Christian beliefs and traditions. Mrs. Pukui was then selected to take her cousin's place.

3. Land ownership. Traditionally, disputed land went to the *'ohana* member who stayed on the land and tilled it. Caring for and living on the land superseded inheritance by seniority or closer relationship.

4. *Hulu kupuna.* From *hulu,* "feather," and *kupuna* "elder" or "elder person." Literally, "feather elder." In usage, "precious elder." Feathers were used in the *kahilis,* the standards of high *ali'i.* There were god images made of feathers. Connotations of rank and religion given feathers made them most precious objects; elders were most precious family members.

leina—a place to leap from; a leaping place.

Deriv: a contraction of *lēhei,* "to leap" and *ana,* a particle which in this case means "there" or "then." Literally, "leap there."

Leina, a place to leap from, is often used as a short form of *leina-a-ke-akua* or *leina-a-ke-'uhane,* the place from which spirits leaped into eternity or *Pō.* It was thought the spirit of man took this leap after death. Certain cliffs or precipices on each island were believed to be the *leina* from which spirits plunged into the ocean, symbolizing *Pō.* See *aumakua.*

luhi—a child cared for temporarily by someone not his parents; to care for another's child.

Deriv: Literally, *luhi* means "tiredness." The adult becomes tired in the necessary work of caring for the child. Simple fatigue is meant; there is no connotation of being "sick and tired" of effort or child.

In traditional practice, *luhi* signified a temporary or part-time arrangement. Though relationships between *luhi* and the adult who cared for him were often warm and lasting, the child's natural parents could reclaim him at will. This was in contrast with the permanency of taking a *hānai* (foster child).

Today, *luhi* is used in connection with foster home placement, day care facilities and any short-term or part-time care provided by anyone besides parents. A child who spends weekdays with an aunt while his mother works is the aunt's *luhi*, for example. It is understood the child will return to its own parents.

When temporary care stretches out for a long time, the *luhi* is sometimes mistakenly believed to be a *hānai* or permanent foster-child. Adult clients sometimes cannot remember or never understood whether they were the *luhi* or *hānai* of a relative. This can affect status and seniority in the family even though many years have passed.

When the young unmarried mother lets her own parents take her baby, the decision whether the baby is to be the *luhi* or the *hānai* of the grandparents must be clearly understood and equated with its modern equivalents of temporary care or permanent legal adoption.

Contrasts between *luhi* and *hānai* are further discussed under *hānai*.

mā'e'ele—sensation of numbness, physical, emotional or both as in psychosomatically caused numbness. The foot that is "asleep;" the numb feeling of shock; numb feeling of being cold; numb feeling of physical passions.

> Deriv: unknown.
> See discussion under *'ili'ōuli*.

make, kanu and **kaumaha**—death, burial and grief.

make—death, to die.

> Deriv: unknown.

kanu—burial, bury.

> Deriv: plant, as a seed. With earth burials and the covering of the body with soil, *kanu* began to be used to differentiate between this burial and *hūnā* (conceal) in which bodies were hidden in caves, but not directly covered with earth.

kaumaha—grief, sorrow.

> Deriv: From original use of *kaumaha* meaning weight or heavy weight, and from use of the separate syllables, *kau* (place, put, set) and *maha* (relief or rest). From the most literal connotation, that holding a physical weight is followed with relief when it is set down, came the abstract idea that grief is a heavy weight followed by relief.

The study group was talking about Hawaiian mourning customs when Mary Kawena Pukui recalled an old friendship.

"I remember your mother so well," she told the Hawaiian matron across the table. "She was such a beautiful wailer!"

Mrs. Pukui had paid tribute to a valued accomplishment. Wailing *(uwē)* was one of the ways old Hawaii grieved for the dead. Perhaps the only times these funeral wails were not heard came centuries ago when a king or chief with powerful rivals died. Silence might be imposed then, and the royal bones hidden in secrecy. This was done so enemies could not desecrate the sacred *iwi* (bones).

na'au'auwā or deepest grief

If such caution was not needed, mourning for a beloved *ali'i* (ruler or aristocrat) might go far beyond wailing. For *na'au'auwā* ("grief within the very bowels") was sometimes expressed in extreme and violent manifestations called *mānewanewa*. These might include:

"... Knocking out front teeth and gashing the head and scarring the body. A man might trim the hair on his scalp in a peculiar fashion. In the old days, the people would abandon themselves to an orgy of passion ... and do such things as dashing about with the *malo* (loin cloth) or *pā'ū* (skirt) about the neck, instead of the loins. At such times, it is said, there was general promiscuous indulgence of sexual passion; a climax and venting of pent-up feelings that was doubtless salutary for the people, and believed to be gratifying to the dead *ali'i* as an expression of the ultimate sentiment of passionate love."[1]

pupule actions were excused

Scarring the body and displaying genitals were neither common nor approved, Mrs. Pukui explains. Such actions were excusable only because the mourner was considered *pupule* (crazy) from grief.

offers to be moe hoa or "death companion"

Not *pupule,* but excessively grieved, were persons who offered themselves as death companions *(moe hoa* or *moe pūlua)** to *ali'i.* One such incident on Maui is described:

"... The Queen Mother, Ke-opu-o-lani, lay dying. At her death, September 16, 1823 ... many persons from the back country came and offered themselves as death companions ... but Hoa-pili† ... refused them all."[2]

Moe pūlua offers were a striking departure from Hawaiian tradition, for suicide was rare and not generally sanctioned. Mrs. Pukui sees the death companion offer more as a ritualized attempt rather than a completed suicide. She points out that,

---

*moe (sleep) + *hoa* (companion) or *pūlua* (two persons together). *Moe* was a frequent euphemism for *make* (death).

†A chief and Governor of Maui. He had been Kamehameha's closest friend and thus was named `Hoa* (companion) + *pili* (close; cling).

"Usually, the *aumākua* [ancestor gods] brought the death companion back to life. The same thing often happened if a young person attempted suicide when he was disappointed in love." (Restoration to life is discussed under *'o'ō-a-moa).*

"take my life instead"
prayer often answered

More widespread was the belief that one person could offer his life so another would live. Such "take my life instead" prayers are common among religious persons almost anywhere. The difference in old Hawaii was the conviction that the offer was accepted. Mrs. Pukui relates a typical example,

"A nephew was awfully sick, and my great-grandmother chose to die that he might live. He lived. She died."

(Great-grandmother made her sacrifice more than a century ago. But in 1971, a young Hawaiian woman, speaking of a family death said, "I volunteered to die instead.")

pela (flesh) once
removed from bones

With the advent of Christianity and exposure to Western ways, two ancient funeral practices of both *ali'i* and *maka'āinana* (commoner) were gradually discontinued. One was removing the *pela* (flesh) from the corpse and sinking it into the sea. The other, often following flesh removal *(pūhololoholo),* was believed to transfigure the bones, or sometimes complete body, into a form of *aumakua.* This is described under *kākū'ai.*

Earth burial in a coffin became accepted practice, though bodies had previously been bound in the fetal position and placed in caves or buried beneath ground, or sometimes deposited, lying prone, in mass burial pits.

Until morticians were generally accepted, only close relatives prepared the body for burial.

Among *ali'i,* the royal person, alive or dead, was *kapu* to all but trusted, blood-related retainers. And for any Hawaiian, the body was exposed only to close family members. And so, just as they did in sickness, family cared for family in death. But because even the corpse of a loved relative was *haumia* (defiling), family members purified themselves after the funeral with the rituals of *pī kai* or *kapu kai.* (See listings).

torches by day for
certain ali'i only

Torches lit in daylight became a symbol of grief, but only for certain *ali'i.* One chief of old, Iwikauikaua, walked all around the Island of Hawaii carrying lighted torches to mourn his wife and child—and possibly to proclaim the shameful deed of his higher-ranking wife who had murdered them. He thus began a tradition for his family line. Mrs. Pukui recalls that:

"When Queen Liliuokalani was buried, my husband was a *kahili* (feather standard) bearer, so we noticed everything very closely. There were torches burning during the day and people talked critically about it. But this was proper. She was a descendant of Iwikauikaua."

134

Chants, dirges and wailing continued through the years. In 1854, when King Kamehameha III died:
"The sound of wailing rose and increased like the clamorous sound of the breaking waves. It beat upon the ears insistently and mournfully, like the reiterative strokes of the tapa stick . . ."[3]

And, 63 years later, as Queen Liliuokalani lay in state:
". . . the body . . . was viewed by a vast procession of people . . . the natives venting their sorrow in the oldtime *olis,* [chants] or the *uwē helu* [lamentation].

". . . devoted attendants and loyal subjects [mourned] in song, chant recitations, *olis,* or the weird, soul-piercing, disconsolate wail of a grief-stricken heart . . .

". . . Early on the [last] day, natives came in for the last opportunity for homage and to voice their grief in their own way. Among them were new arrivals from the other islands whose sorrowful wail at times broke out with wild shriek and abandon."[4]

If such were the lamentations for cherished *ali'i,* what were the *uwēs* with an ordinary family? Less influenced by mass emotion, but just as openly expressive of grief. Family mourning centered around the *anaina ho'olewa* or *kia'i kupapa'u* (wake).*

kia'i kupapa'u
"the wake" held

Mrs. Pukui recalls that:
"Everybody in the *'ohana* (extended family) came, bringing food. The *keikis* [children] came too. They used to fall asleep on the floor, sometimes right under the coffin. The body was placed with the feet toward the door, and close relatives sat around the body, so they could see people coming in. As each person arrived, a relative would say—as if telling the dead person—'Here comes Keone, your old fishing companion.' or 'Tūtū† is coming in now. You remember how she used to *lomi-lomi* [massage] when you were sick.' Then each new arrival would wail in reply."

This wailing, addressed to the dead, was filled with reminiscences. One example is translated:

memories recalled
to the dead one

"Oh, my brother, my companion of childhood days, companion with whom I shared my troubles, companion who shared my woes, Ah, you have deserted me! Beloved are the fishing places we have gone to; the sandy stretches where we sat. Oh, [another mourner is addressed] you shall never more see his face. Oh, . . . my companion has gone on the hidden pathway of Kāne."[5]

The wail might tell of the bereaved person's abandonment. As:

---

anaina (crowd, assembly; to assemble) + *ho'olewa* (funeral). *kia'i* (guard, watch, to guard or watch) + *kupapa'u* (corpse).

†originally *kuku.* Affectionate term for any elder. Often translated as "Aunty" or "Grandmother." A male elder is more recently called *"tūtū* man."

"Oh, my beloved, now that you are gone, there will be no one to help me bring our cows from the pasture. Alas, I am alone, alone to do the many things we liked to do. Alone to rear our fatherless children."[6]

scolding
the corpse

Or more directly, the dead person might be scolded. Mrs. Pukui gives an example:

"The fishing companion might say, 'What do you mean, going off when we had planned to go fishing! Now who will I fish with?' Or a wife might say, 'You had no business to go. You should be ashamed of yourself. We need you.'"

Mrs. Pukui continues,

"You could hear the *uwēs* a long way down the road. There was music, too. Someone would sing the songs and dance the hulas the dead person had loved."

pa'i a uma, the
gestures of grief

There was also the "body language" of grief, called *pa'i a uma*.* Again, we quote Mrs. Pukui:

"Usually three persons at a time took part. They would bring a mat with them and kneel down on it. Then, at the same time, they would clasp their hands behind their necks, then fling arms and hands up in the air, then bend over, slapping the chest and wailing loudly."

(In 1968, a part-Hawaiian community worker was reprimanded by an elderly Hawaiian. The young man's offense: leaning back in his chair, he had clasped his hands behind his neck.)

As the usual day and night of the wake wore on, relatives composed *na mele kanikau* (chants of mourning) or dirges. These were recited beside the coffin. Later, Hawaiians also published these poetic funeral odes in the Hawaiian language newspapers. Up until 1894, newspapers carried whole columns of mourning chants.

spirit near corpse
until the burial

Announcing new arrivals, talking to and scolding the corpse, performing the favorite songs and hulas of the deceased, and the much earlier practice of burying food with the body all point to the belief that the spirit was still very close to the corpse. Hawaii's traditional wake customs were evidently not consciously planned ways to vent personal grief, though they did this admirably. Rather, they were farewell communications to the still-lingering spirit. For it seems, the spirit could hear the wails and lamentations. See the torch flames. Be pleased by graceful hulas and complimentary dirges.

corpse took things
& intangibles to Pō

And so, the time before burial was an extension period for death-bed promises, reconciliations, requests and bequests. The dead body was believed

---

pa'i (to slap) + *uma*, contraction of *um iuma* (chest or breast).

to take both spiritual-emotional matters and material objects beyond the grave and into the eternity of *Pō*. Or, as Hawaii often varied the imagery, "into the sunset"... "intó the West"... "taken away forever into the great eyeball of the sun."

ho'omoe pū—objects buried with dead

This belief was expressed as *ho'omoe pū* ("put to sleep together") and *lawe i ka wa make* ("take in time of death"). *Ho'omoe pū* refers to things; *lawe i ka wa make* to intangibles.

In *ho'omoe pū*, various articles were buried with the body as comfort and sustenance in the mystical world. In long-gone times, this might be food. Later, as Mrs. Pukui says,

"If *tūtū* was especially fond of her kukui nut *lei*, or if a *paniolo* [cowboy] had a favorite saddle, relatives might *ho'omoe pū*, or put it to sleep together with the body."

("I was astounded at the number of things the children wanted buried with their mother," a caseworker relates, following a 1970 client death.)

Ho'omoe pū has its counterpart in most cultures. Ancient peoples, primitive or sophisticated, placed food, utensils and cherished possessions with the dead. Today, a rosary, prayer book or Bible, wedding ring, or child's toy—any may be placed in the coffin. What is being expressed may range from religious comfort to detachment from the dead ("take this ring; our marriage is over") to a refusal to accept the reality of separation ("take this symbol of our life together. We are still together.") Sometimes this may amount to identification with the dead person.

In the Hawaiian tradition, *ho'omoe pū* could also be a bribe or contract for good behavior on the part of the dead.

"When a body is buried, the friend should repeat these words: 'Do not go wandering to houses, but stay quietly here. You have food, fish and clothes,'" so Fornander wrote of an early practice.[7]

Or, later:

"When my grandmother was buried, some of my hair was laid away with her," recalls Mrs. Pukui. "These words were said: 'Take your grandchild's hair with you as a token of something belonging to her. Now you have a part of her with you. So do not come back and disturb the child.'"

Here, the practice seems more a part of detaching oneself from the dead; a way of expressing, "You are dead. We are living. Go your way and let us go our way."

lawe i ka wa make—the corpse removed troubles

In *lawe i ka wa make* ("take in time of death"), the dead person took emotional and mystical entities beyond the grave. Unless he had previously passed on his *mana* to descendants, he took this god-bestowed power back to the *aumākua* in eternity. He could take away family curses, quarrels and grudges, *kapus* (taboos), or a name *(inoa)* that carried harmful *kapu* connotations. This was done in a simple request. (See listing, *'ānai*). Any recently deceased adult relative could do this. The body did not need to be that of the ranking senior *(hānau mua)*.

Names could also be traded with a just-deceased person. A living person might do this if his own name was inappropriate or harmful, or simply to honor the dead person and keep his name alive. (See *inoa*).

quarrels made up
during the wake

With or without *lawe i ka wa make* rituals, Hawaiian families traditionally made up quarrels during the wake. The tears of mourning and the kiss of reconciliation go together in many societies.

The corpse gave no sign that disturbing matters were taken away in death. It was understood that sincere requests to *lawe i ka wa make* were granted. However, the corpse was observed for other *hō'ailonas* (portents). One was that of *ka'aka'a ka maka* (opening the eyes).*

ka'aka'a ka maka:
portent of death

Wrote the historian Kamakau:

"Something to be observed when a person died was whether or not his eyes remained closed, and after several hours, opened again. Those who watched the body knew that in this case, the dead was looking for one of the living. If one of his relatives died afterward, the living then recalled it was because the eyes of the corpse had opened."[8]

"Hawaiians dreaded *ka'aka'a ka maka*," says Mrs. Pukui. "That's why they put flat stones—later, silver dollars—on the eyelids."

(In 1969, Sarah, a teenage girl in the last three months of pregnancy, was terrified by a dream in which almost disembodied eyes kept coming towards her, opening and shutting. She believed the dream meant "something terrible is going to happen to me." She then recalled, "When I was six or seven, Grandmother died, and my father took me up to see the body. As I kissed Grandmother, the eyes flew open. I was so scared! That night I dreamed about Grandmother and I woke up screaming."

Fear of death in childbirth is common in late pregnancy. But as Sarah related other events and predictive interpretations from her past, it became clear that she was also experiencing her pre-existing death fears in the portent of *ka'aka'a ka maka*.)

when spirit is nuha
the corpse is heavy

A corpse conveyed a different message if it suddenly became very heavy during the funeral procession. In the present day, the heavy coffin is thought to mean the deceased "wants something," "doesn't want to go" or is displeased at the funeral arrangement.** A husky Hawaiian described his 1970 experience as pall-bearer:

"The coffin got so heavy we couldn't hardly carry it. Old Charlie sure didn't want to go."

---

ka'aka'a (to open) + *ka* (the) + *maka* (eyes).

**Some Hawaiians believe the body must be buried facing West; others that it must face the ocean, or the mountain. The best "rule" is to follow previously expressed wishes of the deceased.

"Charlie didn't want to go—until he had seen a certain person," adds Mrs. Pukui. "When the body gets very, very heavy, this means there is somebody else the departing spirit wants to see. Somebody not there. So the spirit is *nuha* [sullen; sulking]."

Or, as Fornander wrote more than a century earlier:

"If the corpse is being carried, and the loved one is far in the rear, no progress would be made, for the deceased would demur. The one he loved should be immediately behind, then there would be no demurring... [after the corpse was scolded] the corpse will acquiesce, and it will be light work carrying it to the place of burial."⁹

Even now, there is some feeling that the dead can at least receive communications. In 1965 interviews, "A Hawaiian minister and two Protestant Hawaiian lay respondents said the funeral could make the deceased 'satisfied' or 'happy'."¹⁰ In 1971, a part-Hawaiian staff member attended his uncle's funeral. He reported: "We were putting the casket down in the grave when my father stepped forward and called my uncle by name. 'We are going to leave you now,' he said. 'Is there anything you want to tell us?'"

funeral absentee
a sorcery suspect

Traditionally, living relatives noted with great suspicion anyone absent from the funeral. The belief was that a person who had wronged the deceased never attended the burial. If he did, the wrong or evil he instigated would revert right back to punish him. Usually the absentee was suspected of causing the death by sorcery.

'aha'aina make,
funeral feast

Traditionally, after the burial and the purification of *pī kai* or *kapu kai,* mourners held a feast. This was the *'aha'aina make,* literally the feast *('aha 'aina)* of *make* (death). Mrs. Pukui outlines the philosophy as:

"We have laid away our dead. Now let us, the living, comfort each other... And I think it helped the ones who had lost their appetites to eat something."

(An "empty feeling" and loss of appetite are usual in the early stages of grieving. Hawaiians also recognized the opposite, excessive over-eating. This was believed to be "eating for the spirit." See listing, *'ai akua.*)

'aha'aina waimaka
one year later

Exactly one year later, the same persons got together for a second feast, the *'aha'aina waimaka* or "feast of tears." The translation is misleading. This was a happy occasion, a joyful reunion of all who had previously shed tears together.

Recalls Mrs. Pukui, "There was drinking, eating, singing and dancing. We had a *lu'au* when all the grief was done."

grief period is
normally one year

Hawaii's *'aha'aina waimaka* "when all the grief was done" seems to have anticipated the conclusion of 20th Century Western psychiatry: That grief, fully experienced and expressed, normally proceeds from first impact to recovery and reorganization of one's life in one year. In fact, the practices of many civilizations and religions agree with this timing.

There are other striking parallels between Hawaiian mourning practices and the observations of current Western psychiatry. Here, the terms "grief work" and the "grief process" are used.

requirements of grief process

Modern Western psychiatry agrees that:

Satisfactory grief work requires that the bereaved person emotionally acknowledges the reality of the death and fully expresses his sorrow with its components of guilt and anger. As this process of grieving or "grief work" is completed, the dead one gradually ceases to be, on an emotional level, a "living presence" and becomes instead a fond memory.

the time-table of grief work

Grief work is not static; it is a process. Within flexible limits, there is even a "time table" of stages of this process.

There may be initial "numbness" for as long as a week. As reality of the death sinks in, this "no feeling" reaction is replaced by active grieving. Long previous knowledge that a person is dying may shorten this period; sudden death or heavy sedation of the bereaved may prolong it. Hawaii's emotionally expressive wake may have shortened or virtually eliminated this initial stage.

After the full impact of the death is felt and expressed, there is transition from extreme grief to adaption to the loss. This may be as short as four or as long as ten weeks. An accidental death that gave survivors no time to prepare for the loss may result in the longer period. In general, this stage of grief takes from four to seven weeks.

("The majority of bereaved people on Hawaii Island follow [for varying religious-cultural reasons] some special ritual for four to seven weeks after a death," states a 1967 report.)[11]

characteristics of adaptation period

In this period, there are usually sighing and intermittent weeping spells. Poor appetite, insomnia, apathy and inefficiency are common. Sometimes restless, purposeless activity instead of apathy is noted. Temper may flare up, often at friends and relatives trying to be helpful. There is a protesting against the death, hostility toward the dead, and a great yearning for the deceased. There is much recounting of cherished experiences in life with the one now dead. Guilt is always present, as is ambivalence toward the dead one. Hallucinating the dead, especially for the first month, is common.

"Grief," summarizes the Center's psychiatric consultant, "is a whole conglomerate of emotions."

Hawaii's customs aided grief work

Judging by their mourning customs, Hawaiians have always understood and met many of the requirements of grief work.

140

Certainly Hawaii's ancient separation of flesh from bones drove home the reality of death. So did the later practice in which family members prepared the body for burial. This is still done in some rural areas.* Even before death, family members gradually faced the coming loss when they cared for the sick at home and witnessed the final ritual of *hā* (see listing). Possibly, pre-burial rituals addressed to the yet-hovering spirit also helped make the transition from feeling "he is still with us" to "he is gone."

Requests for the corpse to "take away" curses, quarrels and grudges may have relieved guilt feelings. And surely, "scolding the corpse" met the need to vent hostility toward the dead. Today, Western society, denying anger, teaches, "Do not speak ill of the dead."

And what of the reminiscences of the wake—the songs and the hulas, which turn-of-the-century newspapers called "scandalous"?

Psychiatrist Dr. Haertig, states:

"This recalling of events and memories is a part of the very essence of grief work. 'We did this together . . . we visited this place together . . . you sang this song with us . . . this is the hula you always asked me to dance.' All this is a way of bringing it home to the mourner that these shared moments are ended. It is a way of bringing home the realization of death."

cultural differences in hallucinating the dead

Hallucinating the dead is recognized as a part of grieving in both Hawaiian and Western thought. The great difference is that the Western mourner who sees, hears, or senses the dead person's presence *knows* this is a hallucination.[12] To the Hawaiian, the vision is *real.* Center clients commonly "hear father's footsteps" . . . "see Grandma" . . . "smell my husband's body odor."

In Western culture, these hallucinations are considered entirely normal for about the first month of active grieving. In the Hawaiian, visions may continue much longer without being a sign of pathological grief. For visions are a part of Hawaii's heritage. (See *akākū, hihiʻo,* and *ʻūlāleo*). But in the early stages of grief, the experience is very much the same for anyone. Again we quote Dr. Haertig:

"When the relationship has been a very intense, a close and good one, the sense of the dead person's presence is a common experience. These experiences almost often come at night when one is in a more dissociated stage, when the unconscious is closer to the conscious, and when longing is the greatest. In mourning, usually the most difficult time is when one is going to sleep."

noho may not be pathological

Like visions, Hawaii's *noho* (possession by the spirit of a dead person), which is still common today, may or may not be a symptom of griefwork undone. Viewed outside its cultural context, spirit possession seems to be the ultimate in identification with the dead and, as such, is a symptom of pathological grief. However, *noho,* may be merely a culturally normal occurrence. (See discussion under *noho.*)

---

*Embalming is not required if the body is buried within 30 hours of death—Hawaii State Dept. of Health, 1971.

Hawaiians were, and are, uncommonly sensitive to the supernatural. Communication with the spirit of the dead took many forms. Visions, possession, talking to a spirit—these must be carefully weighed against every other factor before a diagnosis of pathological grief (or of a psychosis) is reached.

old Hawaii allowed
grief expression

In many ways, Hawaii's culture carried the message, "Go ahead. It's all right to grieve." Everybody excused the *pupule* behavior of excessive sorrow. *Uwēs* were loud. The very muscles expressed grief in *pa'i a uma*. Society gave full approval to uninhibited mourning. And the pace of Hawaiian life gave time to grieve.

"Sometimes, quite a while after the burial, a person would go to the grave and throw himself over it and wail and cry with abandon," recalls Mrs. Pukui.

"N_____ did a lot of wailing at the funeral parlor—but he continued to go to the grave and wail for a week," reads a 1970 case report.

today, grief is
hushed, hurried

The client was a fortunate exception. Today grief is frequently hurried up or hushed. The widow may be allowed to "break down" at the funeral, but within hours, well-meaning persons are advising her to "be strong for the sake of the children" . . . "keep busy" . . . "don't dwell on the past." Society is embarrassed at a man's tears. Grief periods are defined by the calendar and the time-clock. Standard union contracts in Hawaii allow three days off without pay loss when death occurs in a worker's immediate family.* Overlooked today is the basic truth: You must first "let go" so you can eventually "pull yourself—and your life—together."

incomplete grief
in Hawaii's past

Though Hawaii's mourning tradition was healthfully expressive, not all Hawaiians of the past grieved successfully.

Hawaii's remedy for prolonged, excessive grief was *ho'olana* (to float—float away) or, less literally, to go away. Relatives took the mourner on a visit, perhaps to another island. This was done specifically so the bereaved person would no longer see the grave of the loved dead one. Hawaii believed that constant yearning and "calling to" the dead kept the spirit hovering near the grave. Whether *ho'olana* was a way of detaching oneself from the dead, or whether it was an undesirable flight from the reality of loss, we do not know.

Hawaii's custom of considering another person, usually a child, as a *pani hakahaka* (replacement) for a dead person, suggests grief work blocked from the start. Often a baby was named for a dead relative and cast in a psychological mold of the deceased's personality. (See case examples in *inoa*.) This exists today—and it is not limited to Hawaii. Everybody knows the

---

*Hawaii Employers Council information, 1971.

142

widowed mother who molds a son or even daughter into becoming the "man of the house."

'unihipili was
griefwork blocked

Hawaii's *'unihipili* was notably a ritual form of denied or deficient grief work.

In *'unihipili,* relatives kept, deified, ritually fed and talked to a bone, other body part or close possession of a recently deceased person. The bone became the means of summoning the relative's spirit, who obeyed commands of the *kahu* (master). (See *'unihipili* listing.)

Without any deification, bones of the deceased might be kept and cherished, usually by a bereaved lover. (Discussed under *iwi.*)

Both practices used objects to represent and reinforce the mourner's denial of separation from the deceased. The survivor, unable to accept reality, retained the dead as a still-existing presence in his mind and emotions. This, in any culture, is a basic of incomplete grief work or pathological grief.

But even the bone-cherishing lover might, more healthfully, complete his delayed grief work. Historian Malo implied this when he wrote, "These parts ... were preserved by the fond lover until such times as love came to an end ..."[13]

'oki, breaking the
tie with the dead

The culture also provided ways to *'oki* (sever) this tie with the *'unihipili* spirit. The immediate rationale was that the spirit could get out of control and harm others. Yet, in incidents when the *'unihipili* tie was more a vague, emotional communication, *'oki* was pronounced, and the spirit of the dead told to go away forever. (See listing, *'oki.*)

Even in the 1970's, an occasional Hawaiian has accused an older relative of keeping an *'unihipili* object. Many Hawaiians, including teenagers, use the phrase in an abstract sense of emotional clinging to or calling back the beloved dead. One woman related:

"... it was in the *ho'oponopono** that I found out that it [emotional-mystic disturbance] was *'unihipili* ... it was my *hānai*+ mother ... My *kahuna pule* [minister] told me to take the silverware and the glass dishes that had been my *hānai* mother's and throw them deep in the ocean. So I did."

If casting possessions into ocean depths shocks the Western mind, then "think Hawaiian" for a moment. Property with *'unihipili* significance (even, long ago, the flesh of the dead) traditionally was put into the sea, or sometimes burned or buried, as a conscious way of breaking the tie between living and the dead.

"You row far out and throw it into the sea—*and you never look back.*" So Mrs. Pukui summarizes the belief.

"There must be a separation, a detachment from the dead one," says modern Western psychiatry. "Without this, grief work cannot be completed."

---

*Prayerful family council to correct wrongs that disturbed health or personal and family relationships.

+Adoptive in all but the legal sense.

Center case files show that many present-day Hawaiians have not "done their grief work." This is not surprising, for repressive ways have largely replaced Hawaii's expressive mourning customs. This may be doubly inhibiting for Hawaiians inter-married with Filipinos, Chinese, Portuguese, Puerto Ricans, Koreans and Samoans.* All once wailed openly in bereavement;[14] many have discontinued the old practice.

therapy: revival
of active grief

Therapy with Hawaiian clients is basically the same as with any ethnic group. The therapist helps the bereaved person to "re-grieve." Memories of the dead person are deliberately revived. Tears and reminiscences are encouraged. Hostility toward the dead and guilt centered around the death are brought out into the open. Much of this can be done by a social worker or nurse trained in these techniques, or by the family physician if he can take the time. Clergymen may be the greatest help—or hindrance—depending on their knowledge of the grief process. As one researcher on grief points out:

"While ... [religious measures] have helped many mourners ... comfort alone does not provide adequate assistance ... He [bereaved] has to accept the pain of the bereavement. He has to review his relationships with the deceased ... he will have to express his sorrow and sense of loss."[15]

Long-existing, deeply buried grief is more apt to require psychiatric help. (Or to rephrase it, often such grief is not disclosed as a trouble-cause until psychiatric therapy is in progress.) One Center client who began therapy about a year and a half ago is just now concluding delayed grief work for his wife who died nine years ago.

Revisiting the grave is sometimes used as a way of stimulating active grieving. Unfortunately, this is sometimes blocked. One caseworker states:

"I've had cases come up when N_____ (a minister) and the whole little Hawaiian congregation have done everything they could to discourage visiting the grave. Instead they tell the mourner things like 'don't talk about it anymore' ... 'try to forget it.'"

Hawaiians often feel
they caused death

Some of the usual components of intense grief seem to be given unusual importance by Hawaiians. One is the "Somehow I caused the death" guilt. Hawaiians have always viewed sickness and death as the result of someone's mistaken or malicious behavior. Statements like "I brought on the stroke that killed him" or "Grandma died because I took her *hānai* child away" are common. The guilt burden is especially heavy when old Hawaiian beliefs are reinforced by a fundamentalist religious faith.

There may be guilt-laden distress over "unfinished business." Examples: The funeral went against the deceased's wishes. The mourner did not change his name *(inoa)* as the deceased had asked. So conscience prods.

Its prodding may even aid effective grief work, as in this case:

---

*Samoans once used professional wailers, and wailing was a formalized part of mourning. Today wailing is often done but only as a spontaneous grief expression.

"I wore Aunty's pretty dresses after she died, though she hadn't ever said I could.* But I felt uncomfortable . . . So I burned them all."

Call it obeying conscience. Call it making peace with Hawaiian tradition. It comes out the same; another step is taken towards detaching oneself from the dead.

**death anniversary
a grief stimulant**

Techniques to stimulate re-grieving may be especially effective on an anniversary of the death. Unfinished grief with all its memories is most apt to be revived then. Says one psychiatrist, ". . . the turning point in acknowledging the symptoms is often an anniversary of the death."[16] Even today Hawaiians sometimes hold the first-year feast. Families of multi-cultural background may combine this with corresponding Filipino, Korean, or Chinese or Japanese Buddhist observances. Center caseworkers have put this period of planning and holding the memorial feast to therapeutic use.

As grief work nears completion, the vivid image of the dead person becomes gradually less clear. A young Hawaiian girl seems to have described this process in the most Hawaiian of ways, a vision.

Her caseworker reports:

"For several months after her mother died, Nalani used to 'call her mother back' and they would talk together. Later, she began seeing a mist. To her this mist was—still is—her mother. In recent months when she sees the mist, it breaks up, fragments itself and scatters. She's very upset about this—not about seeing the mist—but because the mist is breaking up."

**conscious image of dead
fragments as grief ends**

Our psychiatric consultant suggests:

"If all the other indications in the girl's progress validate it, then we can think of this scattering of the mist as one very Hawaiian expression that a healing process is underway. Nalani herself is worried that her mother is going away. Nalani senses this in the changes of her symbolic mist. It is becoming vague bits and pieces. This is how conscious memory of a person is gradually lost. We remember fragments—color of hair or eyes, sound of the voice, a certain trait of personality—but not the total person. And we may struggle to recall exactly how this whole person looked and acted, and we can't. This is a part of the normal ending of grief; a signal that we are about ready to begin living emotionally in the present, not the past.

"All that is emotionally unhealthy in Nalani tries to cling to her mother. All that is healthy in Nalani is ready to make her farewell permanent."

Or, to phrase it within the connotation of our title word for grief, Nalani's *kaumaha* or heavy weight is being replaced by *maha* or relief.

Psychiatry says Nalani's "grief work" is ending.

"Old Hawaii," says Mrs. Pukui, "always sensed that 'weight' is followed by 'relief.' That grief is not perpetual. It must end. But while it lasts, it is a painful—and a necessary—part of life."

---

*Wearing such clothing was against Hawaiian tradition.

attitude toward death
the vocabulary of death

Life's ultimate mystery—death. How did Hawaiians feel about their own personal certainty of eventual death?

Of course, we do not know. We can speculate. Among these speculations are: The probability that among *ali'i* and warriors of old worry about bone disposal may have overshadowed fears of dying. The great concern was that the bones were hidden, so they could not be desecrated. How a man died may also have outweighed death anxiety. For a man must die bravely. Even a slain enemy was honored if he had fought with courage to the end. One theory of the old *kauwā* (slave) caste is that they were cowards who allowed themselves to be defeated and taken prisoner.

How the ordinary man, woman or child faced death is not really known. Handed-down legends, a basis of Hawaii's first written history, are made of heroic events.

Certainly, Hawaii's culture provided ways to dodge or deal with the idea of one's own death. Belief in eternal reunion with one's ancestors in *Pō* must have been vastly reassuring to family-conscious Hawaii. And while portents *(hō'ailonas)* and sorcerer's spells brought death fears into sharp focus, rituals to forestall the death-fate obscured or eased the fears.

Mourning and burial rites had another function besides that of expressing grief. Rituals of detachment from the dead and the comforting solidarity of the funeral feast emphasized the feeling "but we are alive" for the mourners.

Each person's emotional view of personal death was apparently shaped by individuality. One daring young *ali'i* might even wager his own life in the *he'e hōlua* (sled riding) races.* Battles were almost a way of life. Yet the culture never risked death in mutilating puberty rites. One individual might become the "death companion" by deliberately starving to death beside the body of a beloved person. A few Hawaiians committed suicide, usually so they would join another in eternity. Yet many more employed all the arts of the *kahuna* to cure ills and keep death at a distance. Ambivalent emotions, known universally, were expressed in Hawaiian ways.

euphemisms for
death & burial

The idea of death was frequently softened by using the word *moe* (sleep). Phrases like the following were—and still are—used:

"Hiamoe i ka make—to sleep in death."

"Hoa moe—sleeping companion" or, less euphemistically, "companion in death."

"Moe kau a ho'oilo—to sleep summer and winter." The "sleep of death."

"Moe lepo—sleep in earth or earth-sleeper." The term was used to describe death and burial, and literally, a person who went to bed unbathed or with dirty feet and "slept dirty."

Euphemisms alone may not indicate any great shrinking from the idea of death, for old Hawaii spoke in metaphors. Love, friendship, jokes, even insults were expressed in verbal imagery.

---

*Literally *he'e* (slide) + *holua* (sled). The exciting sport of sliding down slopes on sled or toboggan-like vehicles.

Folk customs seem to point more reliably to dread of death. Mrs. Pukui remembers from personal experiences that:

A pit or hole *(lua)* with its reminder of the grave must never be left empty and uncovered. A banana stalk, symbolic of man, was traditionally put in the *lua* before filling it. Today, if the dog digs a hole in the yard, a Hawaiian is apt to fill it promptly.

String games, like making "cat's cradle" with string, were not allowed in the house or after nightfall. The fingers, interweaving string, suggest the motions of a dying person fumbling with the bed sheet.*

Hiding games were forbidden in the house or outdoors at night.

Children were not allowed to "play dead."

Children should fly kites only in open spaces and never at night. The old belief was that Death might seize the kite and thereby claim the youngster.

Pounding of nails should never be done at night. This is reminiscent of making a coffin. Formerly, Hawaiians made the coffin at home, often during the night to prepare for the next day's funeral.

A howling dog means somebody is going to die or is dying.

A scent, smelled out of normal setting, warns of death or danger. Magnolias smelled while one is ocean swimming is an example.

Plus many other *hō'ailonas* or signs listed in the English cross-index.

Traditional or a multi-culture mix, death portents are often mentioned by Center clients. Sometimes they are mentioned lightly; but more often seriously. Sometimes they are related by the culturally-imbued old—and surprisingly often, by the young or adolescent. Sometimes portents are perceived on the conscious level. Sometimes they are disguised in the language of dreams. One person may view a sign as a warning of his own death. Another may use it to project his own death fears onto another.

Sometimes, as in dreams, the obvious death portent may symbolize something quite different.

For the caseworker, physician or psychiatrist, it seems important that these portents are not shrugged off as "just Hawaiian superstition." Rather, they may be clues to be listened to with special attention and an understanding of their Hawaiian significance. For the portent and how the individual himself interprets it may really be a way of saying "I think I am going to die" . . . "I want to die" . . . "I wish someone else would die" . . . or "I am still very much attached to or even identifying with someone who has died."

NOTES AND REFERENCES

1. Pukui. *Polynesian Family System in Ka'u,* pp. 156-157.
2. Kamakau. *Ruling Chiefs of Hawaii,* p. 255.
3. Ibid, p. 422.

---

*A Hawaiian staff member was absent-mindedly fashioning a string design at a night meeting, July, 1971, when another Hawaiian politely asked her to stop. "It's all right in the daytime, but not at night," she was told.

4. "Death, Lying-in-State and Obsequies of Queen Liliuokalani," Last Sovereign of Hawaii. *Thrum's Hawaiian Annual*, 1918. pp. 102-109.

5. *Polynesian Family System in Ka'u*, p. 154.

6. Ibid., p. 155.

7. Fornander. *Collection of Hawaiian Antiquities*, Vol. 5, 2nd Series, p. 572.

8. Kamakau. *Ka Po'e Kahiko: The People of Old*, p. 35.

9. *Collection of Hawaiian Antiquities*, p. 572.

10. Kautz. "Funerals of Hawaii Island, A Study of Cultural Lag in Ethnic Accommodations," p. 94.

11. Ibid., p. 180.

12. Parkes, "The First Year of Bereavement," *Psychiatry*, Vol. 33, No. 4, pp. 444-467.

13. Malo. *Hawaiian Antiquities*, p. 99.

14. Except Samoans, information from "Funerals on Hawaii Island." Samoa—Church College of Hawaii informant, 1971.

15. Lindemann. "Symptomatology and Management of Acute Grief," *American Journal of Psychiatry*, Vol. 101, p. 147.

16. Volkan. "Typical Findings in Pathological Grief," *The Psychiatric Quarterly*, Vol. 44, No. 2, p. 238.

OTHER REFERENCES

Caplan. "An Approach to the Study of the Family Mental Health," typescript of lecture given in Honolulu, 1957, and notes taken at Caplan seminar, 1957.

Hoebel. "The Life Cycle," *Man in the Primitive World*, pp. 285-286.

Malinowski. *Magic, Science and Religion*, pp. 47-51.

Ellis. *Polynesian Researches—Hawaii*, pp. 174-182.

Volkan. "Re-grief Work Techniques in Normal and Pathological Grief Reactions, A Guide for the Family Physician," *Virginia Medical Monthly*, Vol. 93, No. 2, pp. 651-656.

Clayton. "A Study of Normal Bereavement," *American Journal of Psychiatry*, Vol. 125, pp. 168-178.

mālama pū'olo—keeping of bones or other objects, usually wrapped in *tapa* as a wrapped "bundle," for some mystic purpose.

Deriv: *mālama*, to keep or care for.
pū'olo, bundle.
Lit. "keeping a bundle."

Mālama pū'olo in its oldest meaning referred to keeping bones or supernaturally imbued objects for use in recalling and controlling a spirit.

One such practice was the keeping and ritual feeding of the bones of a dead relative or close, loved person. These bones were considered deified. They were cherished and cared for by one keeper *(kahu)* who was able to call forth the spirit and send it forth on portentous missions. This is discussed under *'unihipili*.

Another old practice, usually by sorcerers, was keeping some wood of the "poison trees" of Molokai as a way of summoning the *akualele* (flying god) and dispatching him on errands of death and destruction. See *akualele*.

148

A third mystic, but possibly later, *mālama pū'olo* practice was that of keeping animal bones from a feast or the bones from the first fish caught with a new net and using them to feed, in mystic fashion, a spirit.

Today, "bundle keeping" is sometimes mentioned in its *'unihipili* meaning. More often, vague references are made to "keeping something Hawaiian," or "having Hawaiian things" hidden.

Center clients who report that someone in the house is "keeping Hawaiian things" do so with fear. For them, prayer, blessing of the house, and Mrs. Pukui's traditional directions for *pū'olo* disposal may operate together to lessen fears, associations and memories that surround the "bundle."

"To get rid of a *pū'olo,* you row far out and throw it into the sea," she related.

"And you never look back."

mana, māna and mānā.

mana—power possessed by man, but originating in the supernatural, and thus always imbued with a mystic quality. (Also six other meanings, not within the behavioral science context.)

māna—trait or characteristic.

mānā—dry; desert.

Deriv: unknown.

"Please, would you explain *mana?*" I asked Mary Kawena Pukui, and my "a's" were as harsh and flat as Kansas farm land in a drought.

Mrs. Pukui smiled to soften the needed criticism.

"My dear, which one? *Mānā?* Or *māna?* Or *mana?*"

And so I learned that the first thing to know about *mana* is how to pronounce it.

There are three words spelled alike, but given different meanings by vocal intonation, or by printing symbols, as they now apply to the Hawaiian language.

mānā with two marks is "dry"

One is *mānā* with both syllables given macrons. Make it rhyme with the last two syllables of "marijuana," hold the last "a" the merest trifle—and, as far as the non-Hawaiian tongue can manage, you have it. This *mānā* means "dry," "arid" or "desert." It now bows out of this book.

māna, one mark, means "trait"

The second *māna* has a macron over the first "a". In a rough equivalent of sound subtleties, it rhymes with "fawn-uh". This *māna* first meant an actual practice, that of an adult chewing food, then putting it in the mouth of a

149

young child. Or, similarly, chewing the mass of kava *(Piper methysticum)* to prepare *'awa** or *kava* for drinking. The food or substance so chewed was called *māna*. The close contact of mother or grandmother who put food in a child's mouth led to symbolic connotations. *Māna* took on the more abstract meaning of traits, absorbed by the child, just as he took and absorbed the pre-masticated food.

"If we thought a child got his happy disposition from his mother, or had his grandfather's temper, or if he tilted his head the way an uncle did, then we said he *'ku i ka māna'*, he 'fits into the pattern.'[1] Or we might say 'that's so and so's *māna'* or just 'that was absorbed from the mouth.'" Mrs. Pukui explains.

(Western psychoanalytic terminology describes much the same process of identifying with another as "incorporation"—which is exactly what is done when food is taken in the body.)

Putting food from the mouth of an elder into that of a child also took on the idea of learning imparted. For before they had a written language, Hawaiians passed on knowledge by word of mouth. The word *haumāna* means "pupil," one who so takes in knowledge.†

unmarked mana
means "power"

The third *mana* has no diacritical marking. The "a's" sound about like "o" in "above." This *mana* rhymes, more or less, with "pun-uh." Though the word has at least seven definitions, only its primary, often-used meaning is considered here. We are concerned with *mana,* the concept of "power" bestowed directly or indirectly from a supernatural source. The concept—sometimes with a change of terms—exists throughout Polynesia.[2]

Mana has been defined as the existence of and the very aura of power. As authority, not the petty imposing of will on another, but an inherent quality of command and leadership. As a reservoir of strength. In 20th Century terms, as personal magnetism or a high impact personality. As the charisma of a Roosevelt or a Kennedy—or a Hitler or a Castro. More figuratively, as a magnetic field or a mental-spiritual battery.[3]

primary source
of mana was gods

In Hawaiian belief, *mana* could be emitted from a rock, the bones of the dead, the medicine that cures or the potion that kills. *Mana,* in man or object,** owed its primary origin to the gods. While "personal magnetism" in the Western sense is entirely a human attribute, Hawaii's *mana* was a human quality tinged with the supernatural.

Closest to the gods and imbued with the highest *mana* were the ruling *ali'i* (aristocracy). Kings viewed *mana* as a genetic inheritance from god to king to king's descendant. (Rule by "divine right" was not limited to Europe and Asia.) In Hawaii, says historian David Malo, "It was firmly believed that the genius, power and inspiration [*mana*] of a king was like that of a god."[4]

---

*Hawaii's ceremonial drink.

†More literally, one whom food is laid before. From *hau,* to lay before; *māna;* pre-masticated food.

**mana* in one's shadow is discussed under *aka.*

No ruler wanted this *mana* to be diluted. And so, ranking *ali'i* married ranking *ali'i*, ideally someone within the family. A king's marriage to his sister was not incest as the West knows it, but a positive way to insure that high *mana* was reinforced and passed down to heir and future ruler.

Mana as a personal attribute such as courage, skill or wisdom, might be ingested by a kind of ritual cannibalism. For example, among the *ali'i* of long ago, a man's eye might be scooped out and eaten. In a magical, symbolic way, the *ali'i* who consumed the eye thereby absorbed the quality of the eye, the *'ike* (seeing, knowing). In *lua* (hand to hand) combat, a warrior might eat some part of his brave but defeated enemy, so that he might incorporate in himself some of the man's courage. Legend tells that Kamehameha's mother craved and ate the eye of a shark during her pregnancy, thereby taking in and giving to her infant, the daring and fierceness of the shark.

What became of a person's *mana* after death? Hawaiian tradition answers, both in subtleties and specifics.

Some of one's *mana* lingered on in a man's name *(inoa)*, in his bones *(iwi)*, in the clothing that had been close to his body, in hair or nails or body excretions. But a man took his great "storehouse" of *mana* with him in death—unless he specifically passed it on to a descendant.

In this "death bed" passing on of *mana,* Hawaii made a distinction between two types of powers. One was the diffused, hard-to-define personal power and authority. The other was the specific talent or aptitude, such as the ability to heal, to prophesy, to dance the hula superbly, fish with marked success or build the finest canoes.

Passing on the general, diffused power was done by spoken declaration. As the Hawaiian felt death approaching, he called the *'ohana* (family clan) together. Usually after prayers, the dying person then "willed" his *mana,* much as money, property and family heirlooms are willed to heirs today. To the Hawaiian, the *'ōlelo* (word; verbal statement) was both mystic force and binding contract.

Passing on the more specific *mana* of specialized talent was a quite different procedure. This was called *hā*. Mrs. Pukui describes the old and solemn ritual:

"A person about to die expelled his breath into his chosen successor's mouth. With this, the *mana* that made him an expert in an art or craft passed directly to one particular person, not to the family in general. The *mana* imparted by the *hā* kept the art alive."

The ritual could be varied. "The dying person could *hā* instead, right on the *manawa* [fontanel] of the head."

(*Hā* is discussed under separate listing).

non-specific mana
could be divided

Specific *mana* transmitted by *hā* went to one person only. However, a dying man either could pass on his general *mana* to one person, or he could divide it. Mrs. Pukui explains that "He could say, 'To you, Kimo, and to you, Nani, and you, Pua, I give equal parts of my *mana.'*"

An early legend indicates this parceling out of *mana* was once explained, if not practiced, in terms of dividing the actual body. So goes the story of Hekili, the thunder god who took human form and lived on Maui:

"Everyone knew Hekili as a man who had *mana,* so that everything he said was fulfilled. He had but to speak to the thunder and lighting and they avenged him instantly upon his enemies . . . People believed him to be a man with *mana* of a god and they relied upon him as a man of *mana* and as a *kahu* (keeper or master) for the gods of the heavens . . . when they found that this *kahu* of great *mana* was dead, they took the body and divided it into small pieces and distributed the pieces to various parts around Maui. These became their [the people's] *kuleana* [portion or territory] to worship the thunder god Kānehekili in human form."[5]

Passing on *mana,* specific or general was not obligatory. A dying person could withhold his *mana* and take it with him back to the *aumākua* [ancestor gods].

Tradition held that passed-on *mana* could be increased with prayers and appreciative use. *Mana* of many individuals could be built up as a kind of massed group strength and imparted to a sick or troubled one. This was done prayerfully in *kūkulu kumuhana.* (See listing.)

the "rule of mana":
misuse it and lose it

Conversely, *mana,* abused or misused, could be diminished or even lost. In fact, there was a way to hasten this loss. If an individual so abused his handed-down power that everyone in the family was miserable, the family could pray and ask the deceased *kupuna* (family elder) to take back his *mana.* If a chief used his *mana* to oppress his people, the people might eventually kill him. For *mana* that grew weak could be overcome by others' stronger *mana.*

This "misuse it and you lose it" axiom applied to any kind of *mana,* general or specific, good or wicked. The medical *kahuna* who prescribed carelessly and neglected the ritual prayers over his medicines would find eventually he could not heal. The sorcerer who failed to pray to his sorcerer gods, recited his spells in slipshod fashion, or killed indiscriminately would find his black art could no longer kill.*

Was *mana,* therefore, a conceptual canopy under which gathered many timeless and universal observations?

---

*The sorcerer *(kahuna 'anā'anā)* killed "on assignment." He might be asked to destroy a contender for authority among the *ali'i,* for example. Always he was supposed to kill for a reason. Indiscriminate killing for the sheer lust to kill made the sorcerer a public danger. Sooner or later this danger was recognized and somebody would kill the sorcerer.—M.K.P.

Not entirely. For the unique and essential quality of *mana* was its mystical origin. *Mana* and the purely human power of other cultures operate along parallel lines, but they are not identical concepts. In the Western view, a 15th Century Polynesian uprising against a chief who misused his *mana,* and a 20th Century overthrow of a Sukarno who abused his power seem to be the same process of observing abuse, perceiving demagogue rather than hero, and massing group power to take action. Certainly, the result is the same. The oppressor is deposed. The difference is that in Hawaiian thought the Supernatural took away the misused *mana* and strengthened the *mana* of the oppressed.

Or, as Western culture views it, a specific talent grows rusty or is lost when a writer stops writing or turns out only space-fillers, or when a singer consistently mistreats his vocal equipment. In the Hawaiian view, the *kahuna* who grew careless eventually lost his ability to cure—but it was the Supernatural, his *aumakua,* who took away his special healing *mana.*

Though Hawaii's *mana* was a god-given power, man often attributed it to another man. Sometimes mistakenly. History tells that Hawaiians believed Captain Cook was the god Lono, with all the high *mana* of the god. When he bled they beheld a mere man, subject to injury and deserving of death.[6]

("But the Emperor isn't wearing beautiful new clothes. He hasn't any clothes on at all!". So perceived the clear eye of childhood in the Western world's legendary tale.)[7]

Therefore, does *mana,* like beauty, "exist in the eye [or mind] of the beholder?"

Very often. *Mana* seems to be the attribute of an already strong personality to which others have injected, or projected, their own ideas of or wishes for strengths or powers from a mystic source. Everyone has some *mana.* The Kamehameha's of the world have high *mana;* the Mr. Milquetoasts do not. The strong, integrated personality, the one already endowed with *mana,* is the natural recipient for more *mana* others attribute to him. The unhealthy but dominant personality can also have *mana,* and so catch or manipulate others' imaginations that they invest the warped one with their ideas of magic-tinged power. (See *waha 'awa* for examples.) And, with an important exception, uncertain, indecisive or guilt-ridden persons are most likely to attach or instill *mana* into another person, or even into a place or thing. The exception comes when the culture has "fixed" *mana* to a certain person, place or object. In that case, if Kimo believes a certain person has power, or a certain rock is sacred, this does not say anything significant about Kimo—except that he agrees with an accepted idea.

Today, a considerable number of Center clients talk about *mana* or "power" as a very real influence in their lives. A few assign *mana* to objects. One old lady keeps stones in her home because "they have *mana.*" Several wear or place *ti* leaves in the house, because *ti* has protective *mana.* The old persons take comfort from this *mana*. The social caseworker can show respect by not touching or commenting on objects that might be *mana*-filled.

A few clients reveal that, "I have *mana*, but I don't use it because I could hurt people"... "I have the power to heal."... "My *mana* keeps me safe."

mana and
The Pentecost

Many clients who believe they have *mana* have blended or reinforced the Hawaiian concept with Pentecostal beliefs. "I have *mana*" and "I have gifts of the Holy Ghost" may be said almost in the same breath.

Belief in one's own *mana*, just as seeing visions, may indicate merely a strong identification with the Hawaiian past. An individual may feel the family *mana* has come down to him as a kind of privileged responsibility. This may be a memory, recovered in old age. Or, *mana* claims, together with other symptoms, may point to a delusional state. Often, the person who says he has great *mana* (or Pentecostal gifts) is making an unconscious statement about himself and his relationships with others. His unspoken message may be:

mana claims
and ego needs

"I have a real need to feel powerful. Or wise. Or benevolent."... "Here I am taking charity, on welfare. But I can give, too. I can heal the caseworker's headache; solve the public health nurse's problems."... Or, less nobly, "I really want to hurt, embarrass and diminish others, but I hold myself in check"... Or, "I'm afraid of what I could do if I let loose—so don't pick a fuss with me!"... Or, "It's fun to see the family jump through hoops when I speak out."

These implicit statements inspire some questions: Why this need to feel powerful? Why this desire to hurt or push others around? Why this need to see yourself as divinely inspired healer, rather than ordinary Mrs. Housewife? Who has hurt, deflated or pushed you around?

Belief that one has beneficent *mana* seldom causes anyone to seek therapeutic help. Belief that one has or is the victim of destructive *mana* may.

sorcerer's mana
is often feared

Center clients who fear wicked, harmful *mana* in themselves or others usually think this "came down" in some vague fashion from a sorcerer *(kahuna 'anā'anā)* ancestor. Most often the client believes that some relative is using this *mana* to hurt or threaten him.

"Aunty (or Mother-in-Law or Grandfather) has this *mana*. That's why I am sick (or injured or unsuccessful or in jail)." Such is the *mana* theme with variations that range from alibi for failure or avoidance of testing abilities, to more deeply buried fears and feelings.

When client or patient talks frankly about *mana*, the therapist's cue may be to discuss this fear within the Hawaiian context:

How did Aunty get her *mana?* Through *hā?* Through a deathbed declaration of intention? Did Aunty train and practice to keep her specific *mana* strong? Or is she abusing and thus losing her *mana?* In the light of this traditional information, does Aunty really possess any harmful *mana?*

If the client clings to the conviction that Aunty does indeed possess terrifying *mana,* he can be reminded of the rituals Hawaiians use to make this *mana* go away or become ineffective. *Pule* (prayer), for example, should not be forgotten.

This does not mean that every "Hawaiian problem" calls for "Hawaiian therapy." Rather, Hawaiian remedial measures and the techniques of modern Western psychiatry and social casework often work well together. In fact, they may be pretty much the same thing, given a different external guise. For example, during *ho'oponopono* for anyone under a sorcerer's power, the victim tried to recall any conscious misdeed or innocent error that might have brought the spell upon him. Western therapy seeks the self-realization of both specific guilts and diffused, irrelevant guilt feelings that lead to acceptance of undeserved punishment or submission to undue domination.

NOTES AND REFERENCES

1. *Ku i ka māna,* "he fits into the pattern." The more literal meaning is "the *māna* stands." *Ku in its meaning "stand or to stand" was given the connotation of standing unchanged, needing no changes.* Even a garment might be described as being *ku* or fitting so well that it "stands as it is."

2 and 3. *Mana* throughout Polynesia: *Mana* defined:
Goldman. *Ancient Polynesian Society,* pp. 10-13, 418.
Hoebel. *Man in the Primitive World,* p. 407.
Harding. *Cultures of the Pacific,* p. 210.
Firth. "The Analysis of *Mana:* An Empirical Approach," *Cultures of the Pacific,* pp. 316-332.
Ratzel. *Religion in Oceania,* p. 301.
Fornander. *An Account of the Polynesian Race,* Vol. I, p. 128.
Oliver. *The Pacific Islands,* pp. 72-73.

4. Malo. *Hawaiian Antiquities,* p. 135.

5. Kamakau. *Ka Po'e Kahiko: The People of Old,* p. 69.

6. Kuykendall. *The Hawaiian Kingdom 1778-1854,* pp. 16-19, and *An Account of the Polynesian Race,* pp. 157-200.

7. Anderson. *The Emperor's New Clothes.*

na'au—intestines, bowels, gut. By association, character, intelligence, emotions. Later, also "heart."
Deriv: unknown.

Traditionally, the intellect and emotions were thought to exist in the intestinal regions. (The head was dwelling place for spirits, especially beneficent ones such as the *aumākua* or family ancestor gods.) Therefore *na'au,* used alone or in word combinations, carried abstract meanings such as intelligence, character and emotional states. Though association of emotions with the viscera was a pre-missionary concept, the similarity with Biblical phrases such as "bowels of compassion" is striking. Newer versions of the Bible now use the word "heart;" the Hawaiian language has also added "heart" to the meanings of *na'au.*

In modern terms, "gut emotions" is close to the Hawaiian *na'au* concept.

**"Nāu ke keiki
kukae a na'au"**

When Hawaiian parents gave their child to become the permanent foster child of relatives, they said, *"Nāu ke keiki kukae a na'au."* Translated literally it reads, "I give you this child, guts, contents and all." Actually it carried the idea of "I give you this child with all its present and potential qualities of intelligence and character and all its capabilities for love, hate, fear, courage, grief and happiness." The phrase, said in the hearing of others, made the agreement a permanent and binding one. The child was given outright. (See *hānai.*)

Na'au as the seat of abstract qualities is used in the following word combinations:

na'au ao—light *(ao)* inside the gut; therefore intelligence.

na'au ahonui—great breath *(ahonui)* in gut; patience.

na'au 'auwā—a loud wail *('auwā)* in gut; therefore great, overwhelming grief (usually expressed by wailing).

na'au 'ino—bad, harmful *('ino)* in gut; malicious, wicked.

na'au lua—two *(lua)* in gut; therefore undecided, unstable, inconstant.

na'au pō—darkness *(pō)* in gut; ignorance.

nahu akua—a bruise believed to be a bite inflicted by the spirit of a living member of the family. The bite was thought to foretell the death, not of the one so bruised, but of the relative whose spirit made the bruise.

Deriv: *nahu,* bite.
        akua, spirit, god, ghost.

Late one night, the phone rang in a Honolulu home. The son of the family was calling from his military base on the U.S. mainland. He had found on his skin *nahu akua,* the "spirit bite" that foretells the death of a relative. Now he was calling home to ask the dread question, "Who?" "Which one?"

Back across the Pacific came the answer. The young soldier's father was fatally ill. A question, prompted by a belief so old its origin is lost, had been answered in a message bounced from a satellite in space. *Nahu akua* had occurred in the year 1968.

What is this *nahu* (bite) of the *akua* (spirit)?

Mary Kawena Pukui describes it:

"It is a bruise, shaped like the mouth. Sometimes with teeth marks. And when you discover this bruise on your body, and you cannot figure out where it came from, then it is *nahu akua.*

"The *nahu* was made by the spirit of some relative who is in danger of death. The bite is the message that this relative—not yet identified—needs family prayers. The person bitten is not in any danger.

"But before you can pray," Mrs. Pukui points out, "you have to find out which family member to pray for. Which one is marked for death."

In 1968, the soldier away from home had the question answered by trans-Pacific telephone. In its traditional setting, *nahu akua* was really only the first

156

development in a total ritual for the entire *'ohana* (family, or extended family).

After the bite was discovered, the possibilities were narrowed down. A bite on the right side of the body indicated a male relative; on the left, a female. Above the waist meant a close relative; below meant a somewhat more distant one, perhaps an in-law.

Already members of the *'ohana* were gathering. Once brought together, each relative of the indicated sex would "try the bite for fit," by taking the gentlest of bites over the bruise. The one whose "bite" matched the spirit bite was designated the relative in danger of death.

Relatives who could not come had proxies appointed for them. Recalls Mary Pukui, "I remember when my aunt had the 'spirit bite,' I was the proxy biter."

Because she was then a small child, Mrs. Pukui's bite probably would not have matched any adult relative's bite. It is not known whether this was adult reasoning to spare a senior member this mark of fate. (The explanation given Mrs. Pukui was that because she was little, she could bite very gently.)

After a match of bruise shape and teeth marks pointed out the victim, the *'ohana* began to pray for him. Which, of course, was the ultimate purpose of the ritual. For the family *aumākua*, or ancestor gods, might be able to reverse the decision of doom and spare the victim from death.

Such was *nahu akua* and the concerted family action it precipitated. What caused the bite to appear? Was it something like the subcutaneous bleeding that may be induced by hypnosis, or that sometimes occurs in hysterical persons? Or was it a truly mystical phenomenon? Exactly the same questions have been asked of the stigmata appearing on the bodies of Christian saints. We leave both unanswered.

Mrs. Pukui confines her own interpretation to viewing the spirit bite as "a cry for help. One family member was saying 'I need your prayers. Do something. Act!'"

Certainly, *nahu akua* in its traditional context, accomplished just this purpose. For the entire *'ohana* joined in *kūkulu kumuhana*, the concentrated focus of family prayers, family concern and family support on the individual in need of such spiritual-emotional sustenance.

nīele—to ask seemingly irrelevant questions; annoyance at such questioning; exclamation of reproval to one asking such questions.

Deriv: contraction of *nīnau*, question; *ele*, senseless, "without rhyme or reason."

*"'Eha kēia?"** Does it hurt here?" This question makes sense to the Hawaiian being seen by a physician.

"What is your occupation?" "What did your grandfather die of?"

---

*Literally, "Hurt, this?" accompanied by touch or gesture.

"Where is your husband employed and what medical plan does he belong to?" These questions, unless the purpose for asking them is clearly explained, are *niele*. Just plain nosey. So rude one need not answer them.

"kaula'i na iwi i ka lā"
and
"holehole iwi"

To the tradition-imbued Hawaiian, questions about family relationships and health histories are more than rude. Answering such questions takes on the quality of *kaula'i na iwi i ka lā*, or even *holehole iwi*. Both were once actual practices. *Kaula'i na iwi i ka lā* was "bleaching the bones of one's ancestors in the sun." *Holehole iwi* was the grim preparatory step, literally removing or "stripping" the "flesh from the bones" of the dead body.

Today "drying the bones in the sun" means talking too freely about ancestors to non-family members. "Stripping the bones" is the more serious offense of airing the faults and weaknesses of relatives or ancestors to outsiders.

Traditionally, even the most distinguished *ali'i* (royal) Hawaiian did not chant his genealogy except on formal, specific request or when his "credentials" were needed when he traveled. Today one does not properly boast of *ali'i* ancestors; nor does one disclose the facts of Uncle Kimo who likes his liquor too well. Both fame and shame—in fact all family affairs—are discreetly kept within the family.

Though the traditional *kahuna lapa'au* or medical *kahuna* asked questions, the patient apparently recognized the relevance of questions to symptoms. Even the medical *kahuna's* inquiries into conduct and interpersonal relationships were known to be necessary, not *niele*. For how else could the illness be traced to possible sorcery or to an offended *aumakua* (ancestor god)?

Today's detailed medical histories, socio-economic inquiries and insurance requirement questionnaires are apt to seem inquisitive without cause. For example, a woman may not connect the question "how many children have you had?" with her general health or child-bearing future. She may view it instead as a rude query into economics and personal relationships within the family.

The 1968 *Studies in a Hawaiian Community** stress that Nanakuli residents feel it is better to handle illness within a circle of family and friends, and avoid the direct confrontation with doctor or dentist (and also with employment directors). One of the attributes Nanakuli residents list for a good doctor is that "he knows what your problem is after he gives you a physical examination so he doesn't have to ask you what's wrong." Here *niele* is not mentioned, but the traditional dislike for seemingly irrelevant questions seems to exist.

Mary Kawena Pukui adds her experience:

"Once a year, Eleanor Williamson and I go on a field trip to interview old Hawaiians and record the folkways and legends they tell us. We have learned always to write ahead to an acquaintance in each area who makes contacts for us. By the time we arrive, the persons we interview know who we are, have an idea of the types of questions we are going to ask, and, most impor-

---

Studies in a Hawaiian Community: Na Makamaka O Nanakuli, pp. 123-127.

tant, know *why* we are asking them. This makes the recording sessions easier."

Center caseworkers also find that resistant, evasive attitudes can be changed by explaining in advance why questions must be asked and how they apply to the problem at hand. For when the need for questioning is seen, both interrogator and the questions cease to be *"Auwe,* niele!"*

noho—possession by a spirit; one so possessed.

Deriv: original meanings included seat, or to sit, to dwell or dwelling place. In possession, the spirit "sits or dwells" in a person.

Noho is Hawaii's term for a worldwide phenomenon: the apparent mind and body possession of men and women by spirits, demons, gods, souls of ancestors, or even animals. A hop-skip-jump through time and geography reveals that:

In Mesopotamia around 2,000 B.C. some six thousand separate demons were supposed to possess the unwary. Europe knew possession through the Dark and Middle Ages and witnessed it in epidemic form during the Renaissance. Romans were possessed in Caesar's time. When Apollo entered into a seeress, the Greeks had a word for it. In Egypt, spirit invasion, long unknown, began around 1900. Foxes traditionally possessed the Japanese.** Chinese, with possession records going back to the 19th Century B.C., were visited by ancestral spirits. Indians, Thais, Burmese and Indonesians knew—and still experience—possessing spirits. Eskimos and Melanesians, Micronesians and Russians, Tongans and Tibetans have succumbed to the take-over of god or demon. In Africa, whole groups of middle aged women are possessed by the *saka* even today. In America's deep South, present day group possession is by the Holy Ghost. The Old Testament records possession (that of Saul) only once; the New Testament many times.

Just as man has been possessed down through history, so has the invading spirit been exorcised by Christ himself, by Catholic priest and Jewish rabbi; by Indonesian devil-dancer and Protestant minister; by Nichiren monk and Taoist *bonze;* by drumbeat and lyre, magic potion and whip's lash; by bell, book and candle; and, in 19th Century France, by the combined efforts of religion and the new science of clinical psychology.

In this global overview of spirit invasion and banishment, where does Hawaii fit?

First, a look at old Hawaii. The Hawaiian believed he could be *noho* by good spirits or bad; possession could be total or partial, but always temporary; spirits could possess spontaneously or by invitation.

**Auwe!* can express anything from mild dismay to strong annoyance, disgust or scorn.

**The fox was originally considered a form of deity, and possession by a fox was possession by a god. Later this connotation was lost and possession by a fox became zooanthrophy or animal possession.

haka, the
medium

Traditionally, inviting a good spirit to possess a chosen medium was a planned part of life in every well-run *'ohana* or family clan. Within each *'ohana* was a *haka*, or in Western terms, a "medium". The spirit in these invitational possessions was usually a family *aumakua* (ancestor-god) summoned to speak through the *haka*.

kahu was
spirit master

And here enters another family member, the chosen *kahu* or spirit-keeper who summoned the spirit.* This was done in a ritualized, prayerful ceremony or seance (but not in the darkened room of modern spiritualism). Once the *haka* was possessed, the spirit then spoke through him, using the vocal inflections and speech mannerisms of a departed family member.

The *kahu* could also send a spirit to possess a person without holding the seance ritual. The spirit sent in this case was usually a destructive one. Because it possessed a victim without warning, this was considered spontaneous *noho*.

Spontaneous possession traditionally could be by good spirits or bad. Often one's *aumakua* took possession spontaneously to help the troubled or ill. (See *kīheipua* and *ho'oūlu ia*)

Noho induced in the *haka* during a formal seance is apparently lost in the parade of years. Mary Kawena Pukui was witness to the decline of this possession-by-invitation. She reports:

"When I was about six [in 1901], my uncle thought I would make a good *haka* and tried to get me to be one . . . When I was ten, my mother took me to a session with a *haka* to get advice through this medium on why I would not eat pork . . . When I was around 20, I saw the last seance with *haka* and *kahu* in my personal experience."

What has come down from the past is belief in spontaneous possession. Here are three examples from Mrs. Pukui's family records and personal notes. The time range is a century, from 1850 to 1950. Recalls Mrs. Pukui:

"I have heard many times about the neighbor of my grand-uncle. This happened before I was born. The woman's little nephew had died at the age of nine. Uncle said the neighbor used to go into *noho* spells when she would talk and giggle like a child, and use the mannerisms of a little boy."

Or, after World War II, this incident in a rural, largely Hawaiian community where Mrs. Pukui was visiting:

". . . I could see, through the doorway, a girl about 17. She was looking in a mirror and talking, and it was as if she were two persons talking. She would say 'I don't want my hair combed that way. I want it this way.' Then she went on combing her hair, and then she said, 'I'm going to slap your face.' And with that she'd slap her own face. Then she said, 'You slapped my face. I'm going to slap yours, too.' And then she would slap her face on the other side.

---

*See listings, *haka* and *kahu*.

"Later, her father told me, 'Poor Lucy. She and her sister, Luella* were twins. When they were still very young, Luella died. Lucy was very sick. About two years later—Lucy was three or so then—she made me mad and I told her I felt like chopping off her head.[1] A few days later we noticed she was acting like two persons, herself and her twin sister.'

"The head-slapping, hair-combing behavior, the father said, happened intermittently through the years."

Or, this example, from the late 1940's:

"This happened in Kalihi and it was told to me by a haole Mormon elder," Mrs. Pukui relates. "He was called in when a young woman began screaming and crying and tearing her clothing. He believed she was possessed, so he called for the spirit to come out, just about as it is described in the Bible. The woman became calm, for only a few minutes. Then she became even wilder. The elder thought this must be possession by many spirits and he didn't feel he could handle this. So he sent for an old Hawaiian who was also a Mormon elder. He came and prayed over the woman. Then he asked, 'Where are you from?' And the woman answered 'From Molokai.' 'Why did you come?' asked the elder. 'Because she turned down a marriage proposal from one of our family.' 'We?' inquired the elder, 'How many are you?' 'Nineteen' came the answer.

"And then the elder commanded each spirit, one by one, to come out. And to each one he said, 'Now go back to where you came from. Leave the girl alone.' After this the girl was calm and normal."

All three examples meet what we might call a "cultural criterion" of *noho ia* or total possession: someone else speaks through the person possessed. As anthropologist Martha Beckwith wrote:

"... the person possessed speaks, not as he is accustomed, but in the character and words of the spirit whose medium he is. His utterances are not his own."[2]

A further provision or cultural criterion is told by Mrs. Pukui.

**possession by
spirit of dead**

"A living person cannot possess; only a spirit—either an *aumakua* or *'unihipili* or maybe an *akua*. But a living person can sometimes send a spirit to take possession of a person."

(The *aumakua* was the god-spirit of a remote ancestor. The *'unihipili* was the deified spirit of a more recently deceased relative. The *akua* was an impersonal god. In most cases, the possessing spirit was believed to be in one way or another that of a person, related or emotionally close, who had died.)

The third (1940's) example with its veritable population explosion of spirits points to Hawaiian belief in multiple possession. Mrs. Pukui believes that multiple possession was known here long before the first Bibles with their passages about "possessing legions" were brought to Hawaii.

In this case of the 19 disturbing spirits, both the spirits and the rejected suitor who apparently functioned as *kahu* or spirit-keeper, were believed to come from Molokai. The island was noted for its many occult practices. And so, still within the Hawaiian context, the spirits could have been either

---

*Names are disguised.

'unihipili from the man's own family line, or the poison gods (see *akualele*) who came only from the wood of certain trees on Molokai. And, so goes an early legend, these trees were once men and women.

Possessing spirits, single or multiple, could be beneficent or harmful, but they were never demons or devils. The "devil" was unknown to Hawaii until the missionaries performed the introduction. Good spirits such as the *aumā-kua*, entered into mortals through the head and departed through the tear ducts. Destructive spirits entered the body through the feet, specifically by way of a big toe. From there they worked their way on up through the body. Says one present-day Hawaiian:

"One can feel the spirit coming up through the foot. Depending on the spirit, the feet may feel hot or icy cold. As the spirit goes up through the body, this is partial possession. The person is still aware of what is happening until he is completely overwhelmed."

(One's own spirit also left the body by way of the tear duct, sometimes to wander awhile as the body slept, or to leave more permanently as in death. In cases of "temporary" death or apparent death, one's own spirit returned by way of the big toe. Not really *noho*, this spirit-return is described under *'uhane* and *'ō'ō-a-moa*.)

Hawaiians noted
pseudo-possession

Hawaiians distinguished between *noho*, true possession, and *ho'onoho-noho*, pseudo-possession. It was recognized that a person might *ho'onohono-ho* (pretend to be possessed) to impress or frighten, or as alibi for socially disapproved behavior. Physical illness could be mistaken for *noho*. And though *noho ia*, overwhelming possession, could reach a state of madness, it was a temporary condition, distinct from more lasting insanity. The distinction has been made recently. To quote one Hawaiian:

"This little girl was screeching and acting wild and running around and tearing off her clothes. But I knew she was possessed by a spirit, not *pupule* (insane)."

exorcising
the spirit

Such was, and in more isolated Hawaiian communities, still is *noho*. Today, as in the past, beneficent spirits who come to possess leave on their own accord. Wicked spirits also seem to leave eventually but because they cause so much concern, exorcism rites were worked out long ago to speed their departure. Basically, relates Mrs. Pukui, exorcism went something like this:

"First the family prayed over the one who was *noho*. Then someone asked the spirit 'Who are you? Where are you from? Who sent you?' And then this family member would command the spirit to leave by saying *'Ho'i no 'ai i kou kahu'*. That means 'go back and destroy your keeper.'

"Then it was wise to get the *'ohana* (family clan) together for *ho'opono-pono** to find and correct the wrongs or the bad behavior that allowed the spirit to take possession."

---

*Literally, "to set to right." A therapeutic family council. See listing, *ho'oponopono*.

For someone unable to talk, exorcism could be done by using *ti* leaves or white *tapa* in the ritual of *kuehu* (shaking out).

"The family senior or the *kahuna* made the possessed one lie down with his feet toward the house doorway. Then he struck him lightly with the *ti* from head to feet. Then he shook the leaves in the doorway, just as you might shake out a dust cloth. This was to shake the possessing spirit out of the house. Then *ti* leaves were spread under the sleeping mat to keep the spirit from coming back."

(Mrs. Pukui emphasizes that this gentle smiting was in no way a beating. Present day cases in which parent beats child to "get the wicked spirit out" do not fit in any Hawaiian cultural context and are evidently the parent's alibi for a temper outburst.)

"Or, parents could put *ti* leaves, or *hala* or *'aki'aki* grass, in a little sea-salt water and have the child drink it," Mrs. Pukui concludes.

Today both possession and exorcism beliefs are likely to be a kind of mental-spiritual tossed salad of Hawaiian and Christian interpretations. The ingredients seem to blend nicely, perhaps because the idea of possession has always been worldwide. And so in the tradition-permeated Hawaiian family, the *noho* spirit may announce its presence as one man explained (May, 1969):

"When the spirit enters, it grabs three of my fingers. That means the Father, Son and Holy Ghost."

With the same cultural compatibility, the spirit may be urged on its way by Mormon elder, Pentecostal minister or a religious lay worker given a *kahuna*-like status by devout brethren. The "Brother" or "Sister" in the congregation may add a bit of Filipino, Portuguese or Chinese interpretation to prayers or ritual. No matter. In most cases, at least temporary peace of mind comes when both *noho* victim and the house are blessed and purified.

Whether or not possession in Hawaii is ever a transcendental experience is ultimately the private decision of the one so possessed. In this realm, we do not pry. We limit the discussion to the psychological processes and emotional implications of *noho*.

noho and hypnosis

What are these psychological-emotional elements?

Literature on possession around the globe mentions most frequently the hypnotic trance.

Our psychiatric consultant believes this is true in Hawaii's *noho*. He views the planned *noho* of the old seance as a combination of induced and self-induced hypnosis (see *haka*), and sees the still-existent, spontaneous *noho* as a manifestation of self-hypnosis. And here the cultural and the psychiatric observation that true *noho* must be by the spirit of a dead person (or god) are in agreement. Dr. Haertig explains:

"In the hypnotic trance of possession you are oriented towards someone else. You are 'receiving their sendings,' not in a direct fashion, but by a process of identification. This 'someone else' was once known as a real, living person or was known in fantasy; it is impossible to identify with a blank. (In hypnosis used in therapy, there may be some partial identification with a living person, the hypnotist, but this does not apply in *noho*.) What strikes me in all the re-

163

ported *noho* incidents is that this identification is always with someone who has died. Yet for the living, possessed one, the dead person is retained in the unconscious—sometimes consciously—as a sense of a living presence. Under hypnosis, this identification with the dead one becomes more visibly operative. The possessed or *noho* person then speaks, as far as vocal equipment allows, in the voice of the dead one, using characteristic expressions and mannerisms.

"The woman acting and sounding much like the nine-year old boy is an example. Obviously, she knew the boy intimately and continuously through the nine years of his life.

"In the case of the dead and the living twin sisters, the identification seems to come partly from acquaintance and partly from fantasy. Lucy, the survivor, knew Luella only a short time, not much more than in babyhood. From then on, Lucy evidently 'knew' her twin through family reminiscences, pictures, and her own imagination. In other words, by hearsay and fantasy."

In most modern, client-reported *noho* cases, there seems to be this identification with the dead, but relatives never remember to ask 'Who are you?' of the invading spirit. This is regrettable. Such questioning during the possession episode is equally useful to exorcist or psychiatrist.

Says Mrs. Pukui: "You must find out who the spirit is, so you can send it back."

Says Dr. Haertig: "It is helpful, even essential, to know who is apparently speaking through the possessed one, so you can look into the relationships between the two."

"grief work"
is incomplete

He continues:

"In general, identification with the dead strong enough to manifest itself in *noho* suggests interrupted, incomplete 'grief work'*. This points quite strongly to an ambivalent relationship during life.

"Theoretically, if the woman possessed by the nine-year-old boy were in psychotherapy, the approach would be to look for the reasons the grieving process had not been completed, so the grief could be brought out into the open and consciously worked through to its conclusion. In the case of the twin—and again this is speculative or theoretical because I never saw the case—I would explore ambivalent identification in life of the twins with themselves and one another, and the later mixed feelings of the survivor for the dead twin. I'd investigate why Lucy, the survivor, couldn't get the dead Luella 'out of her system.' For, as this is described, Lucy was really playing a dual role. She was herself and her dead twin.

"I would also try to find the medical histories of both twins. Lucy survived an illness serious enough to be fatal to her twin. I'd want to know the diagnosis, and very probably, have Lucy checked for possible after-effects, such as brain damage.

"With the Molokai woman and her fantasied spirits, I would want to know if the woman could identify these spirits and what they meant to her."

---

*Discussed under listing, *make, kanu* and *kaumaha*.

164

Center files, from 1965 through 1969, show that clients often report as *noho* cases which may not be the hypnotic trance but another state of dissociation. For example, a husband gave this intriguing account of his wife: "Anytime she drinks and gets mad and upset, she goes off into a trance, and then she speaks Hawaiian. But when she is herself she can hardly speak Hawaiian at all. She starts off by wailing and *oli*ing [chanting] and then she talks in Hawaiian. I think she is possessed by her mother or grandmother [both dead]. After it's all over, she doesn't remember a thing. I don't know enough Hawaiian to know what she is saying, but one of the neighbors heard her and said she was speaking pure, very old Hawaiian."

Taken out of total case context with its many problems on the part of both husband and wife, this phenomenon is very probably a trance-like, dream-like state. Dr. Haertig explains how this differs from the true hypnotic trance.

"In this dream-like, trance-like state, the orientation is not toward someone else, but within oneself. Then, as the critical mental functions are suspended, what has been repressed or held back unconsciously can then emerge. But this repressed material comes from one's own unconscious, without any identification with anyone else. Even experiences from early childhood can come to the surface. Thus a language spoken in childhood and consciously forgotten can then be spoken. We do know that Hawaiian was spoken by mother and grandmother during the woman's childhood. Hawaiian may well have been the woman's first language, later totally forgotten as far as the conscious self is concerned."

Episodes of rage and irrational behavior are often termed *noho* by Hawaiian clients. This is a reasonable assumption for, says Dr. Haertig, the whole demeanor may seem to be that of someone else.

"It's quite common for people to dissociate their hostilities and aggression so they are not really conscious of them. They 'shelve them'—thrust them back into the unconscious. Then, given certain stimuli, the operative, in-control self may become dissociated and the person becomes raw hostility. The conscious self, the social self is for the time being 'turned off'; the repressed self almost literally 'erupts' and takes over."

Noho, as the hypnotic trance with orientation away from self, the self-oriented trance-like states, and, in fact, all states of diminished consciousness are valuable and helpful to the psychiatrist because they make the unconscious more accessible.

What, actually, does the patient or client convey when he tells of *noho* happening to himself or a family member?

In the first place, the fact he has volunteered this information means he is ready, and even needs to talk about *noho* as a Hawaiian practice. Reasons for mention of *noho* can range from testing out a social worker for understanding and attitudes to particularly occult Hawaiian beliefs, to deepest concern over who is possessing and why.

**noho is
syndrome**

Fundamentally, *noho* is a syndrome, or group of symptoms. P.M. Yap, M.D., a psychiatrist with rare experience in both Eastern and Western cultures, speaks of "the possession syndrome." His clinical experience, and others' professional observations made in Hawaii agree that: The syndrome must be balanced on its own cultural scale as well as in its own case symptomatology.

Certainly, for a Park Avenue sophisticate who is suddenly "possessed," the diagnostic balance might waver from "eccentric" towards "psychotic." For the Hawaiian still very close to the mystical, *noho* episodes by themselves do not necessarily point to the abnormal or psychotic.

As clients report it, *noho* may be true to its traditional pattern, or it may be a culturally garbled occurrence. *Noho* as the hypnotic trance or the trance-like state with understandable speech may lead to enlightening exploration of emotional relationships; *noho* as incorrectly applied to vague "off in another world" states may signify anything from the hysterical fugue to epilepsy to various neurological conditions. Here a worker's knowledge of authentic Hawaiian "possession" becomes basic equipment in the diagnostic tool chest.

NOTES

1. The father believed nothing could be done to help his daughter because the *aumakua* had been so offended by the voiced thought about chopping off the head. A threat was considered tantamount to action once it was said, and the head *(po'o)* was especially taboo because here the *aumakua* hovered. His guilt and concern about the head may well have been communicated to the surviving twin.

2. Beckwith. "Hawaiian Shark Aumakua," p. 503.

REFERENCES

Erickson. "Deep Hypnosis and Its Induction," *Experimental Hypnosis.*

Beckwith. "Hawaiian Shark Aumakua," pp. 503-517.

Zilboorg, Henry. *History of Medical Psychology.*

"Hypnosis in Perspective," *Experimental Hypnosis.*

Kamakau. *Ka Po'e Kahiko: The People of Old.*

Malo. *Hawaiian Antiquities.*

M.D. Magazine, February 1965, p. 12.

Zilboorg. *Mind, Medicine and Man.*

Pukui. *"Noho."*

Oesterreich. *Possession, Demoniacal and Other, Among Primitive Races, in Antiquity, The Middle Ages, and Modern Times.*

Yap. "The Possession Syndrome," *Journal of Mental Science,* Vol. 106, pp. 114-137.

"Psychiatry Around the World," *Archives of Neurology and Psychiatry,* Vol. 75, pp. 653-655.

LeCron. "A Study of Age Regression Under Hypnosis," *Experimental Hypnosis.*

Lambo. *Transcultural Psychiatry.*

'ohana—family; family clan or extended family.

Deriv: *'ohā,* taro, especially taro grown from the original stalk called *kalo.*

na, plural; many.

"Members of the *'ohana,* like taro shoots, are all from the same root," says Mary Kawena Pukui.

The comparison comes from an ancient tradition. '*Ohā*, the root or corm of the taro plant, was not only the "staff of life" in the Hawaiian diet, but it was closely linked with the origin of the people. Legend tells that the progenitor of the Hawaiians was a mystic man-and-taro named Hāloa.[1]

With Hawaiians, family consciousness of the same "root of origin" was a deeply felt, unifying force, no matter how many offshoots came from offshoots. As Mrs. Pukui explains, "you may be 13th or 14th cousins, as we define relationships today, but in Hawaiian terms, if you are of the same generation, you are all brothers and sisters. You are all *'ohana*."[2]

This close tie among distant cousins indicates that in the past, *'ohana* meant "family clan" more often than "nuclear" or "immediate" family. Today, the word means either.

The ties of *'ohana* as an extended family were closest but not limited to the living or to those born into blood relationship. The core of the *'ohana* were the living *pili koko* (blood relatives). However, non-related persons could be admitted to *'ohana* status. And when a family member died, he remained—as a spirit—very much a part of the *'ohana*.

who were
'ohana

The *'ohana* or extended family of old, included:[3]

Makuas, the parents and relatives of the parent-generation, (such as the aunts and uncles of other cultures).

Kupunas, grandparents and all relatives of the grandparent generation. In this *kupuna* (the broad meaning is "elder") group were great grandparents or their generation-equivalent, all called *kupuna kuakāhi;* the great-great-grandparents and relatives of the same generation, called *kupuna kualua;* and the great-great-great grandparents or other relatives called *kupuna kuakolu.*

Keikis, the children. All, as previously explained, were "brothers and sisters" to each other. These *keikis* might be born within the *'ohana* or *hānai'd* (taken in Hawaii's adoptive practice). Usually, the *hānai* was blood kin, given at birth to grandparents or aunts and uncles. All young children were *keikis* or *kamas*. One's grandchild was, more specifically, one's *mo'opuna*.

"make a son"
by ho'okama

Also family members in nearly every sense were those "adopted in friendship" or made *(ho'o)** son, daughter, husband or any kin. A loved, non-related child could be made a *ho'okama* ("adopted in friendship" son or daughter); a woman could become a man's *ho'owahine* (wife); a woman could take a *ho'okāne* (husband). The relationship was a life-long one of love, loyalty and companionship. It did not include economic support, and the *ho'owahine* and *ho'okāne* status did not include sexual involvement.

puluna and
punalua

Sometimes *'ohana* members and sometimes not were the various in-laws. *Puluna* (parents-in-law) shared no joint relationship until the birth of a grandchild linked the two families. With this happy event, parents of the bride and

---

*Literally, *ho'o* (to make) + *kama* or *kāne* or other kinship term.

parents of the bridegroom joined each other's *'ohana.* If this mutual grandchild should die and no succeeding one was born, the *'ohana* connection was severed or given only courtesy recognition.

However, sisters- or brothers-in-law were automatically related. They were to each other *punalua,* or *lua* (companion) of the same *puna* (source or spring).

Punalua also defined the relationship between two wives of the same man, or husbands of the same woman. Here *lua* was defined as "mate"; each woman was "mate" to the same *puna* or "source".

"In the earliest tradition, the relationships of the wives always seemed to be one of deep friendship," explains Mrs. Pukui. "Later, people realized that jealousy often spoiled the friendship, and *punalua* took on meanings of rivalry or even hatred."

**immortals
also kin**

The *'ohana* also included the immortals; always, the *aumākua* (ancestor gods); often, the *'unihipili,* the deified spirits of more recently deceased relatives. And because the *aumākua* could take many forms *(kino lau),* the *'ohana* roll call also took in named and known sharks or owls or lizards, or the fires of the volcano, or the rocks and pebbles of the stream. (see *aumākua).*

In old Hawaii, one's relatives were both earthly and spiritual. Both were looked to for advice, instruction and emotional support. Thus communication with the supernatural was a normal part of *'ohana* living. Each *'ohana* traditionally had its own dream interpreters, its own *haka* (medium) through which a spirit spoke; and to summon this spirit, each clan had one or more spirit "masters" or *kahus.* Even *mana,* that storehouse of supernatural power, was handed down within the family line. All these mystic practices or communications led back in one way or another to those long dead, always cherished *'ohana* members—the *aumākua.*

The Hawaiian, therefore, had not only a sense of belonging to the supportive, here-and-now unit of family; he also had clear knowledge of his ancestry and an emotional sense of his own link and place in time between his ancestors-become-gods in the dim past and his yet-to-be-born descendants. (This is specifically outlined as "triple *piko*". See *piko.)* Or, to put it in modern terms, we could say the *'ohana* system helped give the Hawaiian a healthy sense of identity.

Only the unfortunate, despised *kauwā* (slaves) lacked this tie with the immortals. It was believed the *kauwā* caste had no *aumākua.*

**functions of
'ohana unit**

Though the *'ohana* of old included mystic beings, it functioned as the most practical of social-economic-educational units.

"Upland *'ohana* took taro and bananas to seashore *'ohana* and received fish," recalls Mrs. Pukui. "And when a man needed a new house, relatives from the whole *'ohana* came to build it."

Within the *'ohana,* elders taught youngsters to fish, raise taro, weave and build. Here proper behavior was taught, and rituals and *kapus* (taboos) memorized. Here family history was maintained in handed-down chants. Here the young boy observed male relatives and learned how to be a man (see *kā i mua)*. Sex education was a family responsibility.[4] Illness and offenses against man or god were family concerns. Birth was celebrated by family feasting. When death came, only *'ohana* members prepared the body for burial.

provisions for
family harmony

Obviously, this closely-knit unit had to function smoothly. Otherwise, chaos would result. And so, provisions and practices to maintain or restore harmony were worked out. We can group these rather loosely as follows:

Physical arrangements of *'ohana* living minimized personality conflicts.

Authority of the *'ohana* senior was clearly recognized and obeyed. (See listing, *kupuna* and *hānau mua.*)

Ways to express and correct hostilities and injustices were established. (See *ho'oponopono* and associated concepts.)

If good relationships could not be restored, a clean break of family ties was done in formalized procedure. (See *mō ka piko* under listing, *piko.*)

Rules of conduct were clearly outlined.

Roles and responsibilities within the *'ohana* were defined and understood.

housing
gave privacy

The very housing system lessened discord. Smaller family groups within the total clan or *'ohana* had their own households or *kauhales*. Given any prosperity at all, each smaller family unit had not one, but several houses.[5] "Togetherness" prevailed at night when everyone slept in the *hale noa* (house free of *kapus)*. Otherwise, everyone could get away from each other. The men ate, enjoyed "man talk" and honored the gods in the *mua* (men's eating house). Women and young children ate in their own *hale 'aina* ("meal house"). There were separate houses for crafts, for storage, even for vacation use. A menstruating woman was restricted to the *hale pe'a* ("unclean house" or menstrual house). There the very isolation of her *kapu* state let her get a good rest.

When the Hawaiian needed privacy he could find it. He also had the restorative balm of quiet. The music of nose-flute or *'ukeke** was soft; the beat of gourd or drum blessedly non-amplified. And especially if *ali'i* were around, night noise was *kapu*. Fornander records:

"Set apart [sacred] is the evening. Work has ceased . . .
It is sacred. Let there be *kapu*.
. . . *Kapued* the voice, the loud talking,
The groaning, the murmuring,
The low whisperings of the evening.
The high chiefs rest."[6]

'ohana roles
and rules

Within the *'ohana,* each one knew where he stood in the family rating system. (See *punahele* and *hiapo* listings.) He also knew pretty much what he must and must not do. Rules, expressed or implicit through custom, governed conduct. A few examples:

---

*Small instrument something like the Jew's harp.

A younger sibling obeyed the older one; the elder child cared for the young one. Young people learning to fish, build a boat—or any skill—were expected to *"nānā, ho'olohe, pa'a ka waha"* ("watch, listen, shut the mouth") —and ask questions *after* the demonstration.

There were rules governing sleeping arrangements. In the 1950's, Mrs. Pukui wrote in her *Polynesian Family System in Ka'u:*

"In the *hale noa,* a man slept beside his wife, and next, but not too close to her, might be her sister . . . a man never slept between two women, unless both were his wives . . . a young son might sleep next to his mother, but not after he had grown up . . ."[7]

"How close was 'not too close'?" I asked Mrs. Pukui in 1971.

"Everyone was separated by the sleeping mat. Every person slept on his own mat and was supposed to stay on it. I slept between my grandmother and my aunt. When I was just a little girl I had a very small sleeping mat. As I grew up I had bigger mats."

The rule of the *poi* bowl contributed to amiable, if sexually segregated, dining. This, based on the belief that *taro,* source of *poi,* was god-given, went:

". . . When the *poi* bowl is open, there must be no haggling, quarreling, arguing . . . nor should any serious business be discussed until the *poi* bowls are covered."[8]

Other customs symbolized and reinforced family closeness and loyalty. Co-author Pukui explains that:

"A man might wear his brother's *malo* [loin cloth] but not the *malo* of anyone else . . . Young people were told to 'behave so you won't shame your family.' . . . If two persons would not end a quarrel, they could break the family tie. But if a person behaved disgracefully, his *'ohana* could not disown him.

"Somebody in the family may be a drunkard or a rascal—even a thief— but he is still a relative. You might not like him—but you cannot cast him off."

And always, linking the Hawaiian family was *pule 'ohana* (family prayer), first to Hawaiian deities; later, to the Christian God. Always this was a part of the major prevention or remedy of discord, the *ho'oponopono. Pule* was so much a part of family living that to this day *"'ohana"* is often used to mean *"pule 'ohana."*

ties of blood
defined 'ohana

'Ohana members of the past often lived in the same area. This proximity undoubtedly made it easy and convenient to maintain family ties; it did not determine *'ohana* membership.

"You are not *'ohana* because you live in the same *kuleana* [area] or community. You can be neighbors and close friends—but to be *'ohana* you must all come from the same root or be linked by the same *piko,"** emphasizes Mrs. Pukui.

It is this blood tie (including its *hānai* and *ho'okama* equivalents) that is the core of *'ohana* in its broad meaning of concept, or emotional force. Or, with concept put into practice, the core of *"'ohana* living" or the *"'ohana* way of life."

---

*the *piko* or umbilical cord of a grandchild was considered the "blood link" between the child an the two pairs of grandparents.

Center staff members and others in the social science fields are now trying to determine to what extent the *'ohana* way of life still exists and whether the *'ohana* concept can be revived and used to benefit Hawaiian families of 1971.*

the concept
of 'ohana

Before we report any current observations, let's *peki i hope* (back up) and try to define *'ohana,* the concept. We could say:

"It is a sense of unity, shared involvement and shared responsibility. It is mutual interdependence and mutual help. It is emotional support, given and received. It is solidarity and cohesiveness. It is love—often; it is loyalty—always. It is all this, encompassed by the joined links of blood relationship."

There is plenty of evidence that this feeling of *'ohana* is very much alive today. Center case records show that a strong sense of family unity and total involvement exists on both conscious and unconscious levels.

One indication comes in the very number of names and intricacies of relationships listed in any case record. Few cases list only Mother-Father-Children. Most take in children, parents, grandparents, aunts, uncles, cousins of varying degrees and generations, and *hānai* children—all involved with the problem at hand.

The same records show extended *'ohana* influence in clients' dreams, visions or experiences with portents, and how they interpret these mystic-tinged messages from the unconscious. Most often the person in a dream or vision is a blood relative; less frequently a wife or husband. In both cases, the person is usually deceased. Only occasionally, clients report dreams about a lover, teacher, employer or film star or entertainer. Though a person dreamed about or envisioned is not recognized, the client often says "this was Grandma or Auntie" or "it means something is going to happen to Mama or Tūtū." Portents, as well, are most often thought to apply to relatives. Sometimes this is the traditional interpretation, as in *nahu akua* (see listing).

Even when dream content or client interpretation is clearly one of denial and projection, the projection is most often directed at a family member. Some of these dreams were, of course, stimulated by day events with deep family involvement.

This day-by-day involvement and interdependence is noted in *Studies in a Hawaiian Community.* Nanakuli Hawaiian families surveyed tended to turn to relatives or friends for medical advice.[9] Nearly two-thirds of the men got their first jobs through relatives or friends.[10]

'ohana concept
in casework

Obviously the *'ohana* "spirit" is not keeping Hawaiian families friction-free today. Center case workers see families-in-trouble as well as cohesive families troubled *about* a member.

---

*The Human Services Center, Governor's Office, is beginning a project in which one caseworker will work with 7 or 8 nuclear families who are all related or members of the same *'ohana.* If one family's house needs painting, for example, paint will be furnished and the *'ohana* encouraged to cooperate in the painting.

What has eroded the emotional structure of *'ohana?*
Sometimes, changed housing conditions. The *'ohana* of old had as many
as 7 or 8 houses. Today, in Papakolea, as many as 12 persons are crowded
together in one house.[11] In low-income housing projects, nature-loving Hawaiians are jammed into concrete high-rise apartments.

Sometimes, the conflicts of inter-ethnic marriage. The individualistic
haole who may have left the mainland to "escape family" marries into a Hawaiian family and views *'ohana* concern as "meddling."

Increasingly, conflicts of generation. The Hawaiian teenager is often
caught between the "do things family way" customs of *'ohana* and the "do
your own thing" of the young culture; the "respect the senior" code he grew up
in and the "don't trust anybody over 30" creed of his peers. Hawaiian parents
may not view the child with the mainland scholarship or the job offer else-
where as "going away to develop his talents" but "going away and leaving his
family." (This is not exclusive to Hawaiian families.)

Very often Hawaiian families-in-trouble cherish the idea that they are
'ohana in the traditional sense—but practice few or none of the traditions that
helped the *'ohana* function smoothly. Specifically: the obligation to forgive
and release *(mihi* and *kala)* when asked for forgiveness; holding family discussions, prayers and, ideally, *ho'oponopono* to prevent and remedy hostilities;
and observing the *ho'omalu* (period of silence) so tempers could cool and
thinking become rational. There were even ways to replace the ranking senior
if the *'ohana's* head became incompetent or autocratic (see *kupuna* and *hānau
mua).* *Mō ka piko,* the symbolic "cutting of the cord" (see *piko*) let individuals sever family ties with the knowledge that they might later be rejoined in
'ohana bonds. All these practices helped preserve the total *'ohana* structure.
All are potentially helpful in present day casework with Hawaiian families.

In current casework or psychotherapy, often a first essential is to help
the Hawaiian family get a good look at itself as a family. Dr. Haertig describes
this process of directed self-scrutiny as going along these lines:

"Are you really an *'ohana?* Or just relatives who quarrel? Do you
really help each other? Care for each other's happiness? Or do you merely
hold each other back? Try to make everyone in the family conform to the
same ways? Do you think *'ohana* means all the family must live together?
Or do you remember that the *'ohana* of old let its navigators and explorers
venture forth—and the *'ohana's* love and prayers went with them?"

When a genuine feeling of family unity and loyalty exists, then the
troubled family—or member in trouble—has a strength to build on. The sure
knowledge that the "family still cares" can help the released prisoner go
straight or provide the glue sniffer or drug taker incentive to *'oki* (sever;
break off) the habit. Here the social worker must sometimes help the family
understand that *'ohana* concept does not mean "everybody under the same
roof."

The sex-offender, the alcoholic or the abusive person usually should not
be taken into the home with young or adolescent children. The caseworker
can point out that job-finding assistance, transportation, frequent visits—
all these are valid ways to demonstrate family loyalty and support. The worker
may need to explain that perhaps this wonderful bond of *'ohana* will be better
maintained if the quarrelsome uncle—or the daughter who wants to live in her
own apartment—does live apart. The goal is to keep *'ohana* affection warm

and communication lines open; not to strain relationships by forcing conformity or subjecting daily living to undue stress.

For the true *'ohana* of old was fundamentally one of relationship, not geography or proximity. As Mary Pukui reminds us,

"The miles or the years of separation do not matter—as long as the blood link is there."

can we "stretch" 'ohana concept?

Today the concept of *'ohana* is often extended to include unrelated persons, community groups, or church membership. In this valid? Is this broader application of the concept successful?

If we want to stay within the bounds of traditional definition, it's stretching the *'ohana* concept pretty far. What is most often meant are the *characteristics* of the *'ohana,* such as cooperation and feelings of cohesiveness and unity.

From the standpoint of human behavior, trying to superimpose the *'ohana* concept on a group that is not *'ohana* has quite a few strikes against it. Perhaps non-related persons may with some success turn a minister into a *makua* (parent) if they themselves want this kind of pseudo parent-child relationship. Hawaiian congregations who call their woman minister "Mama" seem to have family-like feelings.

When the *'ohana* concept is affixed to a non-related group, the family bond is clearly artificial. Efforts of industry and government groups to build "one big happy family" have failed. Says Dr. Haertig:

"For example, when the head of the firm is fashioned into a paternalistic 'father image', then each person reacts to him according to individual memories of and experiences with his own father. A lot of these are going to be negative. 'Father' may have been a tyrant to one, a weak person to be manipulated to another. To other employees, 'Father' may have been a violent, hostile person, a seductive one, or an incompetent whose judgment was not to be trusted.

"In general, when you attempt to 'create a family', you are dealing with each person's past experiences with parents, siblings, even grandparents. Negative experiences may be applied to the 'created' parents and siblings; loving experiences and memories may mean the artificially created relative is totally rejected. It's far better to stay realistically employee-employer, caseworker-client, friends or neighbors.

"The real *'ohana* is a natural phenomenon. The superimposed concept makes a contrived situation."

NOTES AND REFERENCES

1. Mrs. Pukui tells that Wākea (personification of the Father, Sky) and his wife Papa (Earth, the Mother) had two sons, one born in the form of a taro, and one born in the form of a man. Both were named *Hāloa.* The taro-child was buried in the earth and gave forth new shoots; the man-child grew up and fathered offspring. Both merged into the one mythical person *Hāloa,* named from a combination of *hā* (breath) and *loa* (long and continuing). *Hāloa* therefore meant "continuing breath" or "life". Or, because *hā* also means "stalk", *Hāloa,* referring directly to the taro, may be said to mean "long stalk."

Many versions of Wākea and Papa and their offspring are given. Some are found in *Malo,* second edition, pp. 238-244, and Beckwith's *Hawaiian Mythology,* 1970 edition, pp. 293-306.

2. This equation of cousins with siblings had an important exception among commoners. Brothers and sisters could not marry because they came from the same mother or father; cousins were allowed to marry. Only among *ali'i* were blood brother-sister marriages approved.—M.K.P.

3. The vocabulary of kinship terms is vast. For example, "sister" could be referred to or addressed in any of 14 separate terms. Each showed an exact degree of relationship, such as older sister to a brother. Kinship terms are listed in the Pukui-Elbert Hawaiian-English and English-Hawaiian dictionaries. Relationships are explained in detail in *Polynesian Family System in Ka'u*, pp. 40-74.

4. Sex education. Among *ali'i* an elder chiefess initiated a young man in his first sexual experience. In the commoner *'ohana*, sex was freely discussed and the genitals were given special care from babyhood on, so intercourse later would be happy and fruitful.

5. Housing. Seven houses are listed and described in Malo's *Hawaiian Antiquities*, Second edition, p. 126.

6. Fornander. *Collection of Hawaiian Antiquities*, Vol. 6, Series 3, p. 418.

7. Pukui. *Polynesian Family System in Ka'u*, p. 10.

8. Ibid., p. 193.

9. Gallimore and Howard. *Studies in a Hawaiian Community*, p. 124.

10. Ibid., p. 18.

11. Knaefler. "Visit to Papakolea."

'ōkala or **'ōkakala**—goose flesh; goose bumps. Often interpreted as a warning or given mystic significance.

Deriv: *kala,* fish so named because of its rough skin. *'Ōkala* is literally "rough feeling."

For *'ōkala* interpreted as a portent, see *'ili ōuli.*

'oki—to cut, sever, separate in physical or psychological sense; to remove or lessen consequences or effects.

Deriv: unknown.

In the human-with-human, human-with-gods relationship of old Hawaii, nearly every destructive or negative psychological-emotional force had its more positive, hopeful offsetting force. A sorcerer's spell *('anā'anā)* could be cancelled by a counter-spell. A curse *('ānai)* could be returned to its sender. Human ties that stifled could be cut. Supernatural claims that grew oppressive could be nullified. Errors might be corrected; transgressions forgiven. Nearly every emotional wound had its suture or bandage; every psychological dungeon, its escape shaft.

In this psychic balancing act, *'oki* played a star's role. Traditionally, *'oki* could remove a name *(inoa)* that harmed its bearer, or merely separate harmful influences from the name so it could be kept. *'Oki* could release the living from the clinging spirit of the dead. It could remove curse or *kapu* (taboo), or prevent or lessen misfortune forecast in a dream or vision. In these important remedial functions, *'oki* was accomplished by prayer, often coupled with a statement that severance was now being done. Rituals of purification or blessing, sacrifice or feasting sometimes accompanied the basic *'oki* prayer. Traditionally, prayer was addressed to Hawaiian *akuas* (gods) and *aumākua* (ancestor gods). Today, the Christian God is invoked, with occasional spiritual mergers with *aumākua* or Buddha.*

In a secular sense, *'oki* was traditionally a spoken pronouncement that immediately dissolved a union between man and woman. Currently, a legal divorce may be called *'oki male* (broken marriage). In a mundane sense, *'oki* may be nothing more than a handy verb. To get a hair cut is to have it *'oki'd*. Or you can *'oki* the top from a turnip. A surgeon may *'oki* an arm or leg.

But in any context of emotions and relationships, secular or spiritual, *'oki* was always prayerful appeal or decisive announcement in which God or *aumakua* was a silent participant. Often prayer and an almost legal-sounding declaration were used together. Mary Kawena Pukui gives an example from her own life. In this she was involved with *'unihipili,* the attachment of the spirit of a dead relative to a living person.** She recalls:

"I was just a little girl when my aunt lost her daughter. On the grave they built a little house with a bed, a bureau and everything. This was for my dead cousin's spirit to use. My aunt would visit the grave-house and take food offerings ... this kept my cousin's spirit in the world of the living ... I was always being taken to the grave ... the spirit became attached to me. I became part of the *'unihipili.* Finally, my mother decided we just were not going to have this anymore! So first we had an *'oki* ceremony at home. Later, we prayed, right there at the grave-house. There I said to the spirit, 'when your mother leaves this life, go with her. *Because I now sever my connection with you.'*

"And that was the end of it."

The link with the cousin's spirit was broken immediately, Mrs. Pukui explains. This is consistent with Hawaiian belief that words took on existence and function as soon as they were spoken.

The same instant effectiveness resulted when one *'oki'd* a name that exerted an adverse influence. Either the bearer of the name, or a *kāula pule* (priest), a senior relative, or later, a minister could pray and so *'oki* the name. Or the name might be retained, but the possible *kapu* or other unpleasant associations of the name *'oki'd.* The *pule ho'onoa* (prayer to free) might be as simple as "please remove this *inoa* [or *kapu*] and let the *keiki* [child] grow up strong and well."

'Oki of a curse *('anai)* could be done by the victim or by the one who placed the curse. Traditionally, the accursed one went to the person who had pronounced the curse, asked to be forgiven for the wrong† that had called down the curse and asked that the curse be lifted or *'oki'd.* Tradition decreed that if the cursed culprit was sincerely repentant, forgiveness be granted and

---

*Noted with marriage into Chinese or Japanese Buddhist families.

**A major concept. See *'unihipili.*

†The concept of *'anai* included a ritual for refusing a curse and sending it back to the originator if no wrong has been done. Only a guilty person had to accept the *'anai.*

the curse lifted immediately. This was the ideal. It was not always lived up to. Sometimes the curse-pronouncer refused to forgive and *'oki.* Still very much under the curse, the victim could then *'oki* the curse himself through sincere prayers and ritual. (See section on *'ānai.*)

Among Center clients, literally scores believe they are under *'ānai.* Very few use *'oki* or even know about it as a curse-remover. Here the professional worker's knowledge of the *'oki* concept may be helpful.

When a supernatural portent warned that disaster loomed, *'oki* might possibly prevent it or, at the least, scale doom down to discomfort. And so *'oki* was done when a *hihi'o* (vision), a *moe 'uhane* (dream) or *'ūlālelo* (spirit voice) predicted tragedy or trauma. Here the traditional rationale was that because an *aumakua* predicted the trouble, or more probably arranged it for punishment, therefore the *aumakua* should be asked to temper justice with mercy. Faith in the remedy, if not the rationale of *'oki'ing* mystically forecast harm, still exists.

To quote Mrs. Pukui:

"Many Hawaiians still believe in *'oki'ing* an unfortunate dream as soon as possible. Sometimes this *'oki* would not entirely eliminate the foretold *pilikia* [trouble], but it would at least diminish it. So as soon as he awoke, the dreamer would pray to have the *pilikia* cut away or *'oki'd.* Sometimes, then, no *pilikia* would come. But if it did, then the dreamer felt some benefits of *ho'omānalo* [lessening or sweetening]."

The following is a much-condensed account a young Hawaiian woman gave of a 1964 experience:

"My husband and I had a quarrel before we went to bed ... I had this terrible, terrible dream about 2:30 in the morning ... My husband was not in bed with me; instead it was this old lady ... she said she was my grandmother. She really died years ago ... Then this *'uhane* [spirit] changed back to my husband. And then, all of a sudden, our bedroom was filled with this red, red glow ... I couldn't get back to sleep. So I called Reverend _____ and she came over. She said this was an *'unihipili* ... She said every time I quarreled with my husband I would, without realizing it, call the spirit of grandmother to come back."

(Convinced there was an *'uhane* in the house, the couple held *ho'oponopono,* the prayer-filled family meeting in which conduct and conscience are scrutinized to find and correct causes of emotional discord.)

"Then after *wehe i ka Paipala,** the answer came. This *'uhane* could destroy my husband because it wanted me ... this *'uhane* could destroy our life together.

"So we had *'oki.* And from that day to today, even though my husband and I still have problems, we can work them out ... we can talk about them together. And if we don't know the answers, we know how to put things in the hands of God."

Obviously, native Hawaiian and introduced Christian beliefs can co-exist —especially when pre-dawn distress calls are answered by such wise and compassionate clergy as the Reverend _____!

---

*The seeking of counsel by picking passages from the Bible at random. Discussed under *wehe i ka Paipala.*

Christian prayer is used today to *'oki* all sorts of pre-Christian *kapus*. Mrs. Pukui gives the following examples:

"A relative of mine has to live in an apartment house with other people on the floor above her. So I prayed to *'oki* the *kapu* on her head . . . that nobody should be over the head. And now she is free of the *kapu*. It's all right to have people walking around over her head—even the toilet in the bathroom over her head, that's all right now." (See listing, *po'o*.)

And:

"When anyone close to me has to go to the hospital, I *'oki* the *kapu* on wearing other's clothing. This makes it safe to wear the hospital gown." (See listing, *'ili kapu*.)

Or, from Center files and Culture Committee reports:

"We called Reverend _____. He said our daughter's *inoa* had a *kapu* on it. So he *'oki'd* the *kapu* and blessed her and the house."

In general, Mrs. Pukui advises:

"If you know a *kapu* is hurting someone, then *'oki*. And when you know you just can't help breaking *kapus*, then *'oki* ahead of time. The *kapus* are lifted before you are ever forced to break them. You are free."

Such is Hawaii's *'oki*. To the deeply religious, mystically attuned Hawaiian, *'oki* used to alleviate misfortune or supernaturally sent punishment can certainly relieve or prevent specific anxieties, guilts and self-destructive behavior. In this use, the reassurance is internal.

Used to sever relationships or end a quarrel, *'oki* gives a solemn "as God—or *aumakua*—is my witness" endorsement to the pronouncement of severance. For the psychiatrist or social worker, *'oki* in this sense can be a useful tool of therapy precisely because: it is invariably linked with other Hawaiian remedial concepts; it makes its effects felt on inter-personal or personal-psychic relationships; it arises from and crystallizes decision-making.

(In current work with Hawaiian-oriented youngsters who sniff glue or paint or take drugs, an *'oki* ceremony might have some benefit. Here the habit which is harmful would be ritually severed. This use of *'oki* would follow cultural tradition if the youngster felt supernatural forces somehow kept him chained to his habit. In this case, *'oki,* further solemnized with rituals of purification and blessing, could bring a feeling that supernatural strength would help him "kick the habit." The rituals themselves add conviction and dramatic impact to the moment of "swearing off" glue or drugs. So far, this is purely a speculative suggestion with possible application to teenagers.)

'Oki to mend relationships is never a solo performance. It involves other persons and other rituals and concepts. For example: To *'oki* a quarrel, family members may also pray or take positive steps to *mihi* (repent), to *kala* (free from associated rancor and grudge holding), and to undertake reparation, all in the "setting to rights" of *ho'oponopono*. And so the actual prayer or ceremony of *'oki* is surrounded by family efforts—sometimes pressure on the "hold-outs"—to restore friendly relationships.

Even when *'oki* as severance (rather than alleviation of harm) is done in private prayer, it is still a part of a total remedial effort. For the decision to *'oki* is preceded by awareness that something is wrong, that something should be done about it, and, finally, the decision that *something is going to be done about it.* The doorway through which recovery may enter is pretty well opened when the Hawaiian *'oki's* or plans to *'oki* and tells the therapist about it. (Provided the therapist knows what the patient is talking about!)

For example: The patient or client who *'oki's* an *'unihipili* is ostensibly shaking off the all-too-clinging spirit of a dead relative. In reality, a human relationship is being clung to; the living will not let the dead become a memory. Unfinished grief work and previous ambivalent relationships in life are commonly involved in *'unihipili*. The Hawaiian who *'oki's* his *'unihipili* feels, more or less consciously, that here is an unhealthy relationship. Especially when he volunteers information about *'oki'ing* a spirit or *'unihipili*, exploration into past human relationships can usually be made.

Often the *'oki'ing* of a name invites exploration into personal relationships. For the very *inoa* (Hawaiian name) given a child and the reasons the *inoa* was chosen may point to use of the child as emotional replacement, or the forcing of him into a pre-cast mold.

And so Hawaii's ritual-and-belief in *'oki* to sever what is unhealthy has therapeutic potential because it is both an ending and a beginning. An ending to self-denials that trouble exists. An ending to the self-defeating premise that "nothing can be done about it." A beginning to insight. A "fresh start" with its enabling (even if temporary) benefits. A recognition that because old relationships had to be severed, new relationships must be built with some change of behavior and viewpoint.

'o'ō-a-moa—a crowing sound heard when dangerously arrested breathing begins again. Heard in sudden recovery from "near death". Hawaiians believed that the sound meant the departed spirit *('uhane)* had re-entered the body.

Deriv: *'o'ō*, crow.
  a, of
  moa, rooster, chicken.
  Literally, "crow of a rooster."

"When a person died, and the *kahuna po'i 'uhane* [spirit catching practitioner][1] caught the spirit and brought it back, the spirit would come in and up through the big toe and up the body. And when the spirit got close, as the breath filled the lungs, then the person would *'o'ō-a-moa*, like the crowing of a cock." So Mary Kawena Pukui explained in 1971.

"The soul entered the body, up to the chest, to the throat, and Kawelu crowed like a chicken." So Fornander reported in an early legend.[2]

Obviously, Hawaii's *kahunas* had observed the same phenomenon that Western medicine noted: That sudden restoration of breathing was accompanied by this unique, crowing sound. According to Mrs. Pukui, the *po'i 'uhane* also knew how to bring about this welcome sound. For along with prayers, ritual and *lomi-lomi*,[3] he made a significant gesture.

"He took his fist and pressed—pressed hard—against the sole of the foot."

Or, even the non-*kahuna* layman might know another method of spirit catching. Mrs. Pukui gives a 20th Century example.

"This child died . . . and the father took him home. The Hawaiian friend followed. He got some *ti* leaves, chewed them, came up to the child and smacked him right on the seat. The child *'o'ō-a-moa'd.*"

178

A definite cause-and-effect had also been noticed. For there are parts of the body which pressed forcefully or irritated usually stimulate respiration. One is the buttocks. "Smacking the bottom" is a time-honored way to start a reluctant new-born breathing. Another is the sole of the foot. Snap the bottom of the big toe or press hard against the sole of the foot and interrupted respiration may begin again.

The observations of Hawaiian and Western medicine were similar; the interpretations differed. What Hawaii viewed as a mystical occurrence, the West explained as a physiological process. In a "borderline" death when breathing has stopped, respiratory muscles have relaxed, allowing the lungs to collapse. As the person revives, these respiratory muscles go into convulsive contractions. Air is sucked into the lungs very quickly, and the larynx gives a distinctive crowing sound. It is a sound with emotional impact in any culture!

In Hawaiian belief, *'o'ō-a-moa* was an electrifying moment in a life-drama enacted by man and his *'uhane*. For the *'uhane* could leave and return to the body in other ways than death. It caused dreams, went on adventures, and like the soul of Christian concept, existed after death. These beliefs are discussed under *'uhane*.

NOTES AND REFERENCES

1. *Kahuna po'i 'uhane.* There were two kinds of "spirit catchers." One caught the spirit and induced it to return to the body, thus restoring life. The other caught the spirit when it temporarily left the body of a living man and kept it from returning, thus causing death. *Kahuna* in this case can refer to the doctor-priest of old Hawaii or to the death-dealing sorcerer.

2. Fornander. *Collection of Hawaiian Antiquities,* Vol. 5, pp. 188-89. Kawelu was revived by her husband Hiku, according to a legend that probably grew more elaborate with each telling. Hiku first rescued his wife's spirit from deep in the ocean, brought it to shore and when he "reached the house where the dead body of Kawelu was lying, Hiku pushed the spirit . . . into the body from the feet . . ." The legend has Kawelu dead for days, which would make resuscitation impossible. However, the number of different legends concerning spirit-restoring suggests that Hawaiians did practice methods to stimulate interrupted respiration. Mrs. Pukui often heard this discussed in her family.

3. *Lomi-lomi,* massage. In spirit restoration, such massage was done upward, towards the heart. Observation of recoveries may have led to the interpretation that the spirit works up through the body. (Discovery of the circulatory system in Europe, 1618, provided background for the accepted first-aid principle of massage towards the heart.)

pī kai—a ritual sprinkling with sea water or other salted water to purify an area or person from spiritual contamination and remove *kapus* (taboos) and harmful influences.

Deriv: *pī,* to sprinkle.
      kai, sea; sea water.

Probably no ritual of Hawaii's past has merged with Christian sacramentals with less conflict than has *pī kai.* For the use of water in symbolic purification is universal.

**sea salt water
used in pī kai**

In Hawaii's pre-Christian era, fresh water, sea water and even coconut water were all used ceremonially. When the water of purification *(wai huikala)* had sea salt in it and was sprinkled, then the ceremony was basically *pī kai.* *'Ōlena* (turmeric) or *limu kala* (sea moss) might be added to the water. *Hala* (pandanus) leaves, symbolic of cleansing, might be among the ritual objects. *Kahuna* or layman might conduct the ceremony. Such were the variations on the *pī kai* theme.

Pī kai was done when *heiaus* (temples) or specific altars were dedicated, at the dedication of a house or newly made canoe, after contact with a corpse, and sometimes after menstruation or childbirth or contact with a menstruating woman.*

**pī kai in
circumcision**

Two important events that called for *pī kai* were splitting the foreskin of a boy's penis[1] and burial of the dead. Kepelino provides a description of the first, quoted here in part. The excerpt follows an account of the *kahuna's* acceptance of sacrificial offerings and the approach to the altar by the boy's relatives:

"Then the *kahuna* took water with a little salt mixed with it, prayed to Ku, to Kāne, to Lono, and breathed into the water, and the water became *tapued* water, and was called 'the *tapued* water of Kāne,' that is holy water. When all was prepared, then the *kahuna* performed the ceremony of circumcision. Afterward the *kahuna* wrapped white *tapa* about the head of the child and sprinkled him with water."[2]

**pī kai after
corpse contact**

David Malo included the following in his account, "Concerning Dead Bodies":

"... by morning the burial was accomplished. Then in the early morning, all who had taken part in the burial went and bathed themselves with water,** and on their return from the bath, seated themselves in a row before the house where the corpse had been.

"The priest was then sent for ... A sorcerer or *kahuna 'anā'anā* could not officiate at this service of purification. It was only a temple priest, *kahuna pule heiau,* who could purify one from the uncleanness of a corpse or any other source of defilement.

"The *kahuna* brought with him a dish filled with sea water, which also contained a sea moss called *limu kala* and turmeric, and, standing before the people who sat in a row he prayed. [A chant to the goddess, Uli, beginning '... Uli, here is water, water!' was quoted.]

"The *kahuna* then sprinkled the water mixed with turmeric on all the people and the purification was accomplished, the defilement removed."[3]

---

*More common was the *kapu kai,* the ritually (and physically) cleansing bath in the ocean. Legends also give many accounts of ritually purifying baths taken in streams.

**Also probably, *kapu kai.*

180

Such impressive ceremonies are now matters of the past. *Pī kai* itself has continued into the present day. Mary Kawena Pukui remembers this simplified form of *pī kai* used after contact with a corpse:

"A bowl of salt water was set in the doorway before the funeral," she relates. "Then when the mourners came home afterwards, they *pī kai'd* right away."

pī kai done
for vague fears

Present day case reports indicate that *pī kai* is often done because of a vague feeling that "something is wrong." In 1964, one young Hawaiian woman, distraught over dreams and strange visions, called on her church *kāula* (leader, pastor)* for help. She stated:

"Two Reverends came. Then with salt water they went outside and inside the house. They *pī kai'd* every place. All over."

Anyone can *pī kai*. It is not necessary to be a minister. A 1969 report on a household disturbed by apparently supernatural manifestations tells that "My aunt came down to *pī kai* the house."

Pī kai, once accompanied by invocations to Hawaiian gods or *aumākua* (ancestor gods), is today done with Christian prayers. And while originally *pī kai* carried only the meaning of ritual cleansing, in current use it seems intertwined with the idea of benediction or blessing. A present day Hawaiian, relating use of the ritual, will often use the words *pī kai* and "bless the house" interchangeably.

pī kai and
Christianity

Grafting imported credos on to old beliefs is obvious in this excerpt from a social worker's 1968 report.

"The woman told me when she put salt in the water to *pī kai,* she used exactly three grains. One for the Father, one for the Son and one for the Holy Ghost."

A Center caseworker adds another cultural dimension in this 1970 account:

"I went to a funeral a few days ago—the dead man was Filipino—and when we came back from the cemetery, one person was in front of the house holding a bucket of water and some guava leaves. Before I knew what had happened, he grabbed my head and was wetting my forehead and hair! Later on I asked him what this meant. His explanation was almost exactly like *Tūtū's* [Mrs. Pukui's] explanation of *pī kai.*"

pī kai is
not Baptism

Pī kai is not in any sense the equivalent of Christian Baptism. Says Mrs. Pukui, "*pī kai* removes external spirits of evil which surround men or may even have entered within the body. But this evil was not born in the person. Hawaiians did not have the concept of original sin."

Pī kai is also completely separate from old Hawaii's use of urine for ritual sprinkling. *Mimi* (urine) was believed to have an evil *mana* (power) of its own.

---

*originally, prophet or seer.

And so *mimi* was used to *repel* evil in a sort of symbolic battle between two wicked forces. However, there is yet some belief that if water is completely unavailable for *pī kai,* urine may be used strictly as an emergency measure.

Pī kai, today, whether mixed with Christian, Buddhist or, possibly, Taoist concepts, serves both a religious and a psychological function: that of bringing, at least temporarily, a sense of protection from influences felt to be unclean and harmful. As many other rituals do, *pi kai* relieves somewhat the feeling of being helpless in the face of what is unseen, unknown and fearful. Certainly, the very act of doing something believed to be remedial can ease anxiety, even if the ritual is not recognized as being particularly relevant to the fear-filled situation.

NOTES AND REFERENCES

1. Though the Hawaiian operation is usually called "circumcision," the operation actually slit and separated the foreskin, but did not remove it, as in circumcision. Whether or not the operation entailed making a surgical opening into the urethra or urinary canal (subincision) is not clear.

2. Beckwith. *Kepelino's Traditions of Hawaii,* p. 20. Calling this water the "water of Kāne" is often disputed. Use of the term "holy water" may reflect Kepelino's conversion to Catholicism.

3. Malo. *Hawaiian Antiquities,* pp. 97-98.

piko—umbilical cord or umbilicus; genital organs; posterior fontanel or crown of the head; summit or peak. Many other meanings. Many connote attachment: relationships with one's ancestors and descendants; boundary line of adjacent lands; junction of plant leaf to stem. From the literal meanings has come the "triple *piko*" concept of shared spiritual and emotional bonds.

Deriv: unknown.

The individual in old Hawaii viewed himself as a link between his long line of forebears and his descendants, even those yet unborn. Three areas of his body were thought most intimately concerned with this bond that transcended time. They were the posterior fontanel, the genital region, male and female, and the umbilicus and umbilical cord with which he came into the world. All were called *piko.*

triple piko

The Hawaiian observed in thought and ritual, a concept we term today the "triple *piko*". The concept, a fusion of reasoning and the poetry of mysticism, went something like this:

The *po'o* (head) was the place where the *aumākua* (ancestor gods) hovered; where man's own living *'uhane* (spirit) made exit and returned from the sleep-excursions of dreams. Though wicked possessing spirits entered the body by the feet, benevolent spirits took possession through the head. And so the crown of the head (located by the whorl of hair or "cowlick") was the *piko* sacred to the *aumākua*.[1] This was the symbolic "umbilical cord" between mortal man and his ancestors-become-immortals.

umbilical cord piko

The umbilical cord was the obvious link between the infant and the mother. Consequently, this *piko*, the umbilicus, and to some extent the closely associated placenta *('iēwe)* were venerated. The mother-child *piko* was extended symbolically to all blood-kin. Relatives were sometimes called "my *piko*". In dream interpretation, to dream of one's own navel was really to dream about a close relative. Dreaming of injury to one's navel was said to foretell death, illness or injury to a relative.

genitals also piko

The visible, tangible evidences of a bond with descendants were the genitalia, both male and female. These not only provided great pleasure, they made each person a progenitor, a creative link in the long and mystic chain from *aumākua* on through the flesh-and-blood offspring of the infinite future. And so the *piko* of the genitals were both enjoyed and reverenced. The *piko* of ali'i in particular, were paid tribute in *meles* (songs). In these the *piko* might be called *wai'olu* or *ma'i* and the songs called *mele ma'i*.

"Every *ali'i* and many commoners had such a *mele*," says Mrs. Pukui. "We hear *'Anapau'*. That's Queen Liliuokalani's *mele ma'i*. *'U'u'* is the *mele* about Queen Emma's *piko* or *ma'i*.

"Hawaiians never thought of this as being vulgar. Without this *piko*, there would be no children, no descendants."

The genitals, even of young children were given special care, primarily to facilitate later coition. But around the umbilical *piko* were centered symbolism and portentous beliefs. Whether or not actual cutting of the cord was accompanied with ritual depended on family rank and traditions. In a commoner family, the midwife might wield the sharp bamboo knife and tie the cord with *olonā* fiber* without ceremony. In the *ali'i* household, the degree of ritual might depend on sex and status of the baby. A first-born child rated more ceremony than later babies. According to Malo, "if the child was a girl, its navel string was cut in the house; but if a boy, it was carried to the *heiau* [place of worship], there to have the navel string cut in a ceremonious fashion."[2]

navel cord was hidden

For this high-born child, a *kahuna* cut the cord, and the "ceremonious fashion" meant offerings to the gods and chanted prayers. However, the overwhelming concern for Hawaiians of all ranks was proper disposal of the cord (the stump that later dropped off the infant's body). Mrs. Pukui recalls the belief that:

"If a rat found and ate the cord, the baby would have the thievish nature of a rat."

---

*Touchardia latifolia, a shrub with strong, flax-like fibers.

And that:

"In every district on every island were places, usually stones, especially reserved for the *piko*. *Wailoa* was one on the Big Island . . . another was *Moku-ola*. *Ola* means 'life' and *loa* means 'long'. Mothers took the cords to stones with names like these so their babies would live long, healthy lives."

The cords were carefully secured. Co-author Pukui continues:

"They were pushed into the cracks, then tiny pebbles were forced in to hold them in place. A few were wrapped in human hair. These were from babies who had died. The hair was from the head of the mother or grandmother or any relative who had cared for the baby. While wrapping the cord, the relative would address the [spirit of] dead baby, saying, 'Here is a part of my body, my hair. May it be a token of me in the spirit world. Do not come back to hurt me. Do not be angry with us. When you wish to come back to us, come in love to help us.'"[3]

Cords were often kept until they could be disposed of at a planned location. Again, quoting Mrs. Pukui:

"I have seen many old people with small containers for the umbilical cords . . . One grandmother took the cords of her four grandchildren and dropped them into *Alenuihaha* channel. 'I want my granddaughters to travel across the sea!' she told me."[4]

Mrs. Pukui believes that the story of women hiding their babies' *pikos* in Captain Cook's ship is probably true.

"Cook was first thought to be the god Lono, and the ship his 'floating island.' What woman wouldn't want her baby's *piko* there?"

**symbolism of
the placenta**

Symbolic forecasting was also extended to the placenta *('iewe)*. It was always washed. An unwashed placenta meant the child would have weak, sore eyes. In the Puna district, the placenta was put on the highest branch of a *hala* tree, so that the baby's eyelashes would stand out prettily, like prickles on a *hala* leaf.

Usually, the placenta was buried under a tree and the tree became the property of the child. This was thought to keep the child, even through adult life, close to home. Or, yet more mystically, to insure that the child's spirit, after death, would never become that homeless, hungry wandering spirit called *ao kuewa*.

**idols, houses
given pikos**

Early Hawaiians applied the idea of umbilical attachment to their idols. Wrote David Malo:

"They [priests] put a long girdle of braided coconut cord about the belly . . . of the idol, calling it the navel cord from its mother. Then the king and the priest came to perform the ceremony of cutting."[5]

The *piko* concept was extended even to houses.

"The belief that when a house is completed it has a personality goes way back," explains Mrs. Pukui. "The thatch over the doorway was the umbilical cord, and that had to be cut."

Here the Hawaiian idea was quite different from the feeling that a house with its furnishings eventually takes on the personality of its owners. In old

Hawaii, the newly completed house *was* a personality in its own right. As such, it was a candidate for cord-cutting. One beautiful prayer used in the cutting on Molokai went, in part:

"Cut now! Cut the *piko* of your house, O Mauili-ola*
That the house dweller may prosper.
That the guest who enters it may have health.
That the lord of the land may have health.
That the chiefs may have long life . . ."[6]

A more usual prayer invoked blessings "from the four corners . . . from the ceiling to the floor . . ." Nearly identical blessing for a human mentioned the "four corners of the body", meaning the shoulders and thigh bones, boundaries enclosing the vital organs.

mō ka piko
the cord is cut

Cord-cutting was extended symbolically to human relationships. However, the conceptualized *piko* that linked Hawaiian blood-kin was not the mother-and-child "silver cord" of Western thought. The Hawaiian *piko* joined all members of the *'ohana* (family). In Western cultures, "cutting the cord" denotes a beneficial freeing from a dominating, possessive mother. In Hawaii's past, *mō ka piko* conveyed a tragic disruption of loving relationship.

Mō ka piko la ("severed are the umbilical cords") was a clear pronouncement that a family tie was broken. The offended one could make the statement to the offender. Or, a third person (always a relative) whose peace-making efforts had failed could declare the severance. Either way, *mō ka piko* was a last-ditch measure taken for only the most serious offenses. Such as, to quote Mrs. Pukui:

"Helping a sorcerer destroy a family member . . . cruelty to or heartless neglect of a child or parent of the other person . . . refusal to forgive . . . offending another beyond all endurance . . . not saving a life you might have saved."

Mrs. Pukui draws the following distinction:

"If a relative shamed or disgraced you, you could not cast him off. But if he destroyed the family peace and love with quarreling and grudge-holding, then you could *mō ka piko.*"

Though the *piko* was symbolically cut only between two persons, actually the trouble maker was cut off from the entire family. For the *'ohana* system was one of total involvement.

"All the relatives lined up with the one in the right," recalls Mrs. Pukui. "The total family tie is cut away from the offender. There is no more mutual help or love between him and the rest of the family."

In one historic example, *mō ka piko* resulted when family members took opposite sides in a religious-social—perhaps even political—issue. At the time when eating *kapus* were first broken, Liholiho ate with the women, thereby taking a stand for *'ai noa* ("free" eating). His cousin, Ke-kua-o-ka-lani openly refused to give up the eating *kapu*. This led to quarrels. When Liholiho's mother, Ke-opu-o-lani failed to bring about peace, she declared *"mō ka piko la*

---

*God of health, associated with life, source of life, power of healing.

e na hoa hanau" ("severed are the umbilical cords, Oh cousins.") There followed open bloodshed.[7]

Says Mrs. Pukui, *"Mō ka piko* was a terrible thing."

It was. But like so many Hawaiian concepts of disruption or punishment, it carried with it its own remedy. The cord could be re-tied.

retying the cord

This remedial step rested on Hawaii's basic belief that when a sincerely repentant wrong-doer asked for forgiveness, it must be granted (see *mihi* and *kala*). However, the extreme gravity of *mō ka piko* demanded that readmittance to family love be solemnized with ritual. Wrote Mrs. Pukui:

"It was not enough to go to ask pardon . . . and say 'Brother, I have done wrong to you. Please forgive me.' He [offender] had to offer the prescribed sacrifice to him and to their mutual *aumākua.*

"The only way to reinstate himself was to go to an older and trusted relative, preferably a *kahuna,* with the gift of a pig. The two together would then go with the pig to the offended party to ask his pardon and that of the *aumākua* . . . The offended relative could not refuse him then . . . The pig was killed and eaten by both parties . . . The feast was naturally an occasion for rejoicing and merriment, and the night was spent together under one roof."[8]

Both cutting and re-tying of the symbolic *piko* were natural to old Hawaii's expressive society. Relationships were spelled out; feelings were discussed. And when the time came for apologies and forgiveness, there was no need to fumble embarrassingly for the "right approach." Ritual was the Emily Post—and if doubt remained, one consulted the *kahuna.*

piko beliefs of the present

Today—late in 1971—what remains of the old *piko* concept? Of the customs associated with the physical *pikos?*

As far as we know, *piko* folkways have outlived memories of *piko,* the abstraction. Specifically, quite a few women still follow old customs that concern the umbilical cord stump. Here we must take a look at traditions of other ethnic groups. For nearly every culture has given the navel cord and placenta mystic significance. Still-remembered, sometimes-practiced Hawaiian, Japanese, Chinese and Filipino customs are all quite similar. In fact social contact and intermarriage may have increased similarities and strengthened memories.

In 1953-54, Hawaii's public health nurses surveyed young mothers who were public health clients and found that:

Hawaiians still placed great importance on cord disposal, especially keeping the cord safe from rats so the child would not become a thief. (A Hawaiian social work student remembers after her brother was born ten years ago "seeing the cord hidden in the bathroom.")

Filipinas also thought the cord must be safely disposed of, usually by burying. A few mothers saved the cords of siblings and tied them together to insure later close sibling relationships. A few burned the cord stump and put the ashes in a drink given the baby. This was said to save his life in illness, prevent him from cutting himself, and was a way of avoiding a curse that might be placed on him.

Chinese: A few mothers kept the cord as a good luck charm for the baby. Japanese: A few kept the cord until the baby grew up. Some buried the cord. One woman believed the placenta should be cleaned or the mother would get an infection.

All four groups mentioned that the placenta should be buried deep in the ground because: this would keep away devils (Filipino); so harm would not befall the baby (Chinese); so the child would not wander and so animals would not eat the placenta (Hawaiian). Some Filipinas also thought mishandling the placenta would cause the baby to be sick or later to become insane.[9]

Whether concern about the placenta causes some few women to cling to home delivery is not known. In 1971, Oahu hospital nurses remembered no requests to take the placenta home or expressions of concern about it. However, one woman who asked to see the placenta "from intellectual curiosity—to see what it looked like" said she got a "disgusted response" from the nurse. Another woman asked for the placenta "so my son can take it to his science class!"

From Hana, Maui, Milton M. Howell, M.D. reports:

"Our last request for the placenta was in 1963. The request was granted. All placentas here at Hana Hospital were carefully buried among the banana trees in the back until about 1964. At that time, some dogs found the material, dug it up and ate it. Obviously this was greater desecration than burning, so incineration has been in effect since that time.

"At the home of one of our nurses are several fruit trees. After the birth of each child the placenta was buried and a fruit tree planted in that spot.

"Some families continue to save the remnant of the umbilical cord. These are arranged in jars and kept in alcohol."

On Niihau the placenta is called *honua*. There the *honua* was usually buried until recently. Within the last year (1971), the Robinson family (owners of the island) have insisted that *hapai* (pregnant) women go to Kauai and have their babies born in the hospital. The *piko* is still buried or put in a bottle and cast into the ocean. The reason is that "if the *'iole* (rat) eats it, the baby will grow up with *hana keko* [ugly behavior] and bring shame on the family."[10]

Younger women on the major islands sometimes keep the navel cord out of respect for the belief of elders. A Japanese secretary said, "I kept my baby's cord in a jar for years because my mother told me I should use it for medicine if the baby got sick. After Mother died, I threw it away."

The *piko* in its other meanings—and misuses of meaning—is referred to fairly often today. The penis *(ule)* is sometimes called *piko*. The greeting *"Pehea ko piko?"* ("How is your navel?") is used, though many Hawaiians resent this, especially when said by a *haole* (Caucasian). A youth with two cowlicks recently pointed to them saying "two *pikos*—nice, eh?" This probably referred to the old belief that *piko lua* or "two *pikos*" meant a child would be bright, alert and active.

The "triple *piko*" concept seems to survive only in fragments. The *po'o* (head) may be thought *kapu* and not to be touched whether or not the *piko* tie with *aumakua* is yet remembered or believed. The dreamed about *navel* is often interpreted as a dream about a relative.

The total idea of *piko* links that go backward in time to man's ancestors and forward to descendants yet to come has apparently been lost. With the passing of the *piko* concept has gone some of the poetic imagery of Hawaiian thought and Hawaiian language.

NOTES AND REFERENCES

1. Only the posterior fontanel was the *piko*. The anterior fontanel was the *manawa* or the "soft spot" Hawaiians associated with an infant's growth. This *manawa* was sometimes packed with leaves so it would not "close too soon." Mashed sweet potatoes were sometimes put directly on the *manawa* to nourish the infant with the "spiritual essence" of the food, or as some women believed, with the actual food. The *manawa* was the spot through which the dying sometimes transmitted their *mana* to a descendant.—M.K.P.

2. Malo. *Hawaiian Antiquities,* p. 136.

3. Pukui. "Hawaiian Beliefs and Customs During Birth, Infancy and Childhood."

4. Ibid.

5. *Hawaiian Antiquities,* p. 173.

6. Ibid., p. 125.

7. Kamakau. *Ruling Chiefs,* pp. 219-228.
   Pukui. *Polynesian Family System in Ka'u,* p. 51.

8. *Polynesian Family System in Ka'u,* pp. 49-50.

9. "Cultural Beliefs and Practices of the Childbearing Period..." *Hawaii Medical Journal,* Vol. 14, No. 4, pp. 342-346; No. 5, pp. 433-434; No. 6, pp. 539-541; Vol. 15, No. I, pp. 58-59.

10. Personal communication, Niihau resident 1971. *Hana* (activity; behavior) *keko* (monkey; ape). Lit. "ape behavior."

po'o—head as part of body; head as director or leader; many other meanings.
Deriv: unknown.

Po'o as the Culture Committee encounters the word means the head in the physical sense. Around the human head center many traditional beliefs and *kapus* (taboos).

While emotions and intellect were traditionally associated with the gut or intestines (see *na'au),* the head was considered the dwelling place of one's own spirit and the temporary home for *aumākua* (ancestor gods) and other good spirits. These spirits at times took beneficent possession of persons. See *'uhane* (spirit) and *noho* (possession).

This occupation by spirits made the head on down to the shoulders a *kapu* part of the body. Touching, hitting and slapping were prohibited. Where royalty was concerned, no commoner was allowed even to sit or stand in a higher position (over the head) of a ranking *ali'i.* King Kamehameha III ended this particular *kapu* when he approved building galleries directly over the royal pew in Kawaiahao Church.

"I have no objection," said the king, "if the galleries themselves don't fall on my head."[1]

The general "don't touch" attitude still exists. Similar attitudes are prevalent in many Asian countries. Thailand is a notable example. In Hawaii, even today, says Mary Pukui, "the way to start a good fight with a Hawaiian is to go up and slap one on the head."

Slapping or hitting the head or face was a serious offense. One was really hitting the *aumakua* that hovered in or around the head. And because Hawaiians believed that a thought put in words was virtually a thought put in action, even expressing a wish to slap was *kapu*.

"If you say 'I'd like to give you a good slap on the face,' you have given the slap," explains Mrs. Pukui.

At least one classroom of children gave ample evidence of believing a voiced thought amounted to action. The teacher, caught in end-of-the-day exhaustion, said something like, "you all ought to be slapped." Promptly the Hawaiian and part-Hawaiian children burst into tears.

A consultation with Mrs. Pukui enlightened the teacher on the Hawaiian attitude to the head. Later when the children grew unruly the teacher declared, "I'd like to give you all a good spanking."

Tension-relieving laughter filled the room. The spanked '*ōkole*[2] was funny. The slapped face was an outrage.

The tradition-observing Hawaiian does not even pat a child's head in affection. He does not try on another's hat, sit on his bed pillow or rest his head on a floor pillow. (These restrictions are reinforced by other traditional prohibitions on trading clothing and interchanging sitting and sleeping mats.)

For the non-Hawaiian, the social implications are obvious. Even in 1972, check that impulse to pat the head or pinch the cheek of the Hawaiian youngster!

NOTES AND REFERENCES

1. Cunningham. "The Westminister Abbey of Hawaii," *Sunday Digest,* May 15, 1960.
2. Spanking would have meant turning the '*ōkole* (buttocks or backside) to the teacher. This was an insult. Whether the pupils laughed at the piquant situation of having the teacher wish to be so insulted or whether they laughed at the childish aspects of spanking is not known.

punahele—favored child; favorite child.

> Deriv: *puna,* spring or source.
> *hele,* that which continues; goes on.

In the '*ohana* or family of old Hawaii, one or more children might be designated as the *punahele.* Usually this favorite child was the *hiapo* or first born. This child was, by tradition, given *(hānai'd)* to the grandparents, there to be reared for future responsibilities as a family senior.* A non-*hiapo* child might also be earmarked for *punahele* status because of special talents or because of some sign or portent before or at his birth.

---

*See listing, *kupuna* and *hānau mua.*

The derivation of the word makes it clear that the *punahele* was not just the "favorite child" as we know favoritism today. The *punahele* as the "spring or source that continues" was destined to learn the family traditions, genealogy and general lore-of-living so he could in turn pass them on to future generations. He would hold in trust and strengthen the "sense of family" that binds Hawaiian relatives so closely. As an adult he would be the senior member who would guide, counsel and make decisions that would affect family welfare. It was a responsible role. To prepare for it, the *punahele* memorized the family chants, listened to and absorbed the advice of elders, and spent most of his time in a sort of "apprentice for seniority" training course.

With this apprenticeship came certain privileges. Younger children were expected to defer to and obey the *punahele*. He was often given the best food or the finest sleeping mat. In early childhood he might even be carried around and displayed in a sort of *"punahele* beauty contest."[1] These were the trimmings. Basically, the *punahele* was a child in training for an adult position of trust, prestige and authority within his *'ohana.*

Today the obligations of work, learning, and assumption of responsibility seldom accompany *punahele* status. What does exist is closer to ordinary favoritism masquerading under the *punahele* label. Case examples show that many parents or grandparents give *punahele* treatment to one child, yet that child is in no way destined or being trained to become the family's responsible, decision-making senior.

Punahele treatment without *punahele* obligations then results in *lili* (jealousy) and sibling rivalry. Family adults must be helped to realize they have transferred only a fragment of a traditional practice over to present-day living. The fragment does not fit within its modern setting.

REFERENCE

1. Pukui. *Polynesian Family System in Ka'u,* p. 101.

ti leaves—leaves of tropical members of the lily family. Use of green *ti* leaves was thought to protect against harm and invoke protection of the gods. Also used for many household purposes.

Deriv: originally, *kī.* No other origin known.

"Whenever Hawaiian women go to a sacred place,* you see them quietly slipping *ti* leaves inside their brassieres. Then they feel safe." So Mary Kawena Pukui stated in 1969.

Two years previously, local newspapers carried accounts of three young women who were "visited by mischievous spirits." With the help of a Hawaiian policeman, the women used *ti* leaves and sprinkled the rooms with purifying salt water (see *pī kai)* to get rid of the spirit presences.

---

*Site of an ancient temple, for example.

And a Center staff member recalls this 1959 experience:

"We were on the Big Island when *Kilauea Iki* erupted. Everybody was rushing to go see the volcano. One of our party was afraid to go because she was menstruating, and menstrual blood is *kapu* (taboo) and an offense to Pele, the volcano goddess. But there was a school teacher with us ... Japanese, but she knew Hawaiian customs ... and she went out and got a *ti* leaf for the woman to wear so she could go with us. That made it all right."

The three examples demonstrate continuing belief that fresh leaves of green *ti* possess some mystic quality that can protect against spirits, lift *kapus,* and call down the blessing, rather than the wrath of the gods. The origin of this belief is lost. However, it is known that use of *ti* leaves in religious ceremonies once was mandatory under a *kānāwai akua* (law of the gods). Mrs. Pukui relates some of the traditional uses of *ti:*

"Before the greenery of the *hula* altar was put in place, the supporting posts were wrapped in *ti* leaves ... A person carrying food, especially pork, after dark was thought to be endangered by hungry ghosts. *Ti* leaves tied around the food gave full protection ... The *'awa* for offering the spirit in a seance was prepared and served on *ti* leaves. The spirit that possessed[+] the medium dictated the number and arrangement of the leaves."

Hawaiian origin in Tahiti is implied in Mrs. Pukui's mention of Hawaii's fire walking (still practiced in Tahiti) and use of *ti.*

"*Ti* was important in fire walking. No one was able to walk on lava beds cooled just enough to bear one's weight without carrying *ti* leaves. My great-great-grandmother used to walk across hot lava this way and never got burned. Our family line is from the Pele priesthood and Pele is the volcano goddess. So the *ti* leaves invoked Pele's protection."

Mrs. Pukui gives the background for wearing *ti* to remove the *kapu* on menstrual blood.

"*Ti* gave protection when a menstruating woman had to cross Pele's domain. Anklets, wristlets and a *lei* [garland] of *ti* leaves were worn by the woman. On both sides of her walked a man, holding a stalk of *ti* leaves like a *kāhili* [feather standard of royalty]."

Such was the procedure for off-schedule emergencies of travel. Ordinarily, menstruating women were segregated in the *hale* (house) *pe'a* (menstrual) or menstrual house. But even here, *ti* had its role.

"As a sign that they were in contact with *haumia* [defilement], but protected by a plant respected by the gods as a sacred symbol, the women who carried food to those in the *hale pe'a* wore *ti* leaves," Mrs. Pukui explains.

Ti was also used to exorcise an evil spirit, especially when the possessed *(noho)* one was a child or unable to talk. Relates Mrs. Pukui:

"The *kahuna* made the possessed one lie with his feet toward the entrance. Then he struck him lightly with *ti* leaves from head to feet. Then he shook the leaves in the doorway, just as he would shake out a dust cloth. This was to shake the possessing spirit out of doors. The ceremony was called *kuehu* [to shake]. To protect the patient from further molestation, *ti* leaves were spread under the sleeping mat."

Or:

"When a small child was possessed, the *kahuna* or parents could put *ti* leaves in a little salt water and have the child drink this."

[+]See *noho,* "possession."

Such were the sacred and symbolical uses of *ti*. The versatile leaves were also used, completely without irreverence, for all sorts of domestic purposes, ranging from rope to food wrapping to cough medicine. *Ti* also served as a flag of truce in battle. Food cooked in *ti* leaves continues to delight both the Hawaiian and the *lū'au*-loving tourist.*

Ti as a ritual, protective symbol is sometimes used even today by those who identify themselves with their Hawaiian past. This is always the green variety. (Colored *ti* was imported later and has no traditional value of protection. In fact, colored *ti* is used on graves in Western Samoa and some feeling that it is a "funeral" plant has come to Hawaii.) In some fairly well isolated Hawaiian communities, women who are menstruating wear *ti* leaf *leis* in the privacy of the home. And, as one young woman who still speaks and "thinks Hawaiian" explains, "When I get worried or scared and I have this feeling that 'something' is in the room with me, I use [wear] *ti* leaves." Here the *ti* leaves are worn fresh and thrown away without ceremony when they are faded.

As in many of Hawaii's religious concepts, belief in the protective symbolism of *ti* is sometimes mixed or over-laid with Christian interpretations. One example is a Center client, worried about an *'umi* (choking) feeling† in the night , who placed not *ti* but the Bible under the mattress, and so slept without the feeling or fear of strangulation.

However, many more clients who report intense fear because they are seeing ghosts or hearing spirit voices, completely forget about *ti* leaves as protection. This remembrance of what is fearful, and forgetting what is reassuring runs like a *motif* through the major theme of Hawaiian culture today.

'ūhā kapu—a taboo lap; lap so precious to the ancestor gods that a child who wet on it would sicken and die; lap of high ruler, so *tabu* that a child who wet it was killed, or saved by having the ruler adopt him.

Deriv: *'ūhā,* lap.
    kapu, sacred, forbidden, set apart, taboo.

In its most general meaning, *'ūhā kapu* is applied to women who cannot rear children to healthy adulthood. Such women can bear children; they cannot bring them up successfully. The concept is sometimes applied to men as well.

'Ūhā kapu in the present day seems to be confused with a quite different concept, *wahine kapu.* Because of this, it is discussed under the heading, *wahine kapu.*

---

*Lū'au, feast. Originally *'aha'aina.*
†*'Umi,* choking or strangling, was once inflicted by sorcery (see *'anā'anā*). A choking feeling may still have a psychic overlay that adds to the cause-and-effect anxiety of the sensation.

'uhane—spirit; ghost. After introduction of Christianity, soul.

Deriv: *hane,* disembodied person.

Says Mary Kawena Pukui of certain of her ancestral beliefs, "Some things are *'e'epa.* Unexplainable."

Accept that, and it becomes easier to know about *'uhane.* For in Hawaii's religious-mystic tenets, *'uhane* was:

The animating force which, present in the body, distinguished the quick from the dead. And so *'uhane* can be called "spirit."

The vital spark, that, departed from the flesh, lived on through eternity, rewarded for virtue or punished for transgressions in life. Thus *'uhane* is "spirit" in the immortal sense, and the "soul" of Christian concept.

Or, as immortal spirit or soul, the *'uhane* might return to visit the living and so be termed a "ghost."

Or, as immortal spirit, *'uhane* could be more specifically an *aumakua* (god-spirit of a long-dead ancestor), *'unihipili* (deified spirit of a recently deceased person), *akua* (god) or any of the demi-god, nature spirits called *kupua.* Or the "vehicle" that carried a spirit might eventually be known as the spirit itself. *Makani* is a chill breeze—and any Hawaiian knows this breeze means a spirit is present. Therefore, *makani* **is** the spirit.

Or, incorporated into Christianity, an immortal spirit might become *'Uhane Hemolele* or "Holy Ghost"; a wicked being might be called a "demon" or "devil."

Long before "Holy Ghost" entered Hawaii's creeds and vocabulary, some quite specific beliefs centered around *'uhane.* One was that, during life, the spirit could leave the body temporarily and return. (Nobody knew exactly where a man's spirit dwelled, but the head seemed indicated.) The exit point of a living person's spirit was the *lua 'uhane* or "spirit hole." This was the inner corner or tear duct of the eye. Mrs. Pukui recalls the belief, that, "When a person sleeps, the spirit comes out of the *lua 'uhane.* It goes on little adventures, and that produces dreams." Left undisturbed, the spirit returns from its adventures. As it enters the *lua 'uhane,* it awakens the sleeper.

The brief *'uhane* adventures that caused dreams were considered normal. Though a dream might be a nightmare, it might also be useful and beneficial. For in the dream, the *aumakua* or ancestor spirit sometimes communicated needed counsel. But the *'uhane* that became a habitual traveler signified trouble.

"A person who dozed when he should be awake was thought to have a *'uhane hele* or wandering spirit," says Mrs. Pukui. "For this, prayers were said and treatments were given. One treatment I saw given to a member of my family used crushed *ti* leaf.* This was put in water with a pinch of salt. The drowsy person took it every noon when the sun was directly overhead and his shadow had retreated in his body."†

---

*A traditional protective-purifying agent.

†A propitious time for many rituals. See *Kau ka lā i ka lolo, a ho'i ke aka i ke kino.*

po'i 'uhane
spirit catcher
Treatment was needed. For the fear was that a wicked *kahuna po'i 'uhane* (spirit catcher) might snatch the wandering spirit and keep it from re-entering the body. This meant death. When a known, wicked spirit catcher was seen approaching, anyone who was awake promptly roused the sleepers.

A *kahuna po'i 'uhane* could be good or bad. Good ones caught the spirit of the dying and forced it back in the body, thus restoring life. Wicked ones not only snatched living spirits, but even caught and injured spirits of the dead. For, so went the belief, the *po'i 'uhane* could see the spirit and even hold this nebulous, unearthly "something" in his cupped hands. Pursued by a spirit catcher, the *'uhane* might behave with a down-to-earth bravado.

"Some *'uhane* were said to make faces at the spirit snatcher," Mrs. Pukui says. "Maybe even *ho'opohopoho* [expose the buttocks; turn the backside], the worst possible gesture of contempt."

In death, the *'uhane* left the body by some unknown route. Eventually most spirits of worthy men joined other *aumākua* in the eternity called *Pō*. Some, continuously called back by relatives, were the ritually deified spirits called *'unihipili*. Some, penalized for offenses in life, joined the permanently lost and hungry spirits called *ao kuewa*. A few spirits might be returned to the body by a beneficent spirit catcher or the direct action of the *aumākua*.

"When it wasn't really time for a person to go, then the relatives [*aumākua*] might block the way and send the *'uhane* back," Mrs. Pukui states. Such resuscitation is described under *'o'ō-a-moa*.

The spirit was thought to hover near the body for a few days after death. This made spirit restoration easier. It also made possible last-minute requests to the spirit. For the still-lingering *'uhane,* directly appealed to, could take family *'ānais* (curses), *kapus* (taboos) and ill-feelings away with the body into a permanent and peaceful non-existence.

When one's own departing *'uhane* re-entered the body, this was a joy-filled, even miraculous event. When the spirit of another, a deceased, person or god, entered the body, this was *noho* (possession). *Noho* could be inspiring or frightening. It all depended on the possessing spirit.

A good spirit (usually an *aumakua*) was believed to enter the body through the head. But, curiously enough, a wicked possessing spirit entered exactly the same way one's own *'uhane* did when life was restored. Both came up through the big toe and the sole of the foot. When an evil spirit was entering, the feet might feel very hot or extremely cold.*

"We felt Mama's feet and they were icy cold," said a 1969 client, describing her mother's apparent *noho* experience.

In Hawaii's old beliefs, an immortal spirit, whether of god or deceased human, could take many forms and habitations. A man's spirit might rest happily in *Pō,* yet it could still linger in that immortal part of man, his bones. The spirit of a departed one might make its presence known in the shape of a cloud, felt in the rush of cold wind, seen in the flight of a bird, heard in dog's howl or owl's cry. It might inhabit a rock, permeating it with the strange power of *mana*. An ancestor spirit in the form of a shark could keep the swimmer safe; frivolous nature spirits could call to one in the spirit of play. Somewhere and everywhere was an *'uhane.*

---

*This could be a cultural interpretation of circulatory disturbance. Peripheral blood vessels constrict during stress.

194

'E'epa? Unexplainable? Yes. But quite natural and even expected. For in old Hawaii, man and gods and nature were very close, and the curtain between living and dead was woven of cobwebs.

The curtain is still cobweb thin. The *'uhane* is yet a felt, seen, heard and sensed presence for many Hawaiians of today. Most Center clients tell of experiences with spirits, whether they use Hawaiian terminology or not. And though *'uhane,* like the Christian "soul," resists explanation, the reasons for spirit-visits are often quite apparent. Incomplete grief work, guilt feelings, the wishful promptings of the unconscious—all these may be involved. Case examples are especially given in listings: *hō'ailona and hō'ike* (sign and revelation), *akakū, hihi'o and 'ūlāleo* (visions and voices), *noho* (possession) and *nahu akua* (spirit bite).

'unihipili or **'uhinipili**—spirit of the dead manifest in a bone or bones; deified bones through which this spirit was summoned; other body part or close personal possession so used. In the figurative sense, emotionally calling back and clinging to the dead.

Deriv: *'unihi,* bundle.
pili, to cling; clinging; be close to; be related; a relative.

In its original sense, *'unihipili* was a bone or many bones of a relative. The bones, wrapped in tapa or placed in a calabash, were kept in the home, in charge of one family member, the *kahu* or "keeper" of the *'unihipili.** These bones were deified and became, in fact, a "deified ancestor or other relative.

Later, perhaps as burial practices changed, the hair, garment or close personal possession of the dead relative or perhaps a rock, in which was his spirit in changed form (see *kino lau*), could become *'unihipili.* As a supernatural object, the *'unihipili* was cherished, offered food ritually, and was called on by its keeper for help. To some extent, *'unihipili* can be compared to Christian use of the body relic of a saint as devotional aid, or kind of "spiritual pipeline" to supernatural powers. Here the comparison ends.

The *'unihipili* was highly personalized. Here were the bones and hovering spirit of a beloved person, so recently deceased that the curtain between living and dead was still a thin one and easily parted.

Here was a spirit that could be summoned by the spoken wish of its *kahu* and would go on errands of mercy, warning or, regrettably, destruction.

Unlike the *aumakua,* the long-dead ancestor become a god, the *'unihipili* had not been removed from life long enough to attain independent judgment. It obeyed, lovingly but unthinkingly. This placed responsibility squarely on the *kahu.* For if the *kahu* sent the *'unihipili* on an errand of destruction, it might be returned by the prescribed ritual command to "return and destroy your keeper."** (This "as ye sow so shall ye reap" theme of moral-ethical

---

*This was often called *mālama pū'olu* or "keeping a bundle."

**"*ho'i no 'ai i kou kahu*"

responsibility is restated throughout early Hawaiian practices.) Or, sent too many times on vengeful errands, the *'unihipili* might eventually become evil and perform harmful acts on its own volition.

When the *kahu* or keeper felt it was unwise or even dangerous to keep the *'unihipili* as a household presence, he could release the spirit and let it merge into the more tranquil eternity of *Pō*. There were several ways to *'oki* or sever relationships with the *'unihipili*. If a family member died, the *'unihipili* could be buried with the body. If the family gods or *aumākua* were of the sea, such as shark gods, the *'unihipili* could be returned to the sea. Or the *'unihipili* would eventually go to its rest if ritual food offerings were ceased. Prayer rituals included direct requests for the *'unihipili* to "go and do not come back" and ritual pronouncements that the connection was severed.

'Unihipili with actual keeping of a body part is seldom if ever known today. One known case within the last two decades involved a grandmother whose grandson had committed suicide. She immediately collected blood from the dying youth and kept it to use in her announced intention to "bring him back again." This non-client case is known to a staff member.

In another example, a young client told of continuing fear that there were *'unihipili* objects around the family home. Some years ago, the family dug up the yard, found bones which they did not identify as human or animal, and burned them. After that, each time serious trouble came to the family, they looked for and tried to get rid of yet another *'unihipili* in the literal sense. One such search led to personal possessions of a deceased great-great-grandmother. In life she had been a dominating, loved-feared-hated—but never disregarded or forgotten—personality. The family themselves traced much of their abstract *'unihipili* fear-with-fascination to this old lady. Perhaps they were right; ambivalent relationships in life are usually found in extended attachments to the dead. However, the client moved away and the intriguing case was closed.

What are common among Hawaiians today are *'unihipili* experiences in the abstract sense of "calling back" or "holding on" to the deceased. Clients with some knowledge of their culture will themselves call such an experience *'unihipili*. One family reported, without alarm, hearing footsteps of a recently deceased member. Another told of dream visits of her long dead lover. And one young woman realized during the prayerful self-scrutiny of *ho'oponopono** that "I was calling, calling, calling my mother to come back."

All three were enmeshed, without ritual objects, in *'unihipili* as an emotional force. Or, in psychiatric terms, all were engaged in "grief work" not yet completed. The stage-by-stage processes of realization, active mourning and recovery had been suppressed, interrupted or blocked. The living had not yet achieved emotional separation from the dead.

---

*The family conference to find causes of disturbed relationships and, through prayer mutual forgiveness and restitution, "set things to right."

waha 'awa—one who customarily vented wrath on others by making impulsive, vindictive statements. Openly or by implication, the statements conveyed the wish or prophecy that another would meet with misfortune, illness or death.

Deriv: *waha,* mouth.
'awa, bitter, sour, poisonous.
Literally, "bitter mouth."

The rumor had spread through the little fishing community. Kulia's daughter, Hilalia, was almost certainly a *waha 'awa.*

All the little clues had been quietly noted through the years. Now the people were exchanging their long-collected observations. The bold spoke of Hilalia's ways openly, as if to show their defiance or disbelief in *waha 'awa* power. The cautious, fearful that their own words might rebound and harm them, veiled their comments in innuendo and elaborate play on words. Said directly or alluded to, the meaning was clear:

"She was already *lehe 'oi* [sharp-tongued] before she was old enough to carry a child on her back."*

"She left her *lei* on the beach one day and my *mo'opuna's* [grandchild's] dog stepped on it. Hilalia gave my *mo'opuna* a *kokoe ka maka†* look and said, 'You'll catch it. Just for that I hope your dog gets sick and dies!'"

Added another, "A few years ago she told all the children, 'If you touch my coconuts, you'll have a swollen hand!'"

The first speaker continued, "I've never heard her say a kind thing. Always something hateful. Filled with unhappiness."

To which a more perceptive one added, "Hilalia herself has never been a happy person."

The group fell silent. Not even the bravest put into words what everybody remembered. That the dog did get sick and die. That a child mischievously took a coconut and did indeed suffer a swollen hand.

So, except for a few skeptics, the community arrived at an undeclared verdict. Hilalia, now grown to womanhood, was a true *waha 'awa.*** A "Bitter Mouth." As such, her destructive, somewhat prophetic statements, no matter how impulsive, were *hua 'ōlelos,* words which could take on the punishing function of an *'ānai* (curse).

The account is a fictional one, which could very well have happened. We could title it "The Recognition"—or with fair accuracy—even "The Creation of a *Waha 'awa.*"

For the "Bitter Mouth" of Hawaii was fashioned in part by the observer. The resulting creation, like a well-designed dress, was cut to fit the wearer. And the wearer, the *waha 'awa,* seems to have found the costume snug, comfortable and, in fact, just what she had in mind!

---

*Before Hawaiians learned western numerals, age of a child was described by ability to perform certain tasks.

†"dirty look." Literally "eyes scratch."

**Waha 'awa* could, traditionally, be either sex. However, all examples given in Culture Committee sessions are of women.

As the fictionized conversation suggests, the distinguishing marks of a *waha 'awa* were spotted early. Mary Kawena Pukui reports on the old belief that, "Sometimes people were born with *waha 'awa* and it became recognizable as they grew older. You can usually tell when a child is about ten."

Events during early life could also shape the *waha 'awa* character. Mrs. Pukui furnishes this illustration:

"I'm thinking about a *waha 'awa* relative. She was one of twins, but the other child wasn't human.* That child died . . . When this relative was about a year-and-a-half, her father took her on a non-stop, day-long horseback ride. The ride was just too much. The child was crippled and she grew up a cripple . . . Later she went from church to church trying to get rid of whatever influenced her life . . . She became a *waha 'awa* person. She .wasn't cruel to her children in other [non-verbal] ways, but every so often something bitter would come popping out of her mouth.

"I think she resented the fact she was crippled . . . there must be somewhere in the background, some cause, some reasons for resentment . . . then the *waha 'awa* begins to resent herself."

In general the adult *waha 'awa* showed certain distinctive personality traits. Mrs. Pukui sums them up:

"The *waha 'awa* always *ho'omauhala* (nurses a grudge) . . . is not only bitter, but also very *pa'akikī* (stubborn) . . . From the mouth of a *waha 'awa* come no happy words, no enlightening words . . . A *waha 'awa* says things you cringe to hear . . . makes plenty *pilikia* [trouble] . . . feels she is going to 'get even' with all her might."

Whatever the complexities of birth or environment that created or molded the "Bitter Mouth," all the sharp-tongued ones share a salient characteristic. "People who are *waha 'awa*," Mrs. Pukui says, "are always very proud of it."

So far, the description could fit any embittered grouch who enjoys making others miserable. In the Hawaiian pattern, the malicious crank became a genuine dealer-in-doom when, says Mrs. Pukui, "she said nasty things and the nasty things came true."

Let this happen a few times and what may have been mere coincidence was attributed to *mana,* or power, in this case malign and used to make wish-like, prophetic threats come true. With this, the sharp-spoken one saw herself in the *waha 'awa* role and began strengthening and reinforcing this self-image. This operated in the past and continues in the present, as this 1970 report of a Center case-worker shows:

"_____ says she has this power. When she was a child she had an uncle who mistreated her. She used to mutter, 'Someday you're going to die and I'll be glad!' Later, when the uncle died, she felt that she had brought this about.

"She told me, 'This was the beginning of it. This was the sign that I have power' . . . She then told of other times she had said 'I hope you suffer' or 'I wish you'd die' and the persons concerned did eventually die or encounter

---

*Children born with deformities were traditionally thought to be the offspring of a mystical union between human and god or *aumakua* (family ancestor god). Depending on the appearance of infant (or aborted fetus) they were thought to be a *mo'o* (lizard or lizard-like) *manō* (shark) or any of the forms a god could take.

some distress. Right now a relative is in the hospital. She says this shows that it [*waha 'awa* power] is working... 'it's coming true.'"

Even within the same family, individuals might take completely opposite views of a *waha 'awa*. One person might shrug off or merely "half hear" the words of a "Bitter Mouth," reading into the words no personal threat. Here sympathetic insight into the causes that molded the *waha 'awa* personality certainly protect an "intended target" against anxiety. But for those who are more suggestible, perhaps influenced by guilts, and lacking in this insight, the words of a *waha 'awa* are often interpreted to be a curse.

(These interpretive responses are discussed under '*ānai* (curse) *hua 'ōlelo* (vengeful statement), and *hō'upu'upu* (thought implantation).)

Only the troubled ones who accept a *waha 'awa* as an agent of vengeance come to a social worker's attention. The following accounts are from case reports of 1967 to 1970. They not only suggest how family members respond to a *waha 'awa;* they also fill in our "personality profile" of a "Bitter Mouth."

A case worker reports on a current family situation:

"Mrs. _____ is extremely afraid of her mother-in-law. She said, 'My mother-in-law can put the hex* on me, because she has this power'... The son says his mother has 'this tremendous power,' but he won't elaborate... there is a great deal of fear about what she can do. She is a tremendously disruptive factor in the family."

The worker continues:

"This woman's three sons have remained at home, even after they married. They all made attempts to move away, but, always they came back."

In a separate *waha 'awa* case, another social worker reports:

"Her aunt came to Mrs. H_____'s [client's] house and formally asked her forgiveness for the way she had treated her. Mrs. H_____ absolutely refused to forgive† and make-up."

And another staff member comments on the self-directed anger of a "Bitter Mouth" who frequently voices the "I wish you were dead" *hua 'ōlelos:*

"She tells me, 'I get so mad at the kids I'd like to kill them.' And in the next breath she says, 'I wish *I* were dead.'"

And so the word picture of a *waha 'awa* is fairly well rounded out. Here is a strong, dominating personality. Here is a person who is full of rancor and cherishes it. Here is one who is hostile to others, but perhaps even more hostile to self. An astute character who "predicts" only what she is pretty sure will happen. A sadistic character.

In fact, the "power" of a *waha 'awa* seems to be mainly the shrewdness of the sadist. As the Center's psychiatric consultant explains:

"Persons who act out sadism as a regular part of their lives are usually highly perceptive of where another's weak spots, including guilts, may lie. These persons are usually most adroit in reading signals they get back. They know whether they have hit the mark or not.

"It is easy to see how this perceptiveness comes about. If a person, for whatever developmental reasons, has to engage in verbal sadism towards

---

*An introduced word applied to Hawaii's beliefs that one person could gain occult influence over another.

†Hawaiians believed that forgiveness must be granted the repentant. Refusal is completely against tradition.

others, he finds one of two things happening over a span of years. Either he, himself, gets 'clobbered' and stops the verbal attacks, or he becomes so astute that he nearly always sizes up others' vulnerable spots. In fact, to keep on operating as a sadist—let's say to keep on being a *waha 'awa*—he must be a master of his dubious skill. It's absolutely necessary to know what skeletons are hidden in whose closets!"

wahine kapu—sacred woman; supernatural woman; a goddess, specifically Pele.

Deriv: *wahine,* woman.
kapu, sacred; taboo; set apart; consecrated; forbidden. To forbid, consecrate, set apart.

In August, 1970, a Center social worker stationed in a rural, largely Hawaiian community reported,

"A number of women here believe they are *wahine kapu.* This is causing them considerable anxiety."

When he asked the women what they thought *wahine kapu* meant, he got the following answers:

A middle-aged woman: "It means a woman who never should get married and have children. I did—and all my children are sickly. Some of them died. It's because I am a *wahine kapu.*"

A teenage girl: "It means better I stay one virgin. Just like nun. No go out with boys. Never. Me? No, I never have date."

A third woman, late middle-aged: "Some women can't raise kids. They get sick or crippled or maybe die. They shouldn't ever have kids. They're *wahine kapu.*"

The three women are making much distressing ado about a cultural nothing. Mary Kawena Pukui says flatly:

"Hawaii never had such a *kapu* against marriage and having children. *Wahine kapu* simply means 'sacred woman,' usually Pele. Sometimes it may refer to other goddesses. And the goddesses of old Hawaii had husbands or lovers and they did have children. There was no permanent rule against intercourse. There was no prohibition against bearing children. Such a *kapu* never existed."

What seems to exist for the troubled trio we quoted is a confusion of Hawaiian concepts. Some of these placed a premium on virginity. Some designated certain individuals as *kapu.* Some concerned the inability to bring up healthy children. All were traditionally limited to temporary periods or to selected persons, usually the *ali'i* (aristocracy).

The legend of Kapuakaoheloai tells of a beautiful young girl who lost her virginity. After a king fell in love with her, she twice gave symbolic evidence of her earlier defloration. As she mounted the sacred platform where the king sat she "slipped and fell . . . this was due to her dislike of the platform, as she had lost her virginity." Later she bathed in a "bathing pool which was a very sacred place, those having lost their virginity or who were defiled* were not

---

*menstruating.

allowed to bathe in it . . . when she tried to climb the bank, she slipped back, a sign that she had lost her virginity."[1]

rank, genealogy
stressed virginity

Legends usually reflect actual events or attitudes, often in exaggerated, stylized form. The report of a pool reserved for virgins certainly suggests a high value was placed on virginity. However, this was true only among the *ali'i*. (The legend tells that Kapuakaoheloai was found to be of highest rank.) Hawaii's aristocratic maidens were supposed to be untouched, not because of morality or prudery, but because genealogy of a possible child was all-important. Mrs. Pukui sums up the traditional viewpoint:

"Hawaiians placed very high value on virginity when a girl was reserved for the *ali'i*. *Ali'i* were considered to be under the keeping of the gods. After a woman married to an *ali'i* gave birth to the wanted child, then she was not prohibited from having other love affairs. But the genealogy of this important first child must be perfectly clear. There must be no doubt about his blood lines.

"There wasn't any special emphasis on virginity for the ordinary woman. About the only rule for commoners was that people should not be *kiko moa* ('like the chickens'), or promiscuous."

Traditionally, requirements for virginity or abstinence were temporary in nature. Intercourse was forbidden during the menstrual period and after childbirth, during crop plantings and in various ritual periods. Any sexual contact was absolutely forbidden for the hula student. Mrs. Pukui explains:

ritual virginity
or abstinence

"A hula dancer in training was dedicated to Laka, the hula goddess. Hula training was a religious matter.[2] Total dedication was needed. The student, man or woman, was *kapu* or set apart. An unmarried student had to be a *pu'upa'a* or *ulepa'a* [female virgin; male virgin]. A person who had been married could go into training, but he or she had to stay absolutely away from the opposite sex until after graduation. I think this rule prevented a lot of jealousy among the students. They couldn't 'pair off.' After graduation, then the dancer was perfectly free to marry or have a love affair and have children."

The young girl who said she must "stay a virgin . . . just like a nun" is a hula dancer who takes her art seriously. Possibly she has confused this tradition of temporary virginity with a permanent edict.

Or, various personal *kapus* Hawaiians believed in may be mixed up with the erroneous *wahine kapu* belief. A child, a part of one's body, the clothing— all these could be *kapu*. A girl could be *kapu* to all men except the future husband chosen for her. But, again with emphasis, Mrs. Pukui points out that "none of these *kapus* ever meant to stay away completely and permanently from the opposite sex."

'ūhā kapu,
a kapu lap

The belief that *wahine kapu* means one should never give birth to a child is apparently confused with another tradition, that of *'ūhā kapu*.

201

'Ūhā kapu means literally a kapu or taboo "lap" ('ūhā). The old belief was that a woman with an 'ūhā kapu could give birth to perfectly healthy, normal children. However, she could not rear children.

'Ūhā kapu seems to rest on the undeniable fact that if you held a baby (before the era of rubber panties!), sooner or later that baby is going to mimi (urinate) on your lap. Then, went the belief, dire consequences befell, not the woman, but the baby. Mrs. Pukui wrote in The Polynesian Family System in Ka'u:

**inability to
rear children**

"Some women of the ali'i were so kapu that they could not rear children, not even their own. Should they attempt to rear children, the children either died or became crippled . . . inability to rear children is not uncommon among the Hawaiians; the 'ūhā kapu is accepted as a matter of course."[3]

The reason for this? Mrs. Pukui continued:

"The woman who is 'ūhā kapu is precious to an aumakua (ancestor god). The aumakua does not want the person who is precious to be soiled by urine and feces of an infant. Consequently, the aumakua depletes the woman's children's life force and they die. The only way to save them is to give them away to relatives to rear."[4]

Some women can rear only daughters, some only sons, and others cannot rear children of either sex, Mrs. Pukui explains.

Something like the shade of a Polynesian Freud appears as the account continues:

"In the case of the woman who could not raise sons, this was an instance of a male aumakua who was jealous, as a husband may be jealous of sons."[5]

'Ūhā kapu took on a different character within the highest ali'i ranks:

**ruler could claim or
kill child who wet lap**

"Should a child accidentally wet a chief, that child was killed or automatically became his foster-child.* Children were usually kept away from a [highly placed] ali'i unless the chief himself wished to see them and insisted on holding them, in which case parents were not held responsible for the accidental wetting that made the child the property of the chief."[6]

In actual practice, ranking ali'i sometimes picked up a much-desired child and held it until it urinated, thus gaining possession of the baby. Mrs. Pukui was told this first-person account:

"She [high status ali'i] picked up my child. I said, 'Please don't pick up the baby. The baby might do something on you.'

"And as soon as she picked him up, he mimi'd on her. So the baby became hers, and she was very fond of him."

Because every personal possession of high ali'i was kapu, the 'ūhā kapu belief was also extended to the bedspread on a royal bed. Let the baby mimi on the spread, and royalty could either claim the child or condemn him to death.

---

*The 'ūhā kapu could also apply to a man . . .M.K.P.

202

But the royal personage could resolve the dilemma by claiming the baby and then giving him back to the parents. One account suggests that a bed-wetting incident was arranged to give a youngster inner-circle status. Mrs. Pukui relates the report of a mother who took her infant to see Queen Kapiolani:

"The Queen said, 'Lay the child down on the bed—it's all right.'

"But the mother said, 'No, I don't want to put the baby on the bed.'

"'Oh, go ahead. Put her there,' said the Queen. And the baby *mimi'd* on the bed. There was a motto on the bedspread, *kūlia i ka nu'u* ('Strive to touch the highest'), and the Queen said, 'Now she must bear this name. And now I give the child back to you. But she must go by that name and you must bring her to see me often.'"

no permanent kapu
on intercourse

Why—today—have some Hawaiian women confused *'ūhā kapu* and *wahine kapu* and concluded they should neither marry nor have children?

One woman, suggestible to the point of docility, was told this by a self-appointed religious advisor. The "minister" or *kahuna pule,* confusing traditions himself, told the woman she was *wahine kapu* and should, never have married or had her family. In a kind of retroactive attribution of cause, the woman then used the *wahine kapu* indictment as reason for her children's past illnesses (many were minor childhood complaints), her own miscarriages, one infant death, and, indeed, as a curse overshadowing her entire life.

Whether the same minister influenced other women in the community is not known.

Like many Hawaiian beliefs (especially those misunderstood), *wahine kapu* or *'ūhā kapu* can be used to rationalize actual patterns of living, explain natural events, and assuage guilts and regrets. The case rests with Mrs. Pukui's reassuring statement:

"No woman was by any Hawaiian tradition permanently denied intercourse and child-bearing. No woman except a goddess was ever a *wahine kapu.*"

NOTES AND REFERENCES:

1. Fornander. *Collection of Hawaiian Antiquities,* Vol. 5, p. 544.

2. Hula lessons. The head pupil *(po'opua'a)* led in prayer chants and giving offerings to the gods. In his absence, the assistant *(paepae)* officiated. Even in Mrs. Pukui's youth, hula lessons were still invested with religious significance. Mrs. Pukui was graduated at a *hālau* (long house) dedicated to the hula gods. Students were not supposed to attend a funeral. After going to a family member's funeral, Mrs. Pukui was readmitted to the hula class only after ritual purification ceremony and a symbolic offering to the gods.

3. Pukui. *Polynesian Family System in Ka'u,* p. 48.

4. Ibid., p. 49.

5. Ibid.

6. Ibid.

wehe i ka Paipala or **wāhi i ka Paipala**—post-missionary Bible interpretation; to open Bible, select a passage at random and interpret this as help or solution to a problem.
Deriv: *wehe,* open; to open; to solve, as a problem; or *wahi,* to split; to divide.
Paipala, Bible; Biblical.

Faced with worries or perplexed about the meaning of a dream or other sign, quite a few Hawaiians today go to the family Bible, pray, then shut their eyes, open the book and point a finger somewhere on the open page. The passage so selected is thought to indicate the solution to the problem, or the interpretation of the dream or portentous event. If the first passage seems to have no application to the problem, the process is repeated until a relevant selection is found.

Very probably, at the same time the Hawaiian is pointing at random in his *Paipala,* someone in the "Bible belt" of the South is doing exactly the same thing for exactly the same reasons. Finding the solution in the "good Book" is not exclusive to Hawaii. In fact, the practice is not a traditionally Hawaiian one. It began, of course, after conversion to Christianity and was apparently superimposed on the prevalent Hawaiian belief in a *hō'ailona* (sign or portent).

Today Center clients practice *wehe i ka Paipala* themselves, or consult persons they consider *kahunas** to conduct the ritual. For some clients, "pointing in the Bible" provides simple reassurance. For example:

A part-Hawaiian woman, home after years on the mainland, put a *lei* on her mother's grave. The *lei* fell into the shape of a heart, which the woman believed was a *hō'ailona.*

"I went to see 'someone' to have this interpreted," she later related. The "someone" conducted *wehe i ka Paipala.* The passage marked was not told, but his interpretation of words and the heart shape of the *lei* was that the mother had sent a sign to show she truly loved her children. (This is a modern interpretation; traditionally, emotions were believed to be centered, not in the heart, but in the *na'au,* intestines or gut.)

For others, *wehe i ka Paipala* may become an emotional crutch, a delaying device, or a substitute for taking constructive action. For example:

While her son was piling up a record as a juvenile delinquent, one mother periodically pointed in the Bible to find ways to handle him. This delayed for some time her eventual decision to ask for professional counseling.

In the third example, *wehe i ka Paipala* and a preceding dream apparently helped a client to confront and try to solve an immediate problem.

The cast (all names changed): Malia, the worried mother; Kimo, the worry-making son, and Kimo's girl friend, Janet. Malia had been a Center client since her husband became incurably ill some years previously.

As a child, Malia had been *hānai'd* (the traditional adoption) by her much beloved grandparents, now dead. In Malia's adult life, Grandma often (and Grandpa sometimes) appeared in dreams, giving comfort when it was needed. Malia needed just such emotional support when her "hunch" that Janet was *(hāpai)* pregnant became an absolute, though yet unspoken, certainty.

---

*kahunas intensively trained in the traditional manner no longer exist.

"At first I just wanted to yell and scream and run around like crazy. I wanted to run right over to Janet's parents and tell them! I didn't know what to do!"

What Malia did was to "sleep on it." That night, she dreamed that Grandma came, enfolded her in "large, warm and loving arms," and told her, "I brought you up to be strong . . . to handle things. There is a way. There *is* help —and you know where it is."

The next day Malia opened her Bible in the *wehe i ka Paipala* ritual. Her finger marked the lines:

"A foolish son is a grief to his father and bitterness to her who bore him" Proverbs 17:25 (King James version).

(Later Malia paraphrased this to the case worker as a "foolish son is a burden to his mother," leaving out all reference to the father. Actually, Malia had taken over family responsibilities ever since her husband became ill.)

Since the Proverb certainly identified her problem, Malia turned to the Bible again to find a solution. This time she pointed to:

"As one whom his mother comforts, so I will comfort you; you shall be comforted in Jerusalem." Isaiah 55:13.

This passage, she told the case worker, meant "there is help; there is hope." (If she was using the Revised Standard Version published by the World Publishing Company, one widely used in Hawaii, her eye probably fell on the word "hope" in the page heading, "Zion's Future Hope." Lines preceding this on the same page are filled with metaphors that make of Jerusalem a nurturing, consoling mother.)

Seeking guidance and confirmation of her interpretations, Malia then phoned her own mother. With both speaking in Hawaiian, Malia told of the dream and the Bible passages. Her mother agreed that "you've interpreted everything ['there is help and hope'] just right. And," concluded her mother, "you know where that help is."

Just about then Janet came over to see Kimo. Very calmly Malia asked, "You're pregnant, aren't you, Janet?"

"Yes, I am," said Janet.

Still calm, Malia said, "All right, we're going to see _____ (Malia's caseworker). For that is where the help is in this problem."

From there, events moved harmoniously into a joint conference with Janet's family and the making of realistic plans for the coming baby's future.

And so from Grandma to Bible to Mama to warm and encouraging woman caseworker went Malia's quest for problem-solving guidance. All of which makes Malia seem helpless indeed. But seeing a wholly dependent Malia is taking a partial, one-sided view. Dr. Haertig, familiar with the case since Malia's husband became ill, rounds out and balances the picture.

"Malia's recent and similar past dreams of grandparents, and her interpretation of the Bible passages suggest a self-image that says, in effect, 'I don't have any strengths of my own. I must borrow them from the people who reared me.' And when she ascribes the source of strength to everyone else rather than herself, she is undermining herself. Malia does not lack inner resources for working out family troubles; she lacks belief that she has these resources."

Dr. Haertig suggests that Malia be helped to realize she has internalized strengths and has already put them to good use. Grandma in the dream might well be interpreted less as a source of comfort and more as a message-bearer reminding Malia that, "You know where this strength is. It is in *you*."*

If Malia's self-concept can be so shaped, then eventually Grandma by dream, Mama by phone, and caseworker by supportive consultation may cease to be needed sources of "help and hope." When this occurs, *wehe i ka Paipala* as problem-solving ritual will probably be given less importance.

Anyone in the helping professions who works with Hawaiians may find knowledge of *wehe i ka Paipala* useful. Discussion of a client's "Bible pointing" may build rapport, even though the lines quoted or paraphrased by the client may corroborate what the worker already knows. Of more significance is the fact that the client actually controls the apparently random choice of lines. He can keep on pointing until he gets the message he really wants. And for every passage he reads *out* of the Bible, he also reads *into* it his own interpretation, based on his own needs, problems and wishes. There is also the chance that the Bible falls open to an often-read, therefore particularly applicable page. All this may add to the worker's knowledge of the client.

The omissions, additions and changes the client makes in relating the Biblical lines may provide clues to understanding him. For this kind of "word by word" check, the professional worker must know exactly which version and revised printing of the Bible the client has used.

wela—hot sensation of the skin; also, to feel passion; lust.
   Deriv: from original meaning of *wela,* meaning hot, burned, heat or temperature.
   See discussion under *'ili 'ōuli.*

---

*Past records not disclosed here show that Malia has met and with guidance solved numerous problems that might have overwhelmed someone without a certain innate emotional sturdiness.

Bibliography—books

Anderson, Hans Christian. *The Emperor's New Clothes.*

Bach, Marcus. *Major Religions of the World,* Abingdon Press, 1959.

Beckwith, Martha W. *Kepelino's Traditions of Hawaii,* Bernice P. Bishop Museum Bulletin 95, 1932.

Bishop, Marcia B. *Hawaiian Life of the Pre-Missionary People,* Salem, Massachusetts: Peabody Museum, 1940.

Day, A Grove
Hawaii and Its People, New York: Duell, Sloan and Pearce, 1955.
With Stroven, Carl, Ed., *A Hawaiian Reader,* New York: Appleton-Century-Crofts, Inc., 1959.
With Michener, James. *Rascals in Paradise,* New York: Random House, 1957.

Elbert, S. H., Ph.D.
With Pukui, M.K. *Hawaiian-English Dictionary,* University Press of Hawaii, 1965.
English-Hawaiian Dictionary, University Press of Hawaii, 1964.
Hawaiian-English Dictionary (combined), University Press of Hawaii, 1971.

Ellis, William
Journal of William Ellis, Honolulu Advertiser, 1963.
Polynesian Researches—Hawaii, C.E. Tuttle, 1969.

Emerson, N. B., *Unwritten Literature of Hawaii,* Japan: C. E. Tuttle, 1965.

Fairchild, J.E., Ed., *Basic Beliefs,* New York City: Hart Publishing Co., Inc., 1959.

Fornander, Abraham
An Account of the Polynesian Race, Vol. I, London: Trübner & Co., 1878.
Collection of Hawaiian Antiquities, Vols. I, II, III, IV, V, VI, Bernice P. Bishop Museum Memoirs, Honolulu 1917, 1918.
Selections from Antiquities and Folklore, University Press of Hawaii, 1959.

Gallimore, Ronald, with Howard, Alan, Eds. *Studies in a Hawaiian Community: Na Makamaka O Nanakuli,* Department of Anthropology, Bernice P. Bishop Museum, 1968.

Goldman, Irving. *Ancient Polynesian Society,* University of Chicago Press, 1970.

Handy, E.S. Craighill, et al. *Ancient Hawaiian Civilization,* Rutland, Vt: C.E. Tuttle, 1965.

Handy, E.S. Craighill with Pukui, M.K. *Polynesian Family System in Ka'u,* Wellington, New Zealand: The Polynesian Society, 1953.

Harding, T.G. with Wallace, B.J., Eds. *Cultures of the Pacific,* New York City: The Free Press (MacMillan), 1970.

Henry, George W., M.D. with Zilboorg, Gregory, M.D. *History of Medical Psychology,* New York: W.W. Norton & Co., 1941.

Highland, G.E., Ed. *Polynesian Culture History,* Bernice P. Bishop Museum Press, 1967.

Hoebel, E. Adamson. *Man in the Primitive World,* New York: McGraw-Hill, 1949.

Howard, Alan with Gallimore, Ronald, Eds. *Studies in a Hawaiian Community: Na Makamaka O Nanakuli,* Department of Anthropology, Bernice P. Bishop Museum, 1968.

Holy Bible, The, Revised Standard Version, Cleveland: The World Publishing Co., 1962.

Ii, John Papa—Pukui, M.K., translator. *Fragments of Hawaiian History,* D.B. Barrere, Ed., Bernice P. Bishop Museum Press.

Jung, C.G. *Analytical Psychology: Its Theory and Practice,* New York: Pantheon Books, 1968.

Kamakau, Samuel M.
—Pukui, M.K., translator. *Ka Po'e Kahiko: The People of Old,* Bernice P. Bishop Museum Press, 1968.
—Pukui, M.K., chief translator. *Ruling Chiefs of Hawaii,* Kamehameha Schools Press, 1961.

Kamehameha Schools 75th Anniversary Lectures, Kamehameha Schools Press, 1965.

Korn, Alfons L. *The Victorian Visitors,* University Press of Hawaii, 1958.

Kuykendall, R.S. *The Hawaiian Kingdom, 1778-1854,* University Press of Hawaii, 1957.

Lambo, T.A., Ed. *Transcultural Psychiatry,* Boston: Little, Brown and Company, 1965.

Larsen, Nils P., M.D. *Ancient Hawaiian Civilization,* Kamehameha Schools, 1933.

Liliuokalani. *Hawaii's Story by Hawaii's Queen,* Tokyo, Japan: C.E. Tuttle, 1964.

Malinowski, Bronislaw. *Magic, Science and Religion,* Doubleday, 1954.

Malo, David—Emerson, Nathaniel B., translator (1898) *Hawaiian Antiquities,* Honolulu: Bishop Museum Special Publications, No. 2, 1951.

Michener, James with Day, A. Grove. *Rascals in Paradise,* New York: Random House, 1957.

Middleton, J., Ed. *Gods and Rituals,* Garden City, New York: Natural History Press, 1967.

Montagu, A., Ed. *Man and Aggression,* Oxford University Press, 1968.

Mulholland, John F. *Hawaii's Religions,* Rutland, Vt: C.E. Tuttle, 1970.

Oesterreich, T.K. *Possession, Demoniacal and Other, Among Primitive Races, in Antiquity, The Middle Ages, and Modern Times,* translated by D. Ibberson, New Hyde Park, New York: University Books, 1966.

Oliver, Douglas. *The Pacific Islands,* Garden City, New York: Doubleday and Co., Inc., 1961.

Porteus, Stanley. *A Century of Social Thinking in Hawaii,* Pacific Books, Palo Alto, California, 1962.

Pukui, M.K.
  With Elbert, S. H., Ph.D.—*Hawaiian-English Dictionary,* University Press of Hawaii, 1965.
  English-Hawaiian Dictionary, University Press of Hawaii, 1964.
  Hawaiian-English Dictionary, (combined), University Press of Hawaii, 1971.
  With Handy, E.S. Craighill. *Polynesian Family System in Ka'u,* Wellington, New Zealand: The Polynesian Society, 1953.

Reik, Theodore, M.D. *Listening with the Third Ear,* New York: Farrar and Strauss, 1948.

Stroven, Carl with Day, A. Grove, Eds. *A Hawaiian Reader,* New York: Appleton-Century-Crofts, Inc., 1959.

Vayda, Andrew P., Ed. *Peoples and Cultures of the Pacific,* Garden City, New York: The Natural History Press, 1968.

Wallace, B.J. with Harding, T.G., Eds. *Cultures of the Pacific,* New York: The Free Press (MacMillan), 1970.

Westervelt, William D. *Legends of Old Honolulu,* C. E. Tuttle, 1964.

Zilboorg, Gregory, M.D. with Henry, George W., M.D. *History of Medical Psychology,* New York: W.W. Norton & Co., 1941.

Zilboorg, Gregory, M.D. *Mind, Medicine and Man,* New York: Harcourt, Brace & Company, 1943.

Published articles, abstracts and monographs

Abstract. "Mortality of Bereavement," *Psychosomatic Medicine,* 1968, p. 353.

Abstract. "Psychophysiology of Anxiety," *Psychosomatic Medicine,* 1966, p. 189.

Beckley, Fred W. "Voice Culture in Ancient Hawaii," *Paradise of the Pacific,* December 1932.

Beckwith, Martha W. "Hawaiian Shark Aumakua," *American Anthropologist,* N.S. 19, 1917, pp. 503-517.

Brady, John Paul, M.D. with Levitt, Eugene E., Ph.D. "Hypnotically Induced Visual Hallucinations," *Journal of Psychosomatic Medicine,* Vol. 28, No. 4, p. 351.

Clayton, Paula, M.D. et al. "A Study of Normal Bereavement," *American Journal of Psychiatry,* 1968, Vol. 125, pp. 168-178.

"Cultural Beliefs and Practices of the Childbearing Period . . . ," *Hawaii Medical Journal,* Vol. 14, No. 4, pp. 342-346; No. 5, pp. 433-434; No. 6, pp. 539-541; Vol. 15, No. I, pp. 58-59.

Cunningham, Catherine. "Westminster Abbey of Hawaii," *Sunday Digest,* Elgin, Illinois: David C. Cook Publishing Co., May 15, 1960, pp. 1-4.

"Death, Lying-in-State and Obsequies of Queen Liliuokalani, Last Sovereign of Hawaii," *Thrum's Hawaiian Annual,* 1918, pp. 102-109.

Ellenberger, Henri F. "The Ancestry of Dynamic Psychotherapy," *The Discovery of the Unconscious,* New York: Basic Books, Inc., 1970, pp. 3-52.

Erickson, Milton H., M.D. "Deep Hypnosis and Its Induction," *Experimental Hypnosis,* New York: The MacMillan Co., 1954.

Firth, Raymond. "The Analysis of *Mana:* An Empirical Approach," *Cultures of the Pacific,* T.G. Harding & Ben J. Wallace, Eds., New York: The Free Press (MacMillan), 1970.

Handy, E.S. Craighill
"Dreaming in Relation to Spirit Kindred and Sickness in Hawaii," *Essays in Anthropology,* University of California at Berkeley, 1963, pp. 119-127.
With Pukui, M.K. and Livermore, Katherine. "Outline of Hawaiian Physical Therapeutics," Bernice P. Bishop Museum Bulletin 126, 1934, 51 pages.

Hirsch, Steven J., M.D. with Hollender, March H., M.D. "Hysterical Psychosis: Clarification of the Concept," *American Journal of Psychiatry,* January 1969, pp. 81-87.

Huston, Paul E., M.D. "Neglected Approach to Cause and Treatment of Psychotic Depression," *Archives of General Psychiatry,* June 1971, Vol. 24, pp. 505-508.

Jelliffe, E.F. Patricia, S.R.N. with Jelliffe, Derrick B., M.D. "Children in Ancient Polynesian Hawaii," *Clinical Pediatrics,* October 1964, Vol. 3, No. 10.

Johnson, Harold M., M.D. "The *Kahuna,* Hawaiian Sorcerer, Its Dermatologic Implications," *Archives of Dermatology,* Chicago: American Medical Association, November 1964, Vol. 90, pp. 530-535.

Kalakaua, David
"The Cannibals of Halemanu," *Legends and Myths of Hawaii.* Charles L. Webster and Co., N.Y., 1888. pp. 371-380.
"The Destruction of the Temples," *Legends and Myths,* pp. 431-446.

Knaefler, Tomi
Interview with Bessessen, Daniel H., M.D., Nanakuli physician, Honolulu Star-Bulletin, June 24, 1969.
"Visit to Papakolea," Honolulu Star-Bulletin, August 9, 1969.

Larsen, Nils P., M.D.
"Medical Art in Ancient Hawaii," *Fifty-Third Annual Report of the Hawaiian Historical Society for the Year 1944,* 1946, pp. 27-44.
"Rededication of the Healing Heiau Keaiwa," *Sixtieth Annual Report of the Hawaiian Historical Society for the Year 1951,* pp. 7-16.

"Laws of His Majesty, Kamehameha IV," 1860 *Archives of Hawaii.*

"Laws of His Majesty, Kamehameha V," Passed by 1872 Legislative Assembly Session, *Archives of Hawaii.*

LeCron, Leslie M. "Study of Age Regression Under Hypnosis," *Experimental Hypnosis,* New York: The MacMillan Co., 1954.

Levitt, Eugene E., Ph.D. with Brady, John Paul, M.D. "Hypnotically Induced Visual Hallucinations," *Journal of Psychosomatic Medicine,* Vol. 28, No. 4, p. 351.

Levy, Robert I., M.D. "On Getting Angry in the Society Islands," *Mental Health Research in Asia—The Pacific,* Coudill & Lin, Eds., East West Center Press, 1969.

Lidzi, Theodore, M.D. with Smith, D. Clint, M.D. "Interrelated Schizophrenic Psychoses in Fraternal Twins," *Archives of General Psychiatry,* 1964, Vol. 10, begins p. 422.

Lindemann, Erich, M.D. "Symptomatology and Management of Acute Grief," *American Journal of Psychiatry, 1944, Vol. 101, p. 147.*

Livermore, Katherine; Handy, E.S. Craighill and Pukui, M.K. "Outline of Hawaiian Physical Therapeutics," Bernice P. Bishop Museum Bulletin 126, 1934, 51 pages.

Moss, P.D. with McEvedy, C.P. "Epidemic of Over Breathing Among School-girls," (abstract), *Journal of Psychosomatic Medicine,* Vol. 29, No. 4, p. 398.

Norgard, Brian A., Ph.D. "Rorschach Psychodiagnosis in Hypnotic Regression," *Experimental Hypnosis,* New York: The MacMillan Co., 1954.

Parkes, Colin Murray, M.D. "The First Year of Bereavement," *Psychiatry,* November 1970, Vol. 33, No. 4, pp. 444-467.

"Psychiatry Around the World," *AMA Archives of Neurology and Psychiatry,* Vol. 75, pp. 653-655.

Pukui, M.K.; Handy, E.S. Craighill and Livermore, Katherine. "Outline of Hawaiian Physical Therapeutics," Bernice P. Bishop Museum Bulletin 126, 1934, 51 pages.

Pukui, M.K. "Songs (Meles) of Old Ka'u, Hawaii," *Journal of American Folklore,* July-September 1949, pp. 247-258.

Ratzel, Friedrich. *Religion in Oceania* (excerpts), London: MacMillan & Co., Ltd., 1904, Vol. I, pp. 300-330.

Session Laws of Hawaii, 4th State Legislature, 1967 *Archives of Hawaii.*

Smith, D. Clint, M.D. with Lidzi, Theodore, M.D. "Interrelated Schizophrenic Psychoses in Fraternal Twins," *Archives of General Psychiatry,* 1964, Vol. 10, begins p. 422.

Tingling, David C., M.D. "Voodoo, Root Work and Medicine," *Psychosomatic Medicine, Journal of the American Psychiatric Society,* Vol. 29, No. 5, pp. 483-489.

Titcomb, Margaret. "Kava in Hawaii," *Journal of the Polynesian Society,* Wellington, New Zealand, 1946, Vol. 57, No. 2, pp. 105-169.

Volkan, Vamik, M.D.
"Re-grief Work Techniques in Normal and Pathological Grief Reactions, A guide for the Family Physician," *Virginia Medical Monthly,* 1966, Vol. 93, No. 2, pp. 651-656.
"Typical Findings in Pathological Grief," *The Psychiatric Quarterly,* 1970, Vol. 44, No. 2, p. 238.

Watt, Anne S., M.Sc. "Helping Children to Mourn" (Part I) and "When Children Mourn" (Part II), *Medical Insight,* July 1971, pp. 29-39 and August 1971, pp. 57-62.

Williams, Griffith W. "Hypnosis in Perspective," *Experimental Hypnosis,* New York: The MacMillan Co., 1954.

Yap, P.M., M.D. "The Possession Syndrome: A Comparison of Hong Kong and French Findings," *Journal of Mental Science,* England, 1960, Vol. 106, pp. 114-137.

Unpublished material

Aiona, Darrow L. "Hawaiian Church of the Living God: An Episode in the Hawaiian's Quest for Social Identity," Thesis, June 1959, University of Hawaii Library.

"An Enactment of a Psychiatric-Anthropological Consultation Session," Social Work Conference Presentation, 1966, 17 pages, a Committee presentation.

Caplan, Gerald, M.D. "An Approach to the Study of Family Mental Health." Typescript of lecture given in Honolulu. 1957. and notes taken at Caplan seminar, 1957.

Interviews, Taped, with M.K. Pukui and Richard Paglinawan, April 1965. Bones, burial caves, funeral practices, traditions concerning *meles,* etc.

Kaku, Kanae, M.D. "Are Physicians Sympathetic to Superstition? A Study of Hinoe-Uma," June 1971, 11 pages.

Kautz, Amanda Tichenour. "Funerals on Hawaii Island, A Study of Cultural Lag in Ethnic Accommodations," M.A. Thesis, 1967, Sinclair Library, 94 pages.

Lucas, Clorinda. "Queen Liliuokalani, The Poet-Composer," presented at Kawaiahao Church, August 27, 1967, 5 pages.

Minutes of the Hawaiian Culture Study Committee meetings for 1965, 1966, 1967, 1968, 1969, 1970, and 1971 to date.

Pukui, M.K.*
  "*Akua Lele,*" undated, 2 pages
  "Beliefs on Birth, Infancy and Childhood," 1941, 37 pages
  "Bits of Hawaiiana," undated, 21 pages
  "Body Molding," 1957, 2 pages
  "Feather Work"
  "*Hale Naua (Naua), The,*" Bishop Museum Tape H-129 A, recorded May 19, 1964.
  "*Ho'oiloiolo* (Predicting Trouble)," undated, 2 pages
  "*Ho'okauhua,*" undated, 1 page
  "*Ho'oponopono,* an Illustrative Illustration," June 3, 1965, 4 pages
  "*Kahuna Hāhā, The,*" undated, 2 pages
  "*Laulima,*" undated, 2 pages

---

*Most of the material is also on tape at the Bishop Museum.

"Lomilomi," undated, 1 page

"Names," February 19, 1968, 4 pages

"Noho," undated, 4 pages

"Notes and Definitions Concerning Sickness," October 14, 1968, 4 pages

"Notes on Uses of *Ti* Leaves," September 15, 1969

"Offering," undated, 7 pages

"Pahu or *Kiwi,"* undated, 1 page

"Po'i 'Uhane," (Spirit Catching), undated, 2 pages

"Uhane," and Other Notes, January 1968, 16 pages

Also numerous short notes and definitions incorporated into the Minutes of the Hawaiian Culture Study Committee.

Thompson, Myron B. "Queenly Touch of Growth," presented at Kawaiahao Church, August 30, 1964, 5 pages.

English topic index and reference guide

Individual definition-discussion listings and major references are in bold face type.

220